Your
Child's
Growing
Mind

Praise for *Your Child's Growing Mind*

"How do our children learn to read? What can we do to encourage creativity or to help develop math skills? How do we know if our child has a learning problem? From infancy to adolescence, Jane Healy offers us a blueprint for understanding our children. Never condescending and always sympathetic to what is asked of parents, Dr. Healy gives concrete, clear-cut suggestions on what to do and leaves us with an understanding of the ways our children's brains work."

—Kathy Heinzelman,
The Parents League of New York

"Dr. Healy has done it again with *Your Child's Growing Mind*. Nobody makes child development and its practical applications so clear and readable. A must for parents."

—Michael Brody, M.D., American Academy
of Child and Adolescent Psychiatry

"*Your Child's Growing Mind* is an essential book for all parents and educators. Healy offers an impressive selection of scientific brain research and articulates with clarity and passion its relevance to child development and learning. Replete with research-based ideas, recommendations, and resources for parents and educators, this book is a powerful guide for raising developmentally healthy children and adolescents."

—James P. Comer, M.D., Maurice Falk
Professor of Child Psychiatry, Yale Child
Study Center, and Associate Dean, Yale
School of Medicine

"Jane Healy's work has long enjoyed the respect of those who believe that the developmental needs of children are the first responsibility of educators. With the latest edition of *Your Child's Growing Mind,* she makes it abundantly clear that a child's mind is not an immature or outmoded computer, but an integral component of a dynamic, motivated, and rapidly changing organism. In making her case as clearly as she does, she secures her reputation as a constructive contrarian in the current debate about the role of technology in early childhood education."

—Frank R. Wilson, M.D., Clinical Professor of Neurology, Stanford University School of Medicine

"Kudos to Jane Healy on the third edition of her seminal book *Your Child's Growing Mind.* No one writes about the development of the child's brain as succinctly and practically as Healy. This book belongs on the shelf of every parent. I wish it had been available when my own children were young!"

—Patricia Wolfe, author of *Brain Matters: Translating Research to Classroom Practice*

Your Child's Growing Mind

**Brain Development
and Learning from
Birth to Adolescence**

Third Edition

JANE M. HEALY, PH.D.

Broadway Books
New York

Broadway Books titles may be purchased for business or promotional use or for special sales. For information, please write to: Special Markets Department, Random House, Inc., 1745 Broadway, New York, NY 10019.

PRINTED IN THE UNITED STATES OF AMERICA

BROADWAY BOOKS and its logo, a letter B bisected on the diagonal, are trademarks of Random House, Inc.

Visit our website at www.broadwaybooks.com

First edition published 1987

Library of Congress Cataloging-in-Publication Data
Healy, Jane M.
    Your child's growing mind : brain development and learning
from birth to adolescence / Jane Healey.—3rd ed.
        p.   cm.
    Includes bibliographical references and index.
    1. Learning, Psychology of.   2. Child rearing.   3. Educational psychology.
4. Pediatric neuropsychology.   I. Title.

    BF3 18.H4 2004
    155.4'13—dc22

                                                                      2003062558

ISBN 0-7679-1615-8

10   9   8   7

This book is dedicated to all the

parents and teachers who said,

"That's very interesting, but what

should we *do* about it?"

Acknowledgments

As *Your Child's Growing Mind* enters its third edition, I am drawn to reflect back to 1987, as I waited anxiously for the public's response to this, my first literary "child." The immediate outpouring of acceptance from both parents and educators both astonished and gratified me, and I remain increasingly grateful to all those who continue to support the book and tell me stories about how it has helped them. So, thanks first to all the dedicated parents and teachers who regularly confirm my faith that most adults truly care about kids and want to learn more about how to educate them in positive and appropriate ways.

I am boundlessly grateful to the innumerable colleagues who have contributed to the book's success and my continuing education over the years. A lot of wonderful people working in this field have taught and encouraged me, and provided important "wake-up calls" to keep the message on target. Many have taken the time to answer questions—and forced me to ask new ones.

During these years of teaching and lecturing around the world, my greatest reward has been in human terms: new friends everywhere, parents from all walks of life who have said, "Thank you for helping me trust my own judgment," and teachers who told me that "bringing the brain to school" made a difference—for them and for their students. Now, adult former students also reassure me that brain-appropriate teaching methods really do make a difference. Every week parents and children provide the real impetus for my work by bringing to life the implications of the research.

For this third edition, I again thank my agent, Angela Miller, for continuing to nudge my motivation and organize its fruition. Trish Medved, my editor, energized the project even while producing another "growing mind" by becoming a new mom while the manuscript was being completed! Beth Datlowe was invariably responsive and helpful. The staff at the Vail Public Library once more proved an invaluable resource. I remain grateful to friends for putting up with the vagaries of a writer in process and not rhapsodizing too much about the ski runs or hikes they took while I sat at the word processor.

My family, always supportive, now includes a new generation. My most loving thanks to Nicholas, Katherine, Andrew, Nathaniel, Emma, and Sarah Jane for delighting, amusing, reenergizing, and keeping their grandmother up to date with the stages, needs, and joys of childhood. My children, who agreeably consented to appear in the book when it was first written, are now invaluable as informants on the challenges of parenthood in the twenty-first century. "Mano Mac," my mother, who was so proud of the book, is no longer with us, but her spirit is on every page.

I am superfortunate as well to have Tom, my husband of forty-six years, who is my steady bulwark, sounding board, soul mate, and the best friend I could ever have.

Thank you all.

Contents

Part Three
Learning Applied

Figures

Preface

I am delighted to present this third edition of *Your Child's Growing Mind*, with its expanded content, updated research, and a sparkling new face. When I initially wrote this book back in the mid-eighties, no one knew much or had thought very deeply about how brain research might be applied in education, and certainly not to the dilemmas of parenting. Since then, of course, research in all these fields has taken off. The natural result, a deluge of information, is a wonderfully positive development—positive, that is, if the facts are appropriately and accurately applied. As with any newly "trendy" field, interpretations of research in neuroscience and educational psychology are easily caught on the thorns of oversimplification and misapplication.

I have tried here to explain what is accurate in terms of the research and to stick to common sense and proven educational and parenting practice. Inasmuch as I have been a professional educator (and parent!) for more years than it is prudent to admit, I find it quite thrilling to survey the quality and usefulness of what is now available. We have indeed made a lot of progress since the incident that first got me started.

This book originated in a college classroom one gloomy afternoon in 1955 when a psychology professor lost his patience with me. "Jane, for heaven's sake, stop asking questions about children's brains," he exclaimed. "We can't see them, we can't measure them, and for all we know they don't have that much to do with learning anyway!"

I'm glad I didn't take his advice. I've kept asking questions during many years of studying, teaching, and being a mother and now grandmother to little and not-so-little growing brains. My well-intentioned professor was dead wrong. Understanding a child's brain and the way it develops is the key to understanding learning.

For this third edition I have revised and expanded many topics, and added some more. You will find useful current information on attention, reading development, infancy, brain "stimulation" at different ages, stages of brain growth, new definitions of intelligence, creativity, learning differences, and learning disabilities. As always, each is awash with practical suggestions that you can use today at home or in the classroom.

The landscape of childhood is changing almost as fast as are the methods for scanning and measuring the learning brain. More and more children are "out of sync" with school, with attention, with motivation, and with the quiet corners of their own minds. New drugs that affect brain chemistry are now routinely prescribed for children, so I have included new information about the neurochemicals that power learning and personal development, while reemphasizing specific ways in which the home environment can make a positive difference. Likewise, increasing exposure of children and teens to different types of electronic media demand practical approaches. You will receive advice from experts about managing TV, computer time, and video games along with an introduction to helping your children become "media literate."

One thing never changes: Parents want desperately to do a good job, and they struggle to draw the line between too much and too little stimulation, between what is developmentally appropriate and inappropriate. I hope this book helps you respond positively and confidently to the confusing demands of our fast-paced and achievement-oriented world.

No matter how elaborate the technology, our children still desperately need our human presence: as parents and teachers, loving models and mentors. While the human brain is sufficiently "plastic" to accommodate a considerable amount of parental bungling (thank good-ness!), it has its own curriculum of "basics" that must be available at each stage of development. Probably the most important of these is rooted in the needs of the "emotional brain." The newest news in the neurosciences is really the oldest: intellectual and emotional develop-ment are inseparable—as the old song says, "You can't have one with-out the other." The simple fact is that children crave their parents' love and attention far more than anything else. When given the choice of time with parents vs. the most delectable treats, desirable toys, or ex-citing experiences, guess what they overwhelmingly choose. You! If I have done my job here, you will emerge from this book with a better idea of how to meet these needs—and enhance your family's mental ca-pacity at the same time.

In this book you will find stories about many real parents and children, although names and identifying details have been changed. I hope these experiences help you, as they have helped me, to unravel some of the wonderful mysteries of your own child's—or your stu-dent's—mind. If your time is limited, choose the chapters most help-ful to you. For a full tour, however, I recommend you learn the inside story of the growth of intelligence—from the beginning.

Part One

Brain

Development

and

Learning

Chapter 1

Opening the "Black Box"

One evening some years ago, I received a call from a young teacher whom I hadn't seen since she had left school on maternity leave. We had often talked about her hopes and plans for the baby, but tonight she sounded worried.

"Jane, I'm sorry to call you at home, but I just have to ask for some advice about Tony. He seems very advanced, and I'm doing all the things we talked about—playing with him, talking to him, reading to him—but this neighbor of mine has just signed up for a course that advertises ways to raise her child's IQ by increasing his brain development. Should I be doing more? Can parents really help build their kids' brains?"

Amy's call didn't surprise me, since over the years I have gotten the same question in many forms. The pressure on parents becomes more intense all the time. They come to my office wanting to do a "perfect" job despite the constraints of busy schedules, but they are confused by conflicting theories about child development and by omnipresent advertising for products that claim to make children smarter sooner. Confusion and guilt are inevitable: Am I doing enough? How much and what kind of enrichment does a preschooler need? What is the best way to teach reading and math—and what if my child is having difficulty? Should parents help with schoolwork? Can creativity be developed? How can we act as a child's advocate if school personnel aren't attuned to individual needs? What, really, is "attention deficit disorder"? How can we make kids more motivated? What about the child who doesn't "fit the mold"?

These questions have never been easy ones, but now the science of developmental neuropsychology, integrating brain research with children's behavior and learning, offers some answers. We know more about learning, individual differences in abilities, and emotional development than we did even five years ago. Although no two human brains are alike and no one set of answers is right for every child, new information can help teachers do a better job and assist parents in making wise decisions—while confirming the innate wisdom of their own best instincts. An incident much earlier in my career makes me realize just how far we have come.

I met nine-year-old Aaron when he tripped over me as he was entering his science class. As a visiting consultant, I was trying to be invisible, and apparently I had succeeded as far as Aaron was concerned. I began to suspect that this waifish-looking little fellow had a problem when he next bumped into the doorway, scattering a mass of smudged work sheets whose mangled manuscript letters would be an embarrassment to most six-year-olds and which bore the indelible marks of teacher rejection: "Messy!" "F." Ignoring my mission to evaluate the science curriculum, I watched him struggle to organize himself around a desk, dropping his pencil and fumbling through a tattered folder for misplaced homework. A discussion of space exploration immediately attracted his attention, and his skinny arm gyrated in the air, once more knocking his pencil, unnoticed, from the desk. Recognized at last by the teacher, he delivered a stunning exposition of rocket trajectories, fuel needs, and relative astral distances.

I couldn't resist asking the principal about Aaron. "Has he ever had a neurodevelopmental evaluation? It sure looks as if something is misfiring when he tries to translate his good ideas into action."

"Oh, no," he said. "Poor kid has an emotional problem. He's being treated by a psychiatrist. Believe it or not, he still wets his bed! His mother rejected him emotionally when he was born, and he's always had difficulty with schoolwork even though we can tell he's smart."

"Well, you might consider looking further," I ventured. I was quite sure Aaron had some problems that predated the emotional ones, but I was there to evaluate curriculum, not to do diagnosis.

Six months later I received a note in the mail from a woman who identified herself as Aaron's mother. "Thanks to your intervention," she said ("intervention," indeed!), "we took Aaron to a clinic and found that he has had a problem since birth in one of the important lower brain centers." Since the area she described is part of a system responsible for voluntary control of motor movements such as writing, avoiding bumping into people and doorways, and yes, even bladder control, it is not surprising that Aaron was having problems despite an IQ in the superior range. "Now we understand that he isn't lazy or stupid, and he will get special help with this problem," she went on to say. "If you only knew the guilt and the anguish we have been through, you would understand why I am so grateful."

I keep that note, not only because it is the only effortless success story of my career, but also because it is a perfect example of the "black box" view of the brain that prevailed for so long: "If we can't see inside, we'll ignore it." "Emotional problems" became the handiest scapegoat whenever things weren't going well. The unfortunate result became a "blame game" in which the parents, school, and even the child were accused of responsibility for problems in learning. We have come a long way, but the "blame game" is still around—for parents, for children with learning differences, for some whose environments shortchanged them early in life, and too often for educators who can't force unprepared or unready neural systems to mature on a set timetable.

LOOKING INSIDE

Various forms of brain research have been conducted for centuries, but the field has experienced an avalanche of new information since the development of electronic methods of observing and measuring brain activity. Harmless ways of looking directly at the brain in action help teach us about why learning happens—or fails to. The major methods of looking inside utilize either caps of electrodes or computerized scanners. Mapping the brain's electrical activity shows how actively and how quickly brain areas respond to a stimulus; different kinds of scanners display the structure of the brain or the way it functions during normal activities, such as reading or working mental problems. Because these technologies are still difficult to use in real-life situations (in a scanner, for example, the child must lie still for an extended period of time), their findings are combined with behavioral observation and good educational and developmental research to get a bigger picture.

From another angle, work with "artificial intelligence" has also sparked research on how the human brain functions, giving scientists new respect for the capabilities and complexity of even a toddler's brain as they try—and fail—to duplicate human learning abilities, such as building a block tower. Computer brains are terribly good at some things, but terribly bad at others—such as creativity, understanding the nuances of language, or practical problem-solving. Nor can they compete with human caregivers in providing "scaffolds" for a child's social, emotional, and cognitive growth.

The purpose of this book is to bring you up to date by explaining what science has discovered and how we can apply it in real-life situations at home or school. I will be drawing on research in a wide variety of fields and on a background of professional and personal experience. I hope you will also feel empowered to use your own common sense! In this chapter we will introduce two major questions central to the book: Where does brainpower come from, and what can we do about it? The following chapters will apply this basic information to different age groups and to specific aspects of personal development, learning fundamentals, and academic achievement.

BRAINPOWER: UNDERSTANDING THE BASICS
Overview: Brain Structure vs. Function

Frank Lloyd Wright, the famous architect, is said to have used the phrase "form follows function" to make the point that the way a structure is to be used should determine the way it gets shaped. This principle definitely holds true for the human brain. The way your children—or students—use their brains will help determine the shape and power of neural connections.

The basic structure of the brain—its architecture—is composed mainly of cells called neurons and their supporting cells. Its function, on the other hand, is a dynamic process that involves the way these neurons communicate through electrical and chemical signaling. As relays between cells are repeatedly made, they create complex physical networks of connections—which in turn become part of the structure of the brain. In this sense the brain is "plastic," literally shaping itself according to what it responds to.

Where Does It Come From?: Heredity and Environment

"I'm not surprised that Sally is having trouble with math." Her mother, Mrs. Strang, was apologetic. "I was hopeless in math even though I was a good student otherwise." Sally, now a fifth grader who had just won the school spelling contest, was struggling mightily with her math assignments, particularly those involving "story" problems, charts and graphs, and geometric forms. We decided to ask Sally's math teacher to work individually with her after school, and her mother agreed that they would practice together at home with some materials designed to improve concepts of space relationships. As Mrs. Strang left my office, I noticed that she first turned in the wrong direction before she started down the hall, and I recalled a much earlier conversation in which she confided that she didn't let Sally climb trees for fear she would hurt herself.

Did Sally inherit her math problem? Did she pick it up from poor teaching? Can we blame it on a lack of experience with physical and space relationships in her early years? How about her best friend, Megan, who started to read and calculate when she was three and gets straight As with very little effort? Was she born smart or did her parents do something right? Should we switch the "blame game" to parental genes?

Does heredity ("nature") or environment ("nurture") play the major role in development? There is such a constant interaction between basic capacity and experience from the moment of a baby's conception that the question is impossible—and really unnecessary—to answer. Every child inherits a physical brain structure and a timetable for development as well as chemical and electrical response patterns that strongly influence its functioning. A child's personal tempo—the natural pace of responding and the speed of carrying out activities—also seems to be genetically determined.

Other inherited dimensions of personality have their roots in the brain, such as introversion or extroversion. Some children are shyer, while others are more outgoing and people-oriented from the beginning, behaviors that reflect activation in opposite sides of the brain in new or challenging situations. An easy or difficult disposition related to the balances of brain chemicals may also come with the package. The tendency to act impulsively, linked to the function of a specific area of the front part of the brain, seems to be present in some families, although you will learn later how envioments affect this behavioral style. Family patterns for the timetable of physical and intellectual development make some children pass through the stages of growth more quickly than others, although more rapid maturation does not necessarily predict a better final outcome.

Certain constellations of abilities, such as music, engineering, or literary talent, seem to cluster in some families; there are also some types of learning problems, such as developmental dyslexia, which are hereditary and involve specific differences in brain structure and function. Nevertheless, in the case of dyslexia, the language environment at home and the type of reading instruction a child gets can determine the severity of the problem and even how the brain functions during reading.

Studies of identical twins, who have identical genes, have also demonstrated the inherited stability of some aspects of intelligence even when the twins are raised separately. Since many different genes are involved in intellectual ability, it is not easy to pin down this complex phenomenon. Some severe psychological problems, such as depression or schizophrenia, also have a genetic component (both structural and biochemical differences have been found in these brains), although identical twins often differ in whether they become schizophrenic, suggesting involvement of environmental factors as well.

A Two-Way Street

The child's personality and response style also help determine the way he gets treated by those around him. Some children are just plain "difficult," and some are harder for parents to relate to because they are temperamentally very different from the rest of the family. Naturally, their behavior increases the stress, and thus affects the response, of the adults in their life. No doubt Aaron was one of these youngsters. Understanding the problem enables us to help such children while making the parent's role an easier one.

What accounts for Sally's math problem? Undoubtedly a combination of factors. Rather than trying to pin responsibility on genes or early experiences, our job is to appreciate her particular way of learning and provide new experiences to enhance it. In short, neuropsychologists tell us that the human brain comes into the world programmed for certain aspects of learning and behavior, but many of these are susceptible to alteration.

Now, as a prelude to understanding what we can do about helping children develop their own brainpower, let us turn to some basic ideas about how the brain is structured, how it functions and grows, and how it directs learning.

THE DEVELOPING BRAIN
A Tough Start

One of my most poignant recent experiences involved kids who experienced a really tough start in life. I was invited to present a workshop at a conference hosted by an international group of parents of adopted Romanian orphans. The plight of these youngsters has been well-publicized, as it is one of the most appalling examples of child neglect and abuse ever uncovered. Committed to grossly understaffed orphanages by desperately poor parents, these children were fed gruel out of bottles and confined in cribs—sometimes for years. Many lacked even minimal interaction with adults or peers, physical or emotional stimulation, language, toys, or any of the other necessities we normally take for granted.

These cases have provided a tragic study in the developmental consequences of early deprivation. Indeed, depending on the age of adoption and the child's condition at that time, it appears that some aspects of brain functioning may have been compromised beyond recovery. On the other hand, as I made my way to conference sessions through a playful and energetic bunch of kids and parents, I was astonished at the amount of recovery that had obviously taken place. The parents I met, as a group, were singularly devoted to these children; many had provided countless hours and varieties of expert remediation—in some cases starting almost from scratch. Most important, of course, they had also provided vast quantities of love and emotional support—a most inspiring group of people!

I was particularly struck by the parents' reports that, although many of the children were struggling with various types of learning problems, many had overcome major cognitive obstacles. The main barrier to "catch-up" was in the social and emotional realm—particularly the ability to relate effectively with loved ones or friends. Whether or not some of these youngsters will ever be able to overcome that handicap is an unanswered question, since there are "critical periods" early in life for such basic emotional and personal qualities. The good news is that many of these children were still making progress, even after a neural window of opportunity was presumably closed.

One moral here is that we tend to underestimate the awesome possibilities in the human brain, and we should never give up on any child. Another—which is daily confirmed by research—is that meeting a child's needs for nurturing by a loving and dependable caregiver is even more critical than trying to develop intellectual skills. So let's begin our tour of the developing brain with the "nonthinking" areas that undergird the "thinking brain" and may even be able to switch it on and off for learning.

A Lizard Underneath

Recently I heard two preschool teachers discussing a problem that arose when several children established a pecking order for use of the jungle gym and began to "fight invaders." One teacher remarked, "I bet their little reptilian brains are at work here. They're not purposely being mean, but we'd better teach them some civilized ways of managing territory!"

Rather than insulting her students, this teacher was referring to the pioneering work of Dr. Paul MacLean, who gave us a lasting metaphor for understanding both the brain's structure and some of our own more "primitive" characteristics. Although current research has expanded and complexified MacLean's model, I still find it useful for explaining how lower centers and thinking centers interact.

MacLean's "triune brain" model posited three different brains interacting within one: a reptilian, a mammalian, and a human brain. The latter, the cerebral cortex, is the "thinking" brain, the one we hear most about, but the others are constantly on duty. The so-called "reptilian brain," or "R-complex," lies at the base of the brain and of behavior. It produces such instinctive behaviors as foraging for food, grooming, establishing territory, and forming social groups. Deep below the level of consciousness, these tendencies can be hard to change.

Perhaps some of the annoying "habits" of children, such as forming cliques, fighting, imitating peers, or even biting fingernails when under stress emanate from these lower brain centers. Although the topmost,

THREE BRAINS IN ONE

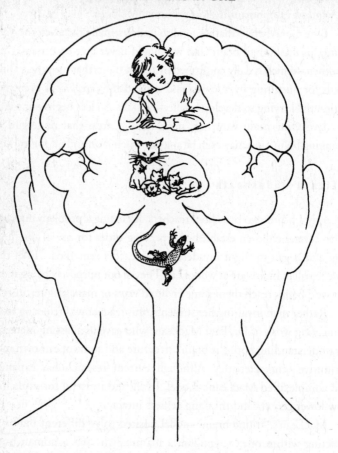

human layer of the brain may find its reptilian neighbor unreasonable at times, anyone who has tried to talk a child out of a seemingly instinctive habit realizes that MacLean may have a point. As an eighth grade teacher, I learned the hard way that my students' self-grooming rituals usually took precedence over use of their higher thinking centers. And I won't mention adults' behavior at social gatherings. . . .

Current research shows that this "R-complex" is linked in ascending and descending loops of connections that extend even to the highest control centers of the cortex. Lower, reflexive brain centers operate to keep us safe; if a child feels seriously threatened, this network may block messages to higher-level centers and respond irrationally; at this point, reasoning usually doesn't work. A firm, calming hand and some quiet time to feel safe once again may help get the cortex back in control.

I recently saw some truly "primitive" behavior at the corner of 73rd and Broadway in New York City. A three-year-old was lying on the sidewalk having the mother of all temper tantrums while his helpless mom stood over him, employing a series of logical arguments as to why he couldn't have any more candy and why he should get back into his stroller.

Meanwhile, totally out of control, the child simply screamed and kicked harder. Now I am a grandmother who prefers to pass screaming children back to their parents, so I restrained my urge to gently but firmly pick him up, give him a big hug, replace him in the stroller, and start moving. I also try to refrain from giving unsolicited advice to strangers, but mom should know that while it is good policy to use words to explain things to children and offer them reasonable choices, we can't expect them to respond to adult reasoning when their lower brain centers are in control. Young children are still very much at the mercy of nonthinking parts of their brains, and they simply cannot muster the intellectual controls that we expect of adults.

Older children, too, can find themselves emotionally out of control when they feel that their own interests or even safety are threatened. My experience suggests that times of rapid neurological change—such as early adolescence—puts them particularly at risk for reptilian-type reactions. (See chapter 5 for guidelines for this age level.) While older youngsters have already developed some feedback loops to put the cortex in charge of irrational behavior, even adults sometimes fall prey to these "lower" brain urges ("Give me chocolate!") and have trouble with rational controls. (Actually, a craving for chocolate may stem from neurotransmitter imbalances, which do affect all levels of brain function, so when I sneak a candy bar I simply imagine that I am enhancing my serotonin levels!) Fortunately, the adult brain has many more control circuits going down than impulsive ones going up, but these take a long time to develop.

At any age, if you want your child to be an effective learner, put the fundamental needs for a safe environment, a sense of having choices, and reasonable limits at the top of your list of priorities. And don't forget the calming effect of hugs, music, exercise, or a friendly hand on the shoulder.

The Mammal's Hidden Agenda

The next level up, MacLean's "mammalian brain," corresponds to the so-called limbic system, also referred to as the "emotional brain." This important collection of organs, lying beneath the thinking brain and below the level of consciousness, participates as well in attention, motivation, and some aspects of memory. It, too, operates in loops with higher and lower centers. The bottom line: emotions are integrally involved with all but the most rote-level learning. Educators can apply this research by getting students personally and actively involved. For example, interesting but intellectually challenging projects—movement, color, music, and other expressive forms—enhance higher-level learning. At all ages, a positive emotional climate, which encourages the student to express feelings and make choices, also helps. In fact, schools' neglect of these needs may account for many problems in "motivation," to be discussed in more detail in chapter 8.

One little gadget in the limbic system, the amygdala, filters incoming experience through a lens of past associations with fear or major stress. Profound negative associations trigger signals of avoidance throughout the brain and body. An example might be a child who is a poor reader repeatedly humiliated in class; subsequently in similar situations, the amygdala sends danger signals to other brain centers, which respond by putting out stress hormones. This reaction can become a vicious cycle that keeps the child from being able to use what he does know. As a learning therapist who works with kids who have had lots of stressful learning experiences, I can guarantee that it takes time and patience to undo these negative connections.

The brain can be physically altered in other ways by chronic emotions. Another limbic structure, the hippocampus, which underlies factual memory, is actually reduced in size by chronic high-level stress.

This does NOT mean, however, that children shouldn't experience "good stress," which enhances learning. Challenge without excess threat is the secret—the positive feeling of tackling a manageable difficulty with the promise of success. This kind of learning energizes the cortex and helps establish memory. Trying to make learning too much easy "fun" robs it of both challenge and joy.

Neurochemicals for Learning

Subcortical areas are continually at work regulating chemical transmitters—generally referred to as neurotransmitters, peptides, or neurohormones—that enable brain cells to communicate with each other and thus direct much of the functioning of the brain. This field is currently one of the liveliest in brain research, as differences in the effectiveness with which each individual's brain creates and uses neurotransmitters account for major shifts in physical, emotional, and intellectual well-being. Insufficient uptake of serotonin by brain cells, for example, is linked to depression; current medications for this condition work by enabling cells to utilize serotonin more effectively. Likewise, some forms of dopamine and other members of the catecholamine family, such as norepinephrine, are associated with risk-taking behaviors and attention deficit disorders, among other things. The mechanism by which this relationship operates is still unclear, but you will find more about attention disorders in chapter 4.

Also unclear is the role of heredity or environment in establishing one's neurochemical balance. Without doubt, your genes account for a great deal, but environmental factors such as nutrition, physical activity, sleep patterns, and emotional state also play a role. The brain may even be able to reset its chemical habits according to experience—especially if it comes during a critical period of development. Alarmingly, some research has indicated that severe early emotional deprivation or abuse may permanently alter the brain's ability to use serotonin for feelings of well-being, sociability, and emotional stability. Since a part of the higher-level cortex (orbitofrontal cortex) that is intricately linked to limbic structures is in a rapid growth phase between eight months and three years, abuse or lack of appropriate face-to-face human interaction at this time may impair a child's long-term ability to relate positively to others. This finding may account for some of the issues found in the Romanian orphans. Likewise, the fact that infants of depressed mothers exhibit a depressed pattern of brain function may indicate that genes and experience are already interacting to set the child up for problems. On the other hand, surging neurotransmitters probably account for the mental "high" that sometimes comes with strenuous exercise, perhaps explaining why teachers have observed elementary students' reading scores rising right after an active play period.

One stunning finding is that the same brain chemicals operate on the heart, stomach, and other body organs. In other words, says Dr. Candace Pert, "When you're teaching a child's brain, you're also teaching her spleen!" The enormous implication here is that education must be a total process, considering all of a student's needs, not just aiming at the intellect. When choosing a school, look for one that is humane and healthy as well as academically minded.

Best for the Brain—at Any Age

To me, this research, although still in its infancy, confirms the value of what we all know is best for children and teens: emotional stability, good nutrition (at least as good as you can persuade them to consume!), plenty of time for play and exercise, attention to sleep schedules, and choice and responsibility within a reassuring daily structure. It also suggests pretty strongly that beating children over the heads with academic "standards" while neglecting more basic needs (such as breakfast, recess, or even art and music) may have very unfortunate long-term consequences.

Building Neural Highways: The Cerebral Cortex

Often referred to as the neocortex, or simply the cortex, the "thinking brain" is composed of six layers of nerve cells (neurons) and supporting glial cells that form a blanket ("gray matter") over the lower areas. The brain's surface area is so large that it must actually fold in upon itself. If your cortex were laid out flat, it would cover an average-sized desk! At birth it is like an untracked plain, but it is already building complex neural highway systems as messages are transmitted from cell to cell. Because the quality of these message systems depends heavily on environmental input, they provide a map for parents to help their children develop strong mental equipment for learning—without pushing.

The geography of thinking does not develop automatically. At birth the brain contains hundreds of billions of nerve cells, but these neurons must become organized into systems for perceiving, thinking, talking, and remembering. The first two years are a period of dynamic change for the cortex.

Amazingly, although the number of cells actually decreases, brain weight can double during the first year of life. How? As neurons respond to stimuli seen, heard, felt, or tasted, they fire off messages that build new physical connections to neighboring cells, linking them into efficient relay systems.

Once neurons form, they must compete to make connections. Each neuron is equipped with a treelike structure of hairlike receptors called dendrites, and a projecting axon, which may vary from a few millimeters to as much as a yard in length. At birth the dendrite spines are sparse and undeveloped, much like the branches of a young tree. During the first six months after birth they become extremely active as sensory messages bombard the infant brain, which must learn to receive them and then pass them from one area to another. Each neuron in a message system picks up signals with its dendrites from the axons of neighboring neurons. It projects this electrical "action potential" down the axon and over

THE DEVELOPING NEURON:
WHERE LEARNING BEGINS

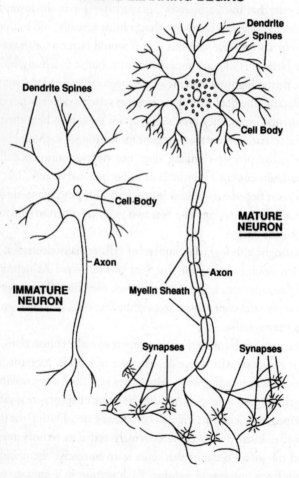

a gap, called a synapse, where the neurotransmitters do their work to complete the connection. Synaptic connections are strengthened by repeated use; if they fail to connect, they die off.

During the first three years, while the brain is constructing this mental infrastructure, it uses an enormous amount of energy—approximately twice the amount used by an adult. If your child is sometimes inconsistent, difficult to reason with, negative, or just plain cussed, it may be partially because her brain is truly experiencing a typhoon of development—and things may seem pretty confusing to her. Those of us with adult brains need to be sympathetic, firm, and as patient as we can. Similar spurts in neural development occur at other times, including early adolescence. Recommendations for appropriate brain-building activities at every age are contained in the following chapters.

Help! My Child Is Losing Brain Cells

It seems logical to believe that the more synapses we have, the better our brains will work. Actually, the human brain has the potential to adapt itself to multiple needs; it develops skill and efficiency by clearing away ("pruning") the dead wood and strengthening those connections needed by that particular child in that particular environment. In fact, some studies of children with autism or retardation suggest that their brains may be overly cluttered with excessive synapses; for some reason these brains did not "prune" themselves effectively.

Cells that are stimulated by picking up and relaying messages become stronger. Dendrite spines are strengthened until each sapling has become a complex, heavily branched tree. This "arborization" of dendrites is one of the main ways in which the brain grows during childhood and adolescence. Parents and grandparents should be encouraged by new research indicating that older adults who keep their brains active and challenged will continue to grow dendrite projections throughout life. Nonetheless, childhood is the period of most dynamic change and the time when the brain is most plastic.

What makes synapses and neural networks form? Active interest and mental effort *by the child* are major factors. Every response to sights, sounds, feelings, smells, and tastes makes more connections. Like a pathway through a forest, the neural traces are at first faint, then, with successive trips, the trail becomes more distinct and easier to traverse. The more exercise the system does, the more automatic and expert it becomes.

Each child weaves his own intellectual tapestry, the quality of which depends on active interest and involvement in a wide variety of stimuli. The home environment provides the raw material for this masterpiece.

"Readiness" and the Brain

The brain's functioning is so complex that multiple areas and systems of neural connections must work together for any task. For example, brain scans of adults doing related language activities—listening, reading out loud, reading silently, and thinking up words—show activity scattered all over the brain, depending on the activity. If a child's brain is not prepared—either by maturation or experience—to function in this complex manner, learning may be difficult and frustrating. This gets us to the important idea of "readiness" for learning.

The brain's readiness to learn anything quickly, efficiently, and enjoyably appears to be predicated partially on the density of synapse formation in the relevant systems and partially on a process called myelination. Myelin is an insulating fatty substance that develops in the brain from before birth until age twenty or thirty. It gradually coats message-sending axons to help them transmit messages more quickly. Before a system is myelinated, messages are likely to travel erratically and may get lost in the shuffle of competing connections. Likewise, in some brain diseases such as multiple sclerosis, myelin is destroyed, interrupting transmission of messages over motor neurons that control movement.

The order of myelination is mainly set by nature, although nutritional factors may influence the amount of myelin laid down. Some speculate that essential fatty acids, particularly those present first in breast milk and then in a healthy diet, are part of this picture, but much is still unknown about this important question. It does not appear to be possible to speed up myelination, although a wide range of physical and mental challenges may pave the way.

Overall, myelin formation starts at the top of the spine and moves up to higher, more complex brain structures at the same time it is progressing down the spinal cord. For example, when the baby is born, structures in the lowest brain centers that are needed for reflexive sucking are well developed, but those for walking, talking, or bladder control are still not myelinated. Common sense tells us that it is useless to try and get a newborn to walk alone, but at about one year, when those connections have matured, it may be difficult to prevent.

"We Had Just about Given Up—and Suddenly He Just Took Off!"

The cycles of myelin formation coincide with the child's mastery of increasingly complex learning throughout the school years and early adulthood. I have worked with many families who struggled for years with a "problem" child who suddenly "got it together," even in his mid-twenties or later. Eventually the efforts pay off when the brain is ready—on its own schedule.

A fine line exists between appropriate support and excess pressure. Although we can certainly stimulate development of cell networks when they are ready, many aspects of this growth cannot be rushed. It is possible to force skills by intensive instruction, but this may cause the child to use immature, inappropriate neural networks and distort the natural growth process. Trying to speed learning over unfinished neuron systems might be akin to racing a limousine over a narrow path in the woods. You can do it, but neither the car nor the path ends up in very good shape! Moreover, the pressure that surrounds such learning situations may leave permanent emotional debris. There is an order in which learning is programmed to take place; while it can be encouraged, it need not be forced. We will take a closer look at solid early foundations for higher-level skills and the issue of school "readiness" in chapter 4.

Since we don't know yet—if we ever will—how to speed up physiological readiness, the best advice is to concentrate on what we do know how to do: provide an array of interesting, curiosity-stimulating objects and experiences, be available to provide a "scaffold" to challenge new learning, and let the growing brain take what it needs. I have seen too many kids who have turned off, tuned out, and even been labeled "learning disabled" because important learning came at the wrong time and in the wrong way.

Recently I met a young mother who was feeling frustrated because her three-year-old daughter had stopped asking for the word cards that had been a part of her life since infancy. "She was reading so well," lamented Mom. "We had just done 'stamen,' 'pistil,' 'filament,' and 'petal' when suddenly she turned off." I resisted my impulse to ask why a three-year-old is reading about flowers when she should be learning about them firsthand, and suggested she have patience. A week later I saw her again and inquired if things had gotten better. "Well, sort of," Mother replied. "Yesterday she finally asked for some new words, but the only ones she wanted were 'poo-poo' and 'yuck.'" Perhaps the limbic reptilian brain has some wisdom after all!

MAPPING THE ORDER OF DEVELOPMENT
The Infrastructure of Intelligence

A better alternative to forcing pieces of adult learning on a system that can't yet integrate or organize them is to follow the natural pattern of brain development—from inside to outside and from back to front. Starting at the top of the spinal cord, the fetal brain first develops brain stem structures for reflexes and basic motor coordination. These important foundations enable us, for example, to hold our bodies upright, stay alert, and execute physical movements such as crawling.

Sensory Experience and Movement Build Brains

Many organs and systems comprise the infrastructure of the "thinking brain" and help illustrate just a bit of its vast complexity. A large organ called the thalamus receives input from the senses and directs it to the appropriate parts of the cortex. The reticular activating system directs consciousness, serving as a sort of gatekeeper to alert the brain, through relays in the limbic system, when it needs to pay attention. Other ascending and descending pathways comprise the basal ganglia, which help direct motor behavior and attention. Although these systems originate beneath the cortex, they are intricately connected to it. As the child matures, she perfects the ability to use these pathways to send messages from the cortex to lower brain areas, for example to voluntarily refocus attention on what the teacher is saying rather than on the kids playing outside the window. In chapter 4 you will find specific suggestions about increasing attentional abilities as your child grows.

Movement, particularly stimulation by rocking, spinning, or hanging upside down, helps develop a large and important area behind the brain stem: the cerebellum, which connects the vestibular system that is linked to the balance mechanisms in the inner ear. The cerebellum also interacts with higher, frontal levels in the brain for cognitive skills such as language, social interaction, music, the ability to perform repetitive activities automatically (e.g., handwriting), and perhaps attention.

During fetal life the infant is rocked as the mother moves about, and its self-initiated gyrations add to the stimulation. The cerebellum has a large growth spurt in the first two years, but continues to grow and change even into adolescence. The fact that most kids love to spin and hang by their knees—and most adults don't—is one more evidence that the brain tends to seek out the activities that it needs at different periods of development. Don't let that hypnotic screen of the TV or computer seduce them from these natural and important types of activities. Real "smarts" start from the bottom and work up—not from some programmer's idea of what needs to be pushed in from the top!

After birth, physical activities are one of the child's main means of advancing physical, intellectual, and emotional growth, so you should encourage many forms of body movement. Most infants and toddlers respond happily to physical stimulation, and you can boost brain integration as you and your child play with rhythms and melody, dance together to music, crawl through tunnels, balance on boards, or climb on playground equipment. "Sensory integration therapy," which expertly uses such activities to rewire circuitry that failed to develop during the earliest years, may help some children who are poorly coordinated, "clumsy," "scattered," or socially inept.

Good elementary schools incorporate lots of hands-on, active learning. Even middle and high school students can profit from physical experience and movement that enhance learning. Hands-on projects, arts experiences, and sports remain important at all grade levels.

CRITICAL PERIODS: A BIZARRE STORY

One important concept in developmental research is that of "critical" or "sensitive" periods. These are times when the brain is in an active period of growth and change. At these times, skills may need a certain degree of stimulation in order to develop fully. You might think of it as a window of opportunity when skill practice or teaching will be most effective.

One of the classic illustrations of sensory deprivation during a critical period for language is the case of Genie, an initially normal girl who was kept locked in a tiny room by her psychotic parents from the ages of twenty months to thirteen years. Rather than conversation, Genie was "barked" at by her father, who punished her severely if she attempted to make noise. Because she had missed all language stimulation during the years before adolescence, a period critical for many aspects of language development, including grammar or syntax, Genie became a source of great professional interest as well as compassion when she was finally discovered and hospitalized. She developed some vocabulary after intensive teaching, but has never been able to form normal grammatical sentences; her "language" is directed from parts of her brain that would not ordinarily be involved.

Stories like this are scary and make us wonder what we may be missing out on that will leave our children with permanent "holes" in skill development. Yet Genie's case is extreme, and critical periods in human development generally allow us some leeway; only the most fundamental emotional, social, sensory, and language skills—which are almost sure to be stimulated by any sort of natural environment—seem to have a strictly closing window of opportunity. In the ensuing chapters you will learn more about applying the notion of sensitive periods to positive development of sensory skills, language, second language learning, attention, and motivation.

Until we learn more, it makes sense to give your child plenty of human interaction and a rich sensory and language environment without bombarding that sensitive brain. Someday we may be able to chart the timetable of neuronal maturation and plan a program for each child. In the meanwhile it is heartening to consider how much the human brain can reroute itself around difficulties.

THE PLASTIC BRAIN
Neurons Need Connections

As raw material for thinking and learning, nature cleverly equips the infant's brain with an excess of neurons. At birth, much cortical tissue is uncommitted, "plastic" in its ability to develop. Even while the brain grows rapidly during the first two years of life, extra neurons are dying off as cells compete to make connections. When an activity is carried out, the brain stimulates itself to repeat the neural relays involved. Thus, lopsided development may result if some groups of neurons are stimulated at the expense of others.

One of the most well-researched examples of this job redistribution occurs in the brains of people who are born deaf. Because their auditory brain systems are never stimulated by sounds, some of these cells reroute their extensions into other parts of the brain, such as the visual system. By the time these people are adults, scans of their brains show that when they see a flash of light, they respond with parts of the brain normally used for hearing as well as with those originally intended for seeing. Another dramatic evidence of "neuroplasticity" comes from the long-term study of children who had an entire half of their brain re-moved because they had intractable epileptic seizures. To everyone's amazement, such children develop the functions normally served by both sides, although competence in each may be diminished.

On a lighter note, one study of London cabbies' brains showed ex-traordinary development in an area associated with navigation and spa-tial memory. It came, however, at the cost of a little shrinkage in some other areas.

While some functions—such as basic sensory skills—are served only by specific groups of cells in the brain, higher thinking processes require interacting systems that can be somewhat rearranged. The prognosis for bypassing damage to early "hard-wired" areas, such as in the motor difficulties associated with cerebral palsy, is not so optimistic as that for later-developing skills.

The brain's plasticity is at a height in the newborn, but even adult stroke victims can develop new connections to bypass damaged areas. Since some degree of plasticity extends even into old age, there is hope for all of us!

We have indeed come a long way in penetrating the "black box," but many myseries remain. Brain theories change, as do the environ-ments of childhood, but the basic necessity of love and caring between adults and children do not. The brain has its own timetable and built-in wisdom.

The next chapter begins our exploration of the ways in which this dynamic process takes place, and how parents and teachers can help develop each child's unique pattern of abilities.

Chapter 2

Intelligent Beginnings: Laying the Groundwork in Infancy and Beyond

In a well-loved children's book, Dr. Doolittle encounters the pushmi-pullyu, a remarkable creature that is a metaphor for indecision. With a head at either end of its body, it has trouble deciding which way to move. Many parents today feel caught on a similar beast as they receive conflicting advice about developing their child's intellectual skills. When should they push, and when should they pull—or should they back off and let mental growth proceed naturally?

During the years when our boys were growing up, I often struggled with these questions, wishing I knew more about what was really happening inside those little heads. Now we have a lot more research, but too often in its journey from scientific journal to the popular press, this information is oversimplified, stressing parents out even more. I see parents now who are so concerned about brain "stimulation" that they are making their kids nervous wrecks and missing out on the natural (and too-brief) joys of childhood! Like everything else, brain research should be taken with a big swig of common sense, since the scientists themselves agree that we are a long, long way from understanding the whole picture.

This chapter will try to clarify what neuroscience is really telling us about early foundations of intelligence and emotional competence. You will have a chance to evaluate the brain-building potential of your home or day-care setting and perhaps see why collaborating with nature's pattern for building brains is a better idea than trying to create "superbabies."

PRENATAL ENVIRONMENTS FOR POWERFUL BRAINS
Laying the Groundwork before Birth

Some interesting news is that pregnancy increases the number of connections in the mother's brain (this finding holds for animals and probably for humans, too). With all this new potential, women must realize that taking care of their health will produce a healthier baby who will be easier to raise. Not everyone knows, however, that Dad should mind his personal habits as well, since his condition—and thus that of his sperm—at the time of conception may also influence the outcome. Just for starters, both parents might abstain from drug and alcohol use for a few weeks before conception. If you are thinking of having a child, you should both check out a complete set of suggestions, such as that found in *What's Going on in There?* by Lise Eliot. One bit of information that not all physicians may yet know about is to have the woman's thyroid levels checked, along with everything else, since maternal thyroid problems may cause a child to have learning disabilities.

Following the rules early on will pay off since your baby's brain cells start to form as early as three weeks after conception, multiplying more rapidly than other body cells. The brain begins life as a tiny plate that closes into a neural tube by twenty-six days to form the brain and spinal cord. If something goes seriously wrong at this stage, the fetus is likely to be miscarried. Certain precautions are important. For example, physicians are now careful to check the mother's diet for possible deficiency of folic acid, which can create problems such as spina bifida by preventing the neural tube from closing properly.

BRAIN DEVELOPMENT BEFORE BIRTH

25 days

40 days

100 days

6 months

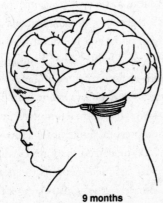

9 months

Neurons, the future "thinking cells," are now produced in abundance. Many migrate to particular sections of the brain as part of subsystems that will later control reflexes, voluntary body movement, perception, language, and thought. Others fail to attach to any area and disappear. This process is assisted by all-purpose housekeepers called glial cells, which form chains on which the neurons can climb to their proper places. Glia also nourish the neurons and keep things tidy.

The prenatal period of cell differentiation and migration occurs in spurts throughout pregnancy. A system is most vulnerable to damage when it is growing fastest, so "insults" at different times may have different effects, depending on what systems are actively developing.

A growth spurt in the formation of brain cells lasts from the second trimester of pregnancy until one year after birth. Since these cell systems are the raw material of a lifetime's intelligence, all women should be informed of the importance of good nutrition and protection from the wide variety of potential toxins present in even a normal environment.*

At least one "old wives' tale" has been proven true. The impact of the mother's emotional state on the baby's brain makes a difference. A pregnancy marked by excessive fear, anxiety, or stress may produce an infant who is more active during pregnancy and more irritable afterward. Stress hormones from the mother's body may be transmitted to the fetus, affecting its brain and behavior. On the other hand, mothers who are blessed with happy attitudes and some degree of tranquility during pregnancy give their youngsters a more positive neurochemical beginning.

Is this another "guilt trip" for women who have inadvertently exposed a child to negative prenatal influences? How about adopted children for whom we lack such information? Fortunately, nature's wonderful gift of brain plasticity gives neurons the potential to make changes after birth. The simple fact is, constructing a fetal brain from billions of cells is a very complex business, and there is bound to be an occasional glitch along the way. Actually, we all probably have a few

---

* For a complete rundown on substances that may harm the growing brain, please see my book *Endangered Minds*.

"gaps" in our brains here and there, but we learn to reroute learning around them, a process called "compensation."

A Head Start on Genius Training?

I have yet to meet parents who do not care about the intelligence of their children. While this concern is natural and important, it is possible to get carried away. Fashionable efforts to hyperstimulate children either before or after birth fall mainly into the "too much too soon" category. By "hyperstimulate," I mean efforts to "teach" children in utero by unnatural means that exaggerate normal input, such as piping in voices or phonics lessons through a megaphone-like device attached to Mom's tummy. (Yes, some people really do this.) Animal studies suggest that hyperstimulation can distort the natural development of the sensory organs and nervous system. Loud noise, for example, can cause early hearing loss; while your fetus adores your talking, reading aloud, singing to it, or listening to soothing melodies (and may even respond after birth as if recalling the stimulus), excessively loud music or piped-in "stimulation" may cause developing systems to misconnect. After duck embryos were subjected to abnormally intense auditory stimulation (noise), they failed after birth to learn their mother's call and showed other signs of abnormal attention and development. When you are tempted to turn up the stereo, remind yourself that "augmented sensory experience" does not make sense for human babies, either.

After birth, trying to press academic skills onto youngsters with devices like alphabet flash cards is not only a little silly (see later chapters for the real foundations of academic skills), but also risks setting up a pressured environment that may ultimately interfere with your child's learning. Children with "pushy" or overcontrolling parents tend to have more problems with motivation, discipline, and personal adjustment than those blessed with parents who can appreciate each stage of growth and follow the child's lead in creating activities.

"Educational" electronic environments in the nursery and computer software "guaranteed" to make your infant or toddler "smarter" should also be viewed skeptically. These unsubstantiated claims have much more to do with selling products than benefiting children. Yes, all these devices keep little ones quiet at a time when you are about as stressed out as you will ever be—but do consider how much you want your baby to imprint his emotional attachments to an electronic device instead of to you. Moreover, good learning habits come from learning to use our brains actively, not from being mesmerized by digital special effects.

One of the infant brain's major tasks is to learn self-regulation, and too much stimulation coming from outside may interfere. Your attentiveness is important because it helps the child develop connections that will eventually enable her to soothe herself and direct her attention independently without the aid of electronic distractions. Don't worry—there is plenty of stimulation available in a normal visual and auditory environment, and the infant's idea of "stimulation" may be very different from yours—such as exercising visual feature detectors by gazing at simple lights, shapes, and patterns. Boring for adults, but essential for infant brains.

Now is a good time to confront a major question: Why did you have this baby, anyhow? If the parents' goal is mainly to produce a child who is smarter and more talented than everyone else's, they—and their child—are in for a tough ride. Trying to put a child "ahead of the curve" begs the question "What curve?"—that dictated by the child's own natural potential or one dictated (or perhaps even forced) by a parent's unfulfilled needs? The growing brain is incredibly complex, and it contains natural checks and balances to ensure proper development of a vast array of skills; it seems very risky to tamper with this program until we know a great deal more about how it unfolds. Moreover, overly pressured kids are harder to raise as they get older.

In my book *Failure to Connect*, I explain why and how the use of "screen time," and especially computer software, for infants and toddlers should be avoided or carefully monitored.

BRAIN-BUILDING ENVIRONMENTS FOR
INFANTS AND TODDLERS

Any wise parent pays attention to a child's nutrition, and breast-feeding is the best start-up brain food you can offer. If this option is not possible, be sure to consult with a professional who can advise you on the best of the available alternatives.

Infant brains instinctively seek stimulation from very simple experiences that help organize the nervous system without overwhelming it. At this age, toys are far less important than a nurturing caregiver. Your child will thrive in a reasonably stable, predictable environment where a concerned and responsive adult is on call. Believe it or not, your infant's motivational systems are already developing; one important aspect is a feeling of "agency," a term used to describe a child's sense that the world is a safe place where her efforts will yield results ("When I cry for help, someone comes.") Babies gradually learn that their own behaviors have consequences, and they prefer those they can control. One study showed that toddlers interacting with a noisy mechanical monkey perceived it as frightening when it moved unpredictably, but enjoyed it when they could control its movements. Children who develop this feeling of "agency" are much more likely to develop positive motivation and become better students.

HOME and Intelligence

A researcher sits in a family living room quietly taking notes while a mother and her toddler play together. She asks the mother a number of questions about their daily life, trying to identify factors that will have long-range effects on intelligence. Studies of this type are remarkably consistent; the same variables are important both for normal development and for reversing the effects of early problems.

The following questions are adapted from a commonly used questionnaire called the HOME scale for families of children from birth to three years of age, which looks at six factors in a child's environment. They can help you evaluate the brain-building potential of your home or day-care center. Whether or not you are the primary caregiver, that person should be aware of the importance of appropriate mental stimulation and be capable of delivering it. Use your common sense to decide how these priorities can best be met in your particular situation—and use this book to help a substitute caregiver understand your child's needs at different ages.

1. Emotional and verbal responsiveness of the caregiver: When the child vocalizes, does the caregiver respond with kind, friendly words rather than gesturing or not responding?

2. Avoidance of restriction and punishment: Does the caregiver refrain from acting angry, shouting at, physically punishing, or needlessly restricting the child?

3. Organization of physical environment: Is the child's world a safe place to be? Does the child have regular contact with other adults? Are television and radio noise regulated and kept to a minimum?

4. Appropriate play materials: Are there toys that the child can manipulate to improve hand-eye coordination (stacking or nesting objects, building toys, blocks, toys with movable parts, creative materials that can be used in a variety of ways)? Are playthings interesting without overwhelming the child with detail? Do the toys require the child to be an active rather than a passive participant? (If you use electronic toys, be a critical consumer—often they do not meet these requirements.)

5. Adult involvement with the child: Does the caregiver know where the child is? Does he or she look at the child often and show interest in the child's activities?

6. Language environment: Does the caregiver use warm and loving language to comment, question, extend the child's experience? Does he or she consistently respond to the child's efforts to verbalize? Is any necessary correction done gently, with words, rather than harshly or without an explanation? Does a loving adult read stories on a regular basis?

7. Opportunities for variety in daily activities: Does the caregiver provide outings and new things to look at and manipulate?

Use of this scale with families of infants who were considered either normal or "at risk" showed that a high score on the HOME index was sufficient to bring some "at risk" children up to normal status on a test of intelligence by the time they were three years old. Infants from homes with lower ratings continued to show delayed development. The amount of adult-child interaction and the interactive quality—not the cost—of the toys provided were particularly important factors. Other studies have shown that praise, prompt attention, and immediate feedback are important as well as the variety of vocabulary used by the caregiver. Children who are talked with frequently, especially about specific objects in their environment, develop better vocabularies and score better on later measures of intelligence and reading.

Enriched Brains

You may have heard that experimental rats raised in enriched cages develop larger and heavier cortical tissue than those to whom little stimulation is available. Did you also know that rats growing up in their natural woodsy environment full of natural challenges have even bigger brains than the lab-enriched rats? Deciding what is appropriate "stimulation" for any brain is tricky, but it is clear that meeting lots of mental and physical challenges are key factors.

Studies show that children who are heavily managed by caregivers may lack both initiative and thinking skills. When adults are overly restrictive in controlling and limiting activities, children show up with poorer problem-solving skills, mental organization, and motivation. Harsh physical punishments, shouting, or sarcasm limit a child's development. But don't throw discipline and structure out the window. Children need safety and protection in order to explore new objects and situations. The security of a set of rules and reasonable limits encourages them to test their developing physical abilities against all sorts of major challenges—climbing, jumping, finding their way around new places, and extricating themselves from surprising situations.

The importance of active involvement for brain development was emphasized by one experiment with identical twin kittens. A revolving bar apparatus was rigged up in a patterned box designed to stimulate the kittens' developing visual systems. Each day the animals were placed in the box, but one had freedom to walk around at will, pulling his brother, who rode in a small basket. Although the visual input was identical for both animals, the active one developed more neural connections. Parents who are tempted to overwork the TV set should remind themselves that children need to be moving, exploring, and independently pushing the envelope on original problem-solving. Self-guided exploration ("How do I connect my arms, hands, and eyes to make that mobile move?" and "How can I get this cupboard door open?") set early skills in place for later problem-solving ("How do I attack this algebra problem on the test?").

How Much Is Too Much?

Beware of the pushmi-pullyu! Finding the fine line between being overly directive and encouraging the youngster's problem-solving abilities is one of parenthood's major challenges. (Teachers confront the same dilemma.) One recent survey found mothers complaining that they were trying so hard to play with their infants that they ended up doing most of the playing while the child sat and watched. If Mom continually takes over, she may add more to the circuits in her own busy brain than to the synapses in her child's.

The bottom line here seems to be that children need safety, love, and conversation from their parents, or from capable, consistent caregivers. They need an environment that stimulates them to do their own exploring, manipulating, and wondering. A calm, caring home with reasonable limits but without excessive fear of punishment is a good one for brain-building. New research also shows that parents who are able to talk about their own mental states ("I'm confused . . ."

"I feel so happy today . . .") help children begin to develop empathy and self-regulation.

As a veteran from the trenches of motherhood, however, I realize that everyone falls short of these ideals sometimes. Don't give up if the word "calm" doesn't always apply! And please don't get so hung up on enriching your child's intellect that you miss the joys of plain old loving.

Guidelines for Brain-Building Play: Infants and Toddlers

Adults who play and talk with their children—often following the child's lead—are the best intellectual and emotional companions. Research again confirms common sense—get down on the floor and get involved when you have the time to be patient, and *let the child be the learner.* Here are some guidelines:

- *Make sure the child is actively interested and involved.*
- If the child seems passive, start a simple activity and then try to "pass it over."
- Remember, at any age, an activity must be repeated many times to firm up neural networks for proficiency. Repetition isn't boring for young children, but if you get sick of "pat-a-cake," think ahead to the days when you will have to share the family car with this little creature. Boredom can be easy by comparison! Besides, "pat-a-cake"–type interactions lay the groundwork for language and social skills.
- For infants, place a selection of interesting toys just far enough away so they can stretch their fingers and grasp the toys.
- *Give the child positive encouragement for active exploration and investigation, which builds motor and sensory pathways.*
- Childproof your home for safety. Encourage attempts at new challenges.
- Carpeting and large pillows make good, safe backgrounds for play.
- Keep playpen time or other restraints to a minimum.

• If possible, provide a window so the child can look outside. Comment on things you both see.

• Provide low, open shelves where a variety of toys, objects, and books is always accessible. Avoid boxes with jumbled toys.

• Bring in new toys or objects one or two at a time. While the brain at all ages responds to novelty, children are more likely to investigate new challenges if they are surrounded by familiar things.

• Interesting visual surroundings with bright colors—pictures, posters, calendars—can be varied to attract visual attention.

• Call attention to specific objects or aspects of the environment. Help the baby focus on one sense at a time for taking in information (look, see, touch, smell, taste, feel).

• Get in the habit of linking language to sensory input. Talk about what is happening, even with babies. Language is the means by which the brain develops its ability to act as control center for thinking, learning, and planning.

• Toys with sound or visual input improve cognitive skills, but it is important that babies and toddlers be able to interact with them. A child banging two pans together is getting far better brain food than one pushing buttons to create noises produced by hidden electronic parts. The child should be able to link cause and effect—and see the parts of the toy at work. With a jack-in-the-box, for example, show a toddler how and why it works by slowly turning the handle until jack pops up.

Appropriate stimulation does not mean keeping your child up longer and putting on the pressure. The human brain needs quiet downtime to organize itself and consolidate learning. Be sensitive to nature's automatic shutoff valves, the signs of overexcitement or crankiness which show that the child has had enough. Exhaustion, anxiety, pressure, or fear may make it impossible for the neurons to send or receive the desired signals. Psychologists voice concern that young children's hectic schedules are causing an "epidemic" of sleep disturbances, which may eventually lead to learning or attention problems. And even well-intentioned parents may unwittingly short-circuit the pathways to skill development by forcing learning.

Forcing the Issue

Should you be trying to teach your child to read, play the violin, or ice skate before age three? Can you indeed accelerate achievement? What are the long-term consequences of such experience? Research showing that the brain at ages two and three is at its height of synapse formation has led some to suggest that we are wasting time and opportunity if we are not "training" skills during that time period. Yes, these are important—perhaps even critical—years for foundations to be laid, not only for academic but also for personal life skills. With such a wide array of neural potential, however, I believe we should be laying a comprehensive foundation rather than training specific skills. This will enable the child to acquire many types of advanced skills more easily later on. In a fast-changing technological world, mastery of new skills—that we haven't even identified yet—will be required. As always, watch your child and try to plug into her agendas. In later chapters you will find information on brain foundations for languages, reading, math, creativity, and basic learning skills.

INFANT TALENTS

Research with newborn babies has shown that they are already very smart in unexpected ways. The "blank slate" concept, which viewed newborn brains simply as waiting for the environment to carve patterns of behavior, has given way to viewing the newborn as a distinct individual who has a distinct personality and certain skills already in place. Some infants are shy, others more outgoing; some are more easily soothed, some more irritable. While these characteristics are partially genetic, any parent of more than one child can tell you that many different combinations of genes are possible within a family.

Most infants instinctively make friends with an adult who cares for them. They show preferences for their mother's voice and can discriminate certain speech sounds (e.g., "la" from "ra"); they also start trying to understand, categorize, and remember speech sounds soon after birth, and they are learning conversational turn-taking with body language and early vocalizations.

Babies come programmed with visual preferences that prepare them for intelligent looking. They like things that are novel or that move or make noise, and already prefer gazing at patterns that resemble real faces rather than at objects or pictures of faces that have scrambled features. A newborn has a strong avoidance reaction when confronted with an approaching object, and will make clutching motions if he feels he is falling. By four months they understand basic shapes and properties of objects (e.g., that one solid object can't pass through another solid object) and already have a sense of mathematics (e.g., showing surprise if two objects with one removed still equals two). By six to eight months they can match the number of objects visually depicted on a display with a number of drumbeats, a major development since it requires connecting information from two different senses. This does NOT mean they are ready for math flash cards, since these basic understandings are not gained from symbols but from experiences with real-life objects.

Parents may be surprised that their infant makes walking motions when held upright, and some discover that the baby can swim, too! Such reflexive talents may last a few weeks, others many months, but eventually the primitive parts of the brain that control these reflex movements yield control to their sophisticated neighbor, the cerebral cortex. Its pattern of growth helps us understand what is important for very young children.

STIMULATING THE RIGHT CIRCUITS

Arousing a baby's interest has to be one of the easiest and most delightful jobs in the world. An active searcher and responder to every

THE GEOGRAPHY OF THINKING

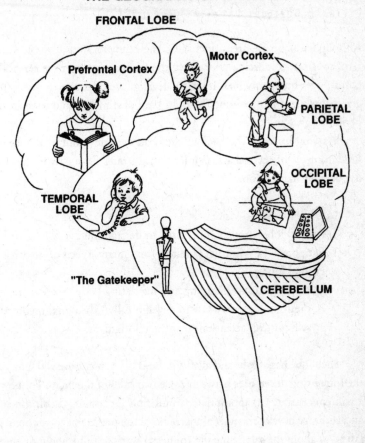

FRONTAL LOBE

Prefrontal Cortex

Motor Cortex

PARIETAL LOBE

OCCIPITAL LOBE

TEMPORAL LOBE

"The Gatekeeper"

CEREBELLUM

element of the environment, the infant thrives on stimulation for all five senses—but not all at once. Elaborate and expensive equipment isn't required, but a loving adult is indispensable as an interpreter, or "mediator," between the child and the confusing demands of the environment. *Your overall goal should be not to "teach" your baby, but to help her discover how to organize experience for herself.* The most active learners are encouraged to choose their own materials for building intelligence.

Dividing Cortical Labor

Although subcortical areas, including the cerebellum and limbic system, continue to develop after birth, the main action is in the cerebral cortex. The order in which its parts develop provides a map for caregivers interested in providing the right kind of stimulation during each period of growth.

Curving up from the back of the head over the front of the forehead, four major cortical areas, or lobes, are arranged roughly in the order of their maturation.

1. Occipital lobe—vision.
2. Parietal lobe—touch and spatial understanding.
3. Temporal lobe—hearing (auditory) and many aspects of language.
4. Frontal lobes.
   a. Motor cortex—planning and regulating body movement.
   b. Prefrontal cortex—last to develop fully: reasoning, memory, self-control, attention, planning, judgment.

Each lobe has a right and a left side, and in chapter 6 we will look at the interesting differences between these two sides of the brain. For now I will concentrate on appropriate stimulation for motor, visual, touch, and auditory development. Major growth of the prefrontal cortex occurs later—at about the same time the youngster starts to think about driving the family car. This "executive center" does have important beginnings in the early years, however, which you also need to know about.

Moving and Touching

Initially, most input for the infant is through visual and motor systems. The motor cortex is developing rapidly at birth; it is responsible for planning and executing complex actions, and it must develop the ability to communicate with the cerebellum as well as with spinal cord connections to muscles throughout the body. Although the baby starts practicing muscle control almost immediately, integrating reflex motor movements into controlled patterns takes a long time. The baby needs many things to see and to touch with body, mouth, and hands. At first the infant's movements seem random, but as he gets the feel of his own body in space, connections build between subcortical areas and the motor cortex to help the child organize his muscles around independent plans of action. Since the development of myelin in the spine proceeds from top to bottom, mouth, eyes, arms, and hands are used adeptly before legs and feet. Likewise, a solid base of concrete learning (touching, feeling, manipulating) should come before more abstract learning (alphabet, numerals).

Infants love to experiment with hands and fingers, attempting to coordinate these fascinating extensions of themselves with objects they can see, getting a lesson about tactile and spatial relationships—how things relate in three dimensions. Bathing, touching, gentle tickling, patting, and games such as peekaboo are natural stimulators. Most children enjoy being stroked with a variety of pleasant textures—for example, velvet, a feather, a soft-bristled brush, or cotton—or having their limbs gently manipulated.

Learning to Explore the World

Motor development is programmed by nature for specific reasons, and efforts to accelerate it may backfire. For example, putting your child in a walker may interrupt the multisensory and visual-spatial feedback the brain gets from the child's view of his feet, and also deprive his cerebellum of critical balancing exercise.

"Tummy time" is also important for a generation of children who sleep on their backs and are frequently carried in seats and pushed about in strollers. This type of exercise develops muscles and neural pathways, possibly even fine muscles in the hands that relate to later handwriting skills. And please don't overwork the stroller after the child is able to walk. Efficiency on Mom's part does not necessarily lead to brain stimulation in a child who passively watches the world go by.

When you go for a walk together, try and gather the patience to let that little growing brain get out of the stroller to explore, investigate, and make connections between lower, upper, and side-to-side brain areas that will lead to later reading comprehension and math skills, among many other things.

Looking Intelligently

Although a newborn's vision is still poor, he is surprisingly skilled at looking. Newborns instinctively imitate certain facial movements such as sticking out their tongues, and two-week-old babies can recognize simple patterns and faces. With practice, the movements of the two eyes become coordinated at around four to six months. Because these are critical periods for various aspects of visual development, physicians are careful to check for early problems such as cataracts or "lazy eye." Babies born with cataracts on both eyes develop near-normal vision if the cataracts are removed prior to age two months, but are permanently impaired if they remain after six months.

Binocular vision—the ability to coordinate the images from both eyes—also needs stimulation between birth and three years, and children suffering from strabismus, or "lazy eye," need treatment before age five for their visual cortex to be organized normally.

The baby's preference for novelty suggests that visual surroundings be changed frequently—a new toy or mobile may be more stimulating than a familiar one—but familiar objects should be kept close at hand. One or two objects at a time are enough, and baby needs to practice reaching and moving toward them. One mother came home to discover that the sitter had literally imprisoned her child with good intentions—there were so many toys in the crib that he couldn't even roll over. When you are tempted to make life too easy for baby, remember the kitten who rode in the basket—and ended up with a smaller brain.

Parents can demonstrate interesting ways to play with new things. Slowly moving objects fascinate the baby, building visual connections as well as knowledge about space. If you talk softly about the toy at the same time, you begin the long, slow process of linking auditory and visual input. Learning to focus on more than one sensory modality requires both neural maturation and practice.

A variety of patterns is important: contours, horizontal and vertical lines, shapes, sizes, and colors, for example. Infants develop an unreasonable attachment to simple black-and-white mobiles that have geometric shapes. Unreasonable, that is, unless you realize that these mobiles are designed specifically to appeal to the developing feature detectors in the brain—one more example that the child's brain may have more understanding of what it needs than do well-meaning adults! These visual feature detectors are forming during the first six months. Starting with simple shapes will later enable the child to discriminate such complex patterns as alphabet letters or numerals when there is a good reason for learning them. Moreover, through such sensory experience, the child begins to gain a feeling of control over a familiar environment and form rudimentary concepts such as "alike or different," "pleasant or unpleasant."

While traditional nurseries were awash with soft pastels and cute figures, vivid contrasts, brighter colors, and geometric shapes may be more effective. It is important to view crib mobiles or other visual stimulators from the baby's perspective rather than from the adult's—they should be interesting, distinct, and not too complex. Combining interesting color contrasts with feelable textures, such as crocheted materials, may help integrate sensory experience—in this case, looking and touching.

Listening

Infants also need to respond to sounds, building auditory pathways in temporal lobe language areas. Although the mechanical aspects of the auditory system are in place at birth, the fiber links to the cortex are sparse and take a long time to reach adult capacity. Newborns can distinguish frequency and pitch; at one to two months infants can tell the difference between sounds and even perceive rhythm. Although auditory pathways continue to develop until seven to ten years, the first year is a critical period for learning the sounds of a language and developing an interest in communicating with others. Sounds from the environment, music, and human speech are all necessary for a well-balanced auditory diet. Although the notion that simply listening to Mozart will raise your child's IQ has been debunked, future musical development will profit by exposing your child to many types of music, since there may be a critical period in the first year for developing a good sense of pitch. Likewise, "mutual rhythmicity," in which you and baby move together to music or a beat, helps lay the foundations for many skills. In chapter 11 we will discuss the development of later music experiences and how they may relate to math abilities.

By eight months the infant brain has entered a critical period for the discrimination of speech sounds and starts to weed out sounds that are not present in the environment. Thus, babies actually acquire the accent and intonation of their native tongue while still babbling.

Soothing, pleasant, and interesting sounds inspire curiosity and a receptive attitude. A variety of sounds is important, one at a time. Music, voices, and even household noises such as refrigerators or dishwashers are good raw material, but a constant background of music or machinery noise makes sound discrimination difficult for babies. Because noise and confusion can be detrimental to development, be sure to monitor the sound level of the TV. Even many children's programs are far too noisy for baby brains.

Likewise, premature babies' exposure to noise in incubators should be as close to the natural sound environment in the womb as possible. Newborns seem to take to the ticking of a clock placed in the crib—reminiscent of the mother's heartbeat.

Some children may learn to screen out human voices because they have been loud or unpleasant. These youngsters have trouble later when they need to listen for information in school or conversation. Simple repetitive nursery rhymes, songs, and loving words help make children eager listeners. Incidentally, there is good evidence that reading real books to the baby will do far more to develop a love of reading than will packs of flash cards or software, especially if reading is associated with a loving lap, a parent's enjoyment, and custom-tailored responses to the child's interests.

Carry on a conversation with your infant. The basis of language—that it is an important way to be involved with someone—is learned from early experiences. Every time you communicate with your child, with words, gestures, or facial expressions, you are teaching a language lesson. "Motherese" is the way we tend to address infants—responsive, higher-pitched, simpler language (not "baby talk") that seems to come instinctively, since even young children adapt their conversation to a baby's level. Of course, it is also important to include good adult language as a model.

Learning to Manage the Brain's Executive

The frontal lobes of the cortex, which help us plan, organize, and carry out ideas and actions, consist of two major areas: the motor cortex, which we have seen starting early in life to learn to manage physical activity, and the prefrontal cortex, which manages mental activity. It is the final control system for personal organization, attention, motivation, and even moral decision-making. Much of its final maturation occurs in late childhood and adolescence, but new research indicates that it has important early beginnings.

Suddenly, at around eight to nine months of age, your child begins to scream when a stranger—or even an out-of-town grandmother—arrives for a visit. This "stranger anxiety" has a very clear cause; the prefrontal cortex has just had a growth spurt in the rudiments of abstract thinking, and baby now realizes that this person is alarmingly unfamiliar. This stage will pass, of course, but in the meanwhile, reassure Grandma that this is a lovely sign of growing intelligence, not a personal rejection. At this same time, prefrontal areas gain other new cognitive skills and begin a sensitive period in social skill development that makes responsive, loving, face-to-face contact especially important.

To learn more about how you can help build the executive brain and its important foundations of attention and motivation, please check out these sections in chapters 4 and 8.

Coping with Problems

Some infants seem to be wired up with better-connected nervous systems from birth. Temperamentally they are termed "easy." Others, who come into the world "jittery," need especially careful handling, but their difficult adjustments to life may leave parents too exhausted to cope.

Because these "difficult" children especially need calm, consistent handling, enlisting the help of relatives, friends, or an outside agency may give everyone's frazzled nerves a break. Fortunately, as the brain matures, many of these characteristics will gradually improve.

All children should be routinely screened by their pediatricians for developmental difficulties that may interfere with learning. Much can be done to forestall problems. Incidentally, premature babies should always be evaluated according to their gestational age rather than their actual birth date. They particularly need special attention in the early months, as they are more at risk for later learning difficulties. Their progress has been closely linked to whether or not the home environment offers appropriate kinds of caregiving and stimulation.

- Make sure your child has ongoing checks of hearing and vision from the early months.
- If your child has recurrent ear infections, be on guard for intermittent hearing loss. Be aware that it may not show up in a onetime appointment; you may need to insist on several evaluations.
- If your child is noticeably delayed in learning certain skills, seek out a qualified professional who can create a special program of remedial activities. Alternate approaches through different sensory pathways are often used for rerouting, and new techniques are continually being developed.
- Don't give up if some types of learning are difficult. Remind

yourself that all brains have certain strengths and weaknesses, and enjoy your child's talents rather than dwelling exclusively on difficulties.

WARNING SIGNALS

Although all children have their unique "quirks," certain warning signals should alert us to the possibility of more serious developmental issues. If you have genuine doubts about your child's development, don't accept "He'll grow out of it." Early detection—or reassurance—is important.

TIPS FROM A CHILD NEUROLOGIST

The presence of any of these warning signs should alert you to seek a professional evaluation:

1. Infant "too good"; sleeps all the time.
2. Habitual poor eye contact with parents.
3. Consistent failure to respond to voices or other sounds.
4. Noticeable asymmetry of limb movements: right and left sides of the body should appear equally strong and active during the first year.
5. Noticeable delay in *many or all* of the commonly accepted milestones for motor development (sitting, creeping, walking, etc.).
6. Noticeable delay in social responsiveness: doesn't participate in pat-a-cake, peekaboo, bye-bye.
7. Failure to develop language within appropriate time limits.
8. Abnormal overresponsiveness to physical stimuli: noises, lights, touch.

NURTURING THE "NEED TO KNOW"

Emerging from all the data is a clear message. Each child must build individual networks for thinking; this development comes from within, using outside stimuli as material for growth. Most babies give explicit clues about what kind of input is needed and let you know when it's overpowering or not interesting anymore. Explaining things to children won't do the job; they must have a chance to experience, wonder, experiment, and act it out for themselves. It is this process, throughout life, that enables the growth of intelligence. Human brains come equipped with the "need to know"; our job is to give them love, acceptance, and the raw material of appropriate stimulation at each level of development. Your own common sense augmented by current knowledge is the best guide.

Chapter 3

Children's Brains at Work:
From Nursery to Schoolroom,
Ages Two to Seven

One morning while I was observing a prekindergarten class in a top-ranked school, a little boy's parents were also taking a look, trying to decide whether they should enroll him the following year. While he delved happily into the sand-and-water table, they circulated around the room. I sensed some skepticism about what they saw, and I guessed the reason. This program for three- and four-year-olds was designed to prepare children for a high-powered academic setting—but it looked like too much fun!

In one corner children intently measured sand and water as they engineered a dam. Nearby, in the block area, two boys and three girls worked on a "White House" with a sliding ramp to capture "bad guys." A teacher in the art corner helped children classify wobbly clay animals for an imaginary zoo, and several youngsters in the dramatic play area discussed their shopping list for a pretend Thanksgiving dinner. No workbooks were present in the literacy area, but an aide read a story aloud and engaged a rapt group of children with questions, predictions, and evaluations. One small boy spent the entire free play time fondling and talking to the class's pet rabbit.

I could see the visiting mother peering hopefully into the five-year-old room next door. When she again found no desks or workbooks, she gave up. Nudging her husband, she whispered, "This school isn't worth the money. They don't do any work here!"

As adults, we have a pretty clear idea of what constitutes "work" and "play." Most of us believe that in order to learn something, we must work hard at it, and too many have forgotten that the process of meaningful learning can be fun, exciting, and even playful. Yet the human brain changes during development, and the "work," as well as the fun, that is appropriate for teenagers and adults is not right for young children. Those who believe that "valuable time" is being wasted or that their children will "get behind" if they are allowed to learn in a developmentally oriented, creative curriculum—which often looks like "play" even when carefully planned—are sadly mistaken. As we shall see later, highly creative and successful adults are often those who once learned to play with objects and now play with ideas and innovations.

In this chapter we will look at the exciting developments that occur during the preschool and early primary years. Parents and teachers who understand the unique and dynamic nature of this age period are best qualified to guide the process.

SETTING THE STAGE FOR LEARNING
Brain-Building Environments for Toddlers

Studies show that the right kind of "enriched" environments promote brain growth and lay good foundations for a lifetime of learning. But what does "enriched" mean at different ages?

First of all, good nutrition continues to get top priority. Various parts of the brain seem to respond to different nutrients; as just one example, recent studies indicate that adequate iron is important both for myelination and for a specific region (*hippocampus*) that contributes to memory. Many such specific relationships will continue to be found, so it is worth the time and effort it takes to help your child learn to make good nutritional choices.

"Enriched" would include stimulating playthings that become increasingly important for cognitive development after age one. Interesting and challenging play materials in children's homes after the first year predict later IQ and school achievement in reading and math. As in infancy, a child's firsthand involvement with objects and experiences is a catalyst for brain growth.

In a market of numbing electronic glitz, the fact remains that simple, open-ended toys are still best. A toy should encourage the child to manipulate, interact, or figure something out. When there is only one "right way" to play, or if toys try to "teach" routine academic skills, opportunities for experimentation and new discovery are limited. Common household objects such as tools, cooking utensils, and gadgets provide great possibilities for creative problem-solving and imaginative play. Nesting and stacking toys or objects, containers for dumping and pouring, art materials, and stringing or sorting different sizes of beads and buttons, for example, all require active handling by the child and teach about relationships: top, middle, bottom; small, big, bigger, biggest. Wooden unit blocks in graduated sizes and shapes are all-time winners.

Toys that encourage manipulative play help higher levels of the brain develop fine motor control and sequencing, which are related to later attention and self-control skills, handwriting, and proficiency in the arts. Large muscle activities integrate hands, eyes, and muscles (as in throwing and catching a ball, or climbing a jungle gym) and promote coordination of both sides of the body—important for building intellectual skills based on connections within and between the two sides of the brain. Activities involving balance, spinning, or somersaults exercise the cerebellum, which also contributes to academic learning later on. Between the ages of two to four, the motor cortex has a major spurt in activity, so this is a time for new physical challenges—as long as they're manageable and fun.

Look also for toys that encourage children to pretend, such as a dress-up box, toy tools and utensils, or small play figures. It is discouraging to hear reports from early childhood teachers that many of today's media-saturated youngsters are so full of other people's plots and images that they can't pretend or imagine. Don't let this happen to your child!

Guidelines for Caregivers

Other factors are also critical in determining the quality of preschool environments. In a day-care setting, research shows the most positive outcomes, both for intelligence and behavior, are related to small group size; a close, affectionate relationship with the caregiver and other adults; language stimulation; and the level of education of the caregiver. Here are further research-based ideas that any adult caring for your child should heed:

- Maintain reasonable rules so that the child's safety needs can be met without discouraging exploration.
- Child-sized furniture, easels, and chalkboards give a comforting feeling of control.
- Try for emotional consistency and a reasonably stable emotional climate.
- Avoid harsh physical punishment or overly restrictive discipline, and help the child feel successful.
- A positive emotional climate also includes giving children insight into the feelings of others ("Tim is crying because you took his ball." "Sarah feels sad because her puppy is sick, and we should be especially kind to her today.") Children with better developed emotional and social competence at ages three and four show better adjustment in kindergarten. This "theory of mind" also helps children manage their own emotions; it should be evident by about age five.
- Let the child take the lead in play. Show and guide; don't direct or boss. Be open to new ways to play or use materials.
- Don't "protect" your child from making a few mistakes—and learning from them. Compliment process ("You're trying hard") rather than outcome ("You won!").
- Even toddlers can make simple decisions. "What color Play-Doh would you like today?" "Which book do you choose to take in the

• Child-sized furniture, easels, and chalkboards give a comforting feeling of control.

• Try for emotional consistency and a reasonably stable emotional climate.

• Avoid harsh physical punishment or overly restrictive discipline, and help the child feel successful.

• A positive emotional climate also includes giving children insight into the feelings of others ("Tim is crying because you took his ball." "Sarah feels sad because her puppy is sick, and we should be especially kind to her today.") Children with better developed emotional and social competence at ages three and four show better adjustment in kindergarten. This "theory of mind" also helps children manage their own emotions; it should be evident by about age five.

• Let the child take the lead in play. Show and guide; don't direct or boss. Be open to new ways to play or use materials.

• Don't "protect" your child from making a few mistakes—and learning from them. Compliment process ("You're trying hard") rather than outcome ("You won!").

• Even toddlers can make simple decisions. "What color Play-Doh would you like today?" "Which book do you choose to take in the car?" Offer uncomplicated choices that you both can live with—and then stick to them.

• At this age it is appropriate to start suggesting that the child do some self-evaluation. "How did I do?" "Did I finish?" Encourage the child to make positive statements about himself. "I stuck with it." "I thought of a new way and it worked." "I did it on my own."

• Provide varied sensory stimulation and many opportunities for active movement and exploration. Allow plenty of free play as well as planned and meaningful play experiences.

• The sensory aspects of play can be linked with language. "How does that look/sound/smell/taste/feel?" This is a good opportunity for vocabulary building (e.g., smooth, bumpy, sharp, delicious).

• Encourage the child to talk about her play. Show that you are interested by listening and asking questions. Encourage her to guide her play by talking about what she's doing.

• As the child gets older, select a weekly topic for play exploration. For example, you might put out a magnifying glass, collecting jars, sorting boxes, and picture books for nature study. Let the child's interests guide you.

• Ideas for creative projects may be found in many magazines. Focus on the child's involvement, not on the finished product.

• Avoid workbooks or other purchased "learning" materials that "teach" rote-level academic tasks of letters and numbers. These will come later.

• Keep electronics to a minimum. Real intelligence and social competence come from real experiences and real people.

• Easels and paints, clay, sand, Play-Doh, fingerpaints, water, construction paper, glue, and mud are examples of materials that help refine and organize sensory intake systems. If you tend to be a fanatic about cleanliness, close your eyes and imagine synapses connecting inside that muddy head.

I once saw a little boy who became almost panicky when he spilled some milk on the table in his day-care center. Later his teachers told me they were worried about his learning. "He's smart," they said, "but he's so afraid of making a mistake that he never tries anything that looks hard."

Help your child risk the adventure of learning.

Security to Learn

Children who feel safe because they can depend on an adult are able to reach out to new experiences. Children who are secure as babies and toddlers tend to be better learners later on: more playful, more curious, more responsive to adults, and able to focus attention more effectively. In our zest for stimulating children's minds, we shouldn't forget that a loving and safe home is always the first order of business. If you find your concerns about your child's intellect getting in the way of simple affection, stand back and ask yourself, "What's really important?"

HOW DO CHILDREN THINK?
Ages and Stages from Two to Seven

Children's thinking ability undergoes several major changes along the route to adult-level reasoning, paralleling the maturation of new networks in the brain. The years from two to seven are characterized by cycles of myelination and synapse refinement that lead to new stages of learning, so dramatic shifts in understanding can seem to occur very quickly—although a child may regress until the connections are firm. Different types of studies have indicated so many different "spurts" or "waves" of growth that it is hard to find a time when this brain is not actively developing some sort of ability. By age seven, sensory systems have become more integrated, language has made major leaps, and maturation of higher-level association areas enable the child to reason more logically and reflect on questions and ideas. By the end of second grade, we hope to have basic foundations in place for reading, math, and handwriting as well as an ever-expanding grasp of facts and concepts and a solid basis of attention, motivation, and independent problem-solving.

At each stage in this process, certain types of experience are important. Since later development builds on earlier experience, a child who gets the brain food he needs at each stage has a better chance of reaching the top of his cognitive ladder. The speed of this climb is partially related to innate intelligence, but life experiences and individual developmental timetables also play major roles. According to well-known theorist Jean Piaget, the child creates his own intelligence at each level by puzzling out inconsistencies between his bits of knowledge, or "schemas," and the reality of his daily experiences.

Different Hooks

If you and your child watch a TV program on the workings of the brain, chances are each of you will learn very different things from it. An adult can "get more out of it" by hanging the new information on to previous pieces of knowledge—mental "hooks" about biology, psychology, and years of practical experience with one's own brain. The term "schemas" was used by Piaget to describe these mental hooks, the bits of learning that combine to form each person's structure of thought. The better the framework and the bigger the hooks, the more we can remember and learn from each new experience.

Since your child's frameworks are small and immature, her learning in any situation is qualitatively different from yours. You can try to lend her your schemas by explaining them, but if she lacks the personal experience, your words will fall right off her incomplete hooks. This theory may explain why each generation seems to have to make its own mistakes instead of taking the good advice of its elders!

When you talk with your child or student, you can help bridge the schema gap.

1. As you solve problems together, talk through your own questions. "I wonder how I should start." "Are these two alike?" "Could I put them together?" "Is it working?" "What's going to happen?" "How did I do?"

2. Ask your child similar questions.

3. Give the child plenty of time to think and answer.

4. Let the child reenact each solution several times in order to understand it.

5. Encourage understanding. Ask, "Why do you think that happened?" "Why did/didn't that work?"

6. As a teacher, I learned that if things weren't going well, I needed to ask myself, "What am I assuming about this situation that the child doesn't yet understand?" It helps to ask what the child is thinking or seeing, and then listen carefully to her answer.

A Small Piece of Learning

I once had a conversation with a six-year-old that taught me about one child's mental "hooks." During the first snowstorm of the year, the level of classroom excitement rose steadily until dismissal time. As the day ended, Marcy lingered behind, staring at the still-barren grass outside. "Why isn't the snow sticking on the ground?" she asked. Not wanting to deprive her of the chance to do some thinking (and learning) for herself, I replied, "What do you think?"

"Well," she replied, "I don't know because snow is supposed to stay there after it comes down—why isn't it?"

"It does seem to be disappearing," I acknowledged. "Do you know anything that would make snow disappear?"

Marcy thought for a moment. "Not really. Snow is cold and it stays. Well, maybe if you put water on it."

At this point I realized that Marcy's notion of snow was both inaccurate and incomplete, so there was no way she could grasp the principle involved. Instead of trying to explain it to her, I took her outside, grabbed some snowflakes as they fell, and we watched them turn into water. Finally we felt the ground temperature and Marcy drew her own conclusions. She enlarged her "snow" schema to include her observation that warmth makes it melt, and she was forced to change her ideas to accommodate this new information. It is through countless such firsthand experiences that children develop knowledge and the ability to manipulate it mentally. *For this type of learning, parents or thoughtful caregivers are the first and best teachers.*

As schemas develop and enlarge, they are combined into mental *operations*, or patterns, that enable the child to think about relationships in more abstract ways. For example, a two-year-old must line up blocks in order to see what they look like; an eight-year-old can think about lining them up without actually doing it, and a fifteen-year-old may be able to make combinations in his mind to test scientific relationships among them.

Levels of Processing

Does experience alone account for these changes? A child's ability to combine new ideas also results from maturation of three special systems in the brain that neuropsychologist Alexander Luria called "functional units." As the child handles millions of bits of experience, chains of neurons link together—first within and then between different brain areas. In a sense, the thinking child makes his own brain fit together.

Lower-level networks come first. At the bottom are reflex responses and *directing attention*, then comes the *reception* of countless pieces of incoming information and *association* of the pieces with each other for understanding. When enough pieces have been taken in, the child finally begins to *interpret* them and *plan* responses.

How does Luria's model work in a real situation? Let's say you are trying to get your child to leave the TV set.

The *first functional unit* regulates consciousness and initial attention. To be consciously processed and remembered, the information must cross the attention threshold.

"Oops, I hear Mom's voice."

Once the message gets into conscious awareness, it is directed to a specialized reception area where the *second functional unit* converts it into a meaningful signal and sends it to the appropriate part of the cortex, in this case the centers for auditory processing. First it must be received and sorted out from other auditory stimuli:

"What did she say?"

then sent to higher-level systems to be analyzed and organized into some sort of meaning:

"What does she mean, 'Clean up your room'?"

and finally, associated with information from other senses or from memory for complete understanding:

"Oh, I remember, I left my clothes and toys all over the floor and she's having company tonight."

Only after all these steps are completed can the *third functional unit*, corresponding to the prefrontal lobes of the cortex, do its work of evaluating the information and planning behavior:

"Guess I'd better pick up that stuff as soon as this program is over."

For most parents this particular example proves Luria's point that the mere presence of a neural structure does not guarantee that it can (or will) be used! Practice is the essential ingredient, and it takes all of childhood and most of adolescence to perfect and connect all the systems.

EARLY LEARNING: THE PRESCHOOL YEARS
Making Connections

A child's first months lay the groundwork for consciously directing attention, taking in bits of information to each of the senses, and practicing with body movements. During this "sensorimotor" period, the brain is not ready to deal with much beyond immediate physical experience. As we saw in the last chapter, at around eight to nine months of age the prefrontal cortex begins its long march toward maturity, and the child suddenly starts to use memory to link past and present experience: "Oops, here comes the sitter—time to cry!"

By eighteen months, most children begin to understand and associate experiences in much larger frameworks. More complex patterns of movements (motor programs) are mastered, and—most exciting of all—language develops. Children with poor foundations in reception areas may fall behind when they have to start associating ideas. The higher levels at which understanding occurs are probably the most sensitive of all to environmental stimulation.

With an increasing base of neural connections, the toddler sees the world in new ways. The development of language and symbolic play represent the beginning of abstract thought. A child talking to Granddad on a toy telephone shows that she has a mental representation of both Granddad (out of sight) and the general function of real telephones. When she asks for a cookie that you have previously put in a cupboard, she shows that she has organized and associated ideas one step beyond cookies she can only see or touch. Many believe that the roots of creativity also lie at this junction of concrete and symbolic experience where pretend play arises. Children who are good at pretend play also get along better socially.

Until sometime around age six or seven, children's "work" is to develop the basis for abstract thought by mastering their physical environments, and by learning to use language. The preschooler is mainly caught in present reality with only a vague concept of past, present, and future. He is "stimulus bound," which means that his attention is easily drawn to any new stimulus. Thus he has genuine trouble keeping his mind on any one task or idea. He has difficulty with other people's points of view. The ability to "decenter," or move out of his own perspective, occurs very slowly, as any mother who expects a child to see *her* point of view can confirm! For this reason, preschool learning must arise from firsthand experience and interest. Perhaps the most important thing to remember is that the child comes at any situation with a different set of hooks than yours. Parents and teachers who respect the unique quality of early intelligence have the best chance of helping it grow.

What Should Preschoolers Learn?

After years of studying young children's learning, I am increasingly convinced that *patterns* are the key to intelligence. Patterning information really means organizing and associating new information with previously developed mental hooks. "Gifted" children have an unusual ability to pick up all kinds of patterns and relationships in everyday experience. One bright little three-year-old, who was being tested for admission into a competitive prekindergarten, had impressed everyone with her huge vocabulary and outgoing personality, but she completed the sales job when she surveyed the artwork on the wall and said, "Look! The patterns in that picture are the same as the ones in my dress."

Children who can "see" relationships and organize input at a sensory level seem to have an easier time organizing thoughts and ideas. Some youngsters come into the world with nervous systems that are better equipped for this assignment than others, but while the brain is still developing rapidly, you can help any child. Focus on helping the child make physical and mental connections through lots of self-organizing play activities rather than emphasizing specific bits of information. Because of immaturity in parietal lobe areas that connect sight, sound, touch, and body awareness, it is still difficult for young children to combine processes from more than one modality, such as in looking at a letter form and copying it, or simultaneously dancing and singing while listening to music.

Even babies can be conditioned to associate two stimuli that are presented repeatedly together, but this learning lacks real meaning for the child and may use inappropriate parts of the cortex instead of those best suited for the job. In fact, forced learning of any type may result in the use of lower systems since the higher ones that should do the work have not yet developed. The "habit" of using inferior brain areas for higher-level tasks (such as reading) and of *receiving* instruction rather than *creating patterns of meaning* causes big trouble later on.

Children who don't learn to search for meaning are often good "technicians" in the first and second grades because they can deal with isolated data, but when the demands for comprehension increase, they "hit the wall." They have difficulty organizing information into more abstract ideas. "I don't get it" becomes their theme song.

Helping Children Create Mental Patterns

During preschool years, our job includes being intellectual challenger for both boys and girls. Some Dads in particular tend to challenge sons and expect more thinking from them than from daughters. No fair! Here are some commonsense guidelines for everyone:

• Remember that the brain at twenty-four to thirty-six months is buzzing with extra connections that are desperately trying to get sorted out into concepts, relationships, and patterns of meaning such as cause and effect, time sequences, and social rules of getting along with others. This is sometimes a difficult brain to live with—for both you and the child—so be patient.

• The brain needs downtime to firm up all this work. Make space for quiet reflection and pondering. Appreciate your child's wisdom as well as her skills.

• Help your child figure out meanings and relationships in daily events; his continual "Why?" questions are a way of expressing his need to make these connections. Often, "why" simply means "I need more explanation about this."

• Introduce skills of sequencing—arranging objects according to size, or remembering words or events in order. It is beneficial to talk about abstract sequences such as "If you go outside without your shoes, your feet will get cold because it's winter"; "If you don't take your nap this afternoon, you might fall asleep at dinner"; but preschoolers must stick to objects and immediate experience if they are expected to put things in order themselves.

• Mental patterns are built on networks of sensory connections. Call the child's attention to patterns in the sensory world: "What does that taste like?" "Do these look alike?"

• Visual patterns are present all the time. "Look at the tree branches against the sky. Doesn't it look as if the tree has arms? Maybe we could draw a picture."

• Puzzles and commercial materials can be helpful in visual patterning. Parquetry blocks, dominoes, and kaleidoscopes are examples. "What is wrong with this picture?" links visual and cognitive skills.

• Patterning in stitchery activities is fun for both sexes, and links visual and motor development.

• Encourage auditory patterning with rhymes, instruments, tunes, familiar stories, or attention to sounds around the house. Tap out a simple rhythm (long, short, short) and see if your child can imitate it. See chapter 7 for tips on language patterning.

• When children are old enough, simple carpentry tools, wood, large nails, screws, nuts, and bolts are excellent materials for making perceptual and motor connections. Measuring, cooking activities, and gardening all involve patterns of relationships.

• Motor patterns need to be practiced over and over—using utensils and tools; cutting; catching and throwing a large, soft ball; or playing games of copying finger or body movements, for example. Self-help skills and household jobs are very important for the child to master—help your child, but encourage him to do it himself even if the job isn't done exactly your way! I have worked with children who are afraid to attempt even simple tasks because Mom has always jumped in and done the job for them. They often appear inept and even disabled when they start school.

• If a child truly needs help with a motor pattern, scaffold the learning by gently guiding her body through the action sequence several times in order to lay the neural path, or divide the action into a series of smaller activity units. Don't expect a child of this age to copy complex actions (kinesthetic) that you show her (visual)—allow her to learn with one sense at a time (in this case, her body). If your child has serious problems with coordination, consider consulting an occupational or sensory integration therapist.

• Give your child time to organize his own play. Mothers who hover may impede the child's ability to form mental patterns of his own; one study even showed that too-frequent offering of food and drink to toddlers was negatively related to later school achievement.

• Be sure to let your child make reasonable choices whenever possible. Learning to make simple decisions—and minor mistakes—is hard but necessary. Children's conception of reality needs to include close personal experience with cause and effect. ("If I press too hard on the crayons, they will break." "If I pull out the bottom shirt from the pile, the others will fall on me.")

• Read aloud frequently and look for patterns in stories. How is this character alike or different from that one? What parts should stories have?

• Eliminate or set clear limits on screen time, and choose a day-care center where children do not watch much—if any—TV or video. Occupational therapists tell me they are now treating many "video kids" who have missed out on some of the most basic motor patterning, and the attention skills and intellectual growth that accompany it.

What about Sports?

How did we get the idea that we have to start training our children for the Olympics before they can read? At a meeting of a parents' counseling group in a large metropolitan area, I recently heard one mother assert: "If you don't have them in organized soccer lessons by the time they're five, forget it!"

When I pressed her a little, she acknowledged that she got her information from a coach who was trying to sell her a program for her son; she also admitted that what she really hoped for was to have him be good enough to win a soccer scholarship to college.

Is it true that all is lost if kids don't receive early training in one or more sports? It is true that because the motor strip in the cortex matures early, most young children can master some large-muscle activities fairly easily, including some of the basic moves of soccer, such as kicking. Many preschoolers can swim, ski, and do creative dance movements such as Dalcroze with enjoyment—if they aren't forced. Ice skating may even fall into this category, depending on how it is taught. These activities do not require intricate combinations of visual and motor skills. Sports such as tennis and baseball—as well as understanding the rules, field positions, and directionality of soccer, however—add fine visual-motor, visual-spatial, and abstract thinking challenges. Competence and enjoyment of such sports is far beyond most children until age seven or so.

"But she wants to do it!" is a frequent parental cry. As always, children will try hard if they sense their parents care a lot about an activity. What a shame, though, to saddle them with expectations they can't meet or pressure for competition before they have the physical coordination or mental perspective to deal with it.

Expert soccer coaches who are not pushing programs agree that it is "foolish" to feel that a child must be in lessons or a league at age five; some have told me that a motivated child can become a good player even as late as seventh grade. They do agree that the best way to prepare for any sport is to play, informally and without pressure, with the basic skills of catching, throwing, and kicking a large ball, moving the body rhythmically and bilaterally, running, hopping, skipping, climbing, following directions, learning that games have rules and that you can't always win, and all the other subskills that eventually make someone an athlete. You can certainly hire a professional to do this, but even if you're not an athlete yourself, your child would prefer your attention and the closeness that ensues from playing together. As to placing expectations—such as college—on an activity that is meant to be fun . . . don't be a parental spoilsport!

A few rare youngsters are "naturals" at almost any age, but if an activity doesn't take, back off and wait until that little brain and body are ready to exercise together.

Intellectual Building Blocks

"Play" is considered so important by child development experts that huge books of research studies have been published about it. During the preschool years, manipulative and symbolic fantasy play are particularly important. Remember the children building the White House with wooden unit blocks? They were manipulating and pretending, but their teacher pointed out that they were also "actively involved in testing two important scientific ideas: 'systems' and 'interactions,' as well as getting a solid understanding of mathematical concepts" ("We only need half as many of these." "The living room should be a rectangle, not a square."). Early physics lessons were also much in evidence ("Don't make that tower too tall or it'll fall over!").

Children playing with blocks also enlarge and change their schemas of relative space ("How do I get this block to bridge these other two?"), numerosity (each block is some multiple of the basic unit), symmetry and proportion, balance, stability, and gravity. One child, attempting to construct a roof to bridge four walls, soon discovered that the walls were too far apart and tried out a number of hypotheses before mastering the relationships involved. Fortunately, no one interrupted her or stole her chance to learn by "showing" her how! Another youngster was busy constructing some mental schemas about number. He lined up eight blocks in a row and counted them in one direction, then backward to see if they were the same. Then he stacked them up into a tower and counted them again—up and down. Convinced that "eight" is "eight" from all directions, he skipped off, unaware that he had just mastered an abstract mathematical idea.

The Power of Pretending

Fantasy play with others gets children to enlarge their mental frameworks, get outside their own minds, practice using language, and gain information about other values and points of view. In a "pretend" household in the classroom, for example, they were also using symbols: blocks as "food," an empty can as a "telephone," and a ball as a "yucky baby." This level of learning separates human thought from that of all other species. Play, in this sense, is the gateway to metaphor, to scientific insight, and to invention. Choose a school that will encourage children to open this gate before expecting them to perform advanced mental operations.

PLAYTIME AS A GATEWAY TO LEARNING

- Playtime should be relaxed and pressure-free. Constructive play usually begins only after a child feels familiar and comfortable in a setting. Activities should not be switched too often as long as the children are satisfied.
- The best play materials suggest imaginative uses rather than being too literal—materials for building a "pretend" house, for example, rather than one already fitted out with perfect furniture and accessories; lengths of fabric rather than costumes; large empty boxes, etc.
- Children use play to gain important feelings of mastery and control or to deal with issues that may be troubling them.
- Children should be able to express "forbidden" feelings in play at school about real events in their own lives. For example, a child with a new baby at home may temporarily adopt rough play with baby dolls at school. She gets rid of some of her feelings without doing any damage to the real baby, and sensitive adults may encourage her to "use words" to help resolve the conflict.
- Rule-governed games are fun for adults and children and promote many kinds of learning, as long as they do not substitute for exploratory and pretend play. You should know that one of the best predictors of your child's first-grade math achievement is how many board games and card games you have played together. Learning to move a marker a certain number of spaces in order, sequencing moves, recognizing whether 10 is bigger than 3, taking turns, following rules, applying strategies, and learning that the world won't end if you lose—all are great lessons for math and for life. One study showed that a computer couldn't simulate this learning, mainly because the verbal "coaching" of the adult was the critical aspect.
- Children playing together often make up their own "rules," which may seem incomprehensible to an adult. As long as the children are satisfied, adults should stand aside. They don't have our schemas for rules, and we have forgotten theirs.
- Dramatic play teaches social skills more effectively than any type of instruction.

- Creative pretense activities are often used by a child to firm up new understandings about the world; good schools allow time for a child's emerging thought.

THE EARLY SCHOOL YEARS
New Challenges in Learning: The "Five-to-Seven Shift"

From ages five to seven or eight, the brain is in one of its most dynamic states of change as it practices combining sensory patterns from different modalities and moves into new forms of symbolic thought. Up until now the child has been creating her own concrete symbol systems such as using words, developing ideas about numbers, and making pictures of things she knows. Now she starts to deal with more formalized symbol systems—words in books, math equations, mental images for thinking and remembering.

Neuropsychologists talk about the "five-to-seven shift" because so much change occurs in the brain during these years. One study found that a specific area involved with language and spatial awareness had changed 85 percent between ages six and seven in one girl's brain. So your seven-year-old is really seeing things from a new and different viewpoint!

By age seven or eight, growth in the higher association areas enables more flexible intersensory communication (e.g., reading for meaning, writing sentences from dictation, reading music while playing), and during this period most brains are avid learning machines. Also by about age eight, the two sides of the brain have developed firmer communication links with each other, enabling better bilateral (two-sided) control of the body (as in holding a paper with one hand and writing on it with another), and the ability to form images or thoughts in words inside the head—fundamental for later creativity and mental planning. (Not all children follow this exact timetable, however. Check out the next chapter to learn more about different developmental timetables.)

Still to come is the real flowering of tertiary areas, so it's unfair to expect much forward planning or serious decision-making. Information still needs to be presented mainly with concrete, hands-on, and personal materials. Challenging projects and theme-based curricula can excite young intellects while still emphasizing basic skills. Children need important and interesting topics to think about at a time when the brain is eager to guzzle up every bit of learning that comes along. A second-grader recently stunned me at a dinner table by spontaneously retelling several of the tales of the Greek myths, complete with multisyllablic names, which he had been studying through storytelling, reading, writing about, and dramatizing them. He doesn't realize that he will be very grateful for this base of information in both high school and college—right now he just thinks it's interesting and fun.

Now is the time when parents first get involved with helping with assignments that have to be done at home. Some also need to cope with the challenge of choosing an elementary school. Let's deal with the school choice first.

Choosing an Elementary School or Homeschooling

I get many questions from parents who face a serious dilemma when they have a choice of schools for their child. My main suggestion is that the parent first become familiar with each school, what each one stands for and their basic philosophies about how children should learn. Ask for an appointment with the principal, if possible. Every school—public or independent—has its own character, differing even within the same district. Montessori or Waldorf schools are specific examples of schools founded on a philosophy and methods derived from the thinking of one individual: Maria Montessori or Rudolph Steiner in these cases. Each has clear ideas about the importance of curriculum and teaching that conform to a child's developmental needs.

Whatever your options, sit in on a class if possible, and decide whether the environment "feels" right to you. If it does, your child may have a better chance of feeling comfortable there. Talk to other like-minded parents for a candid appraisal. My general advice also is to choose what is best for your child at any given age period; for example, I wouldn't advise picking an elementary environment with which you're uncomfortable just because the associated high school has a good record for college admissions. Changes can come later.

Some parents feel that their child might benefit from home-schooling, an option that has become increasingly viable for many families. I continue to gain respect for homeschoolers as I am privileged to speak at some of their conferences and meet the children as well as the parents. Reasons for and implementation of homeschooling (or even "unschooling") are as varied as the families involved. One of educators' major criticisms—that homeschooled children are deprived of peer relationships—is met by forming groups with other homeschooling families for social and educational activities. Many families also supplement homeschooling with enrichment activities and traditional school courses when the child outstrips a parent's knowledge in particular subjects, such as science or math.

Many excellent guides for alternative approaches to schooling have been published; I have included some in the bibliography.

Helping with Schoolwork at Home

I am not the only educator who is concerned about the amount and quality of what passes as "homework" in the early grades. At these ages, it is a shame to let schoolwork and extracurricular activities deprive children of active playtime after school. If you are concerned that your school is overdoing it, ask for a meeting with parents and teachers to discuss the issue together and determine some age-appropriate ground rules.

Specific guidelines for helping with homework will be found in chapter 5. Remember that lots of repetition will be necessary before a child's skills become automatic, as they are for you (e.g., writing, spelling, using the multiplication tables, following directions—even setting the table and playing ball). It helps if you model thinking skills in everyday situations as well as with schoolwork. Here are some steps to help a child "get it together":

1. Before you try to work on anything together, make sure you have the child's attention. Your child will absorb your level of enthusiasm (or lack of it). If possible, let the child ask you for help rather than hovering. This is her work, after all.

2. Link new information to old with illustrations, analogies, and examples; help your child make the associations. ("This looks like a problem you had yesterday. . . ." "Could you make the same kind of study cards for math that you made for your spelling words?")

3. Help the child pretend to act out or draw the idea ("If Mary had eleven oranges and ate two . . .").

4. Show connections, common themes, or organizing principles of new material ("These all seem to be types of flowers, even though they look different." "What vowel pattern do all those words have?")

5. Try to get the child to think up personal connections. ("Did you ever feel the way José did in the story?")

6. Tie abstractions to concrete experience. ("Let's see if we can cut this paper in thirds. What if we cut each third in half?")

7. Pictures or diagrams help organize many types of material. Help your child make charts, maps, or lists of things in categories, or draw "cartoon" sequences to get information into manageable form.

8. Remember that the child still needs many specific instances before generalizations can be made.

Moving toward Abstract Thought

As children start to put ideas together in new ways, they begin to get beyond the immediate physical characteristics of an object and understand the principle involved. For example, the reversible equation $4 + 5 = 9$ is the same as $9 = 5 + 4$, and even $9 - 4 = 5$, and $9 - 5 = 4$. A younger child has a great deal of difficulty with a problem like this; he believes that these things are different because they *look* different. He cannot pull out the essential relationship and thus he cannot "undo" and turn around the sequence in his mind.

How do children get to the stage where they understand these relationships? I am willing to blame a certain amount of neural readiness, but it is clear that they must practice and experiment with hundreds of examples. The mother visiting the class at the beginning of this chapter didn't realize that her son was working on this important type of learning as he played at the sand table.

Another major area of growth is in categorizing, classifying, and class inclusion. Many school tasks contain subtle requirements for classification; outlining is one example of a job that is difficult for students who don't get the idea of subtopics being part of one large, more abstract topic.

Many things that seem ridiculously obvious to adults are not clear to children. We can explain until we're blue in the face, or we can insist the child memorize what we want her to know—and wonder why she has "forgotten" it the next day. One task that is difficult for primary students is the "missing addend" so popular in early math books (3 + ? = 8). Teachers and parents alike are frustrated because, at this age, most students can learn to perform this operation only by rote—the minute they have to remember or organize it themselves, they "forget" because they never really understood it.

I also remember having a near argument with a six-year-old I was tutoring one summer about whether "bigger" meant "older." She was convinced that her daddy was older than her mommy because he was "bigger," and I couldn't change her mind. Having tried to make my point by every pedagogical method at my command, including waking my (large) grown son from a nap for a firsthand demonstration, I finally accepted the fact that I was dealing with a literal thinker who was convinced that "taller" was "more." This experience reaffirmed for me the fundamental truth about learning—you can lead the child to the problem, but you can't make the mental leap for her. *She has to be ready, and she has to do it herself.*

Promoting Cognitive Conflict

How can we prepare youngsters to fit those connections together? As I learned the hard way, attempts to explain to children why their reasoning is incorrect are doomed to fail. The trick is to give them lots of firsthand experiences with the subject in question, then get them to see the inconsistency in their reasoning and to *want* to figure it out. When something doesn't "fit," a state of "cognitive disequilibrium" sets in, and the child can be pulled toward new levels by an adult *asking the right questions.* Try these ideas:

• Ask questions rather than explaining what is "correct." (Child says, "This lemonade straw is broken." Parent, seeing that the straw is blocked, asks, "Is there anything in the straw that is keeping the lemonade from coming through?" rather than, "That straw isn't broken. Here, let me clear it out for you.")

• When the child asks you a question, respond with a question that is just hard enough to make him wonder, but not so complicated that it will frustrate him. Use the child's response as your guide.

• At any age, hands-on experience is the first step. For example, if your child is gaining concepts of classification, you might suggest sorting the family laundry or magazine pictures into piles and then combining them with a general category label. More suggestions are included later when we discuss math and science.

• Ask yourself, "Exactly what is it I expect this child to do, and what is her frame of reference for it?"

• Help the child identify the relevant aspects of a problem. ("What would you have to do to make that track long enough to reach the other one?" instead of "Here, put this piece in there.")

• If you don't know an answer, admit it. Now you have the most exciting opportunity of all—to show your child how you ask yourself questions and seek information.

• Help your child see the discrepancies between his language or mental operations and actual reality. (Child says, "It is snowing because I put my boots on." Parent asks, "Let's think about that for a minute. Pretend we're at the lake in the summer. You have your bathing suit on. Now, let's pretend you put your boots on [child acts out the scene]. Will that make it snow? Is it snowing *because* you put your boots on?")

• As in the above example, many of a child's inconsistencies in reasoning are a result of faulty interpretation or use of language ("because" in this case). Be alert for situations in which you can use real experience to model language concepts. ("Why did the paint spill? Because . . .")

• Be tolerant of "wrong" answers if they are part of a process of new learning and mental exploration.

• Remember that rules can be taught, but understanding can't.

• Make sure that playing with peers is a regular part of your child's life. Children often ask each other the questions that promote positive cognitive conflict.

• Try to present your child with manageable problems rather than constantly providing solutions—it is her struggle with the available data that sparks cognitive growth.

• Piaget suggested that we stop worrying about how fast we can make intelligence grow, and concentrate on how *far!* When people asked him whether we could accelerate children's progress through each stage, he scoffed at what he termed "the American question."

A Boss for the Brain

How long does the brain's childhood last? Mature reasoning does not occur until sometime after age eleven or twelve, and can even come as late as thirty, when the frontal lobes finally become the "boss" of the brain. Until then, thinking has certain limits. It is natural for children to be literal thinkers, stuck in their own point of view. Preschoolers have trouble telling reality from fantasy and may appear to "lie" because of an inability to sort out the difference between what really happened and what was imagined. Children of ages five to ten tend to become very literal and rule-bound in their moral judgments, but they are also notorious for their difficulty in imagining consequences. A pleasure at hand is much more pressing than some future punishment!

Late-maturing areas also control much of what we call "motivation." A young child usually has trouble planning for far-off goals or developing and executing a plan of action. As you will see later, there is a lot we can do throughout the early years to put motivation on track, but we need to be realistic. I frequently see parents (and teachers) who lament, "I don't understand why she is so unmotivated—she doesn't seem to be able to see why this is so important!" One family promised their eight-year-old son a new bike in June if he got "good grades" all year. Unfortunately, these terms were far too vague, June seemed very remote, and the plan failed.

Children of this age need help in planning, organizing, and following through on small intermediate goals. Be wary of dispensing rewards; ideally, the child's reward is his own feeling of satisfaction in a job well done. It is never too early to establish the idea that we are each responsible for aiming at our goals *and* for feeling good about ourselves when we reach them.

Likewise, young children cannot objectively evaluate moral issues or even put heavily emotion-laden material into perspective, and parents may have to stand in to protect them and interpret input they can't handle—even at higher grade levels. I once worked with a group of nine-year-old girls who were sent to me in desperation by their teacher. Although they were all bright children, they were unable to concentrate in class and seemed to be in a perpetual state of excitement. It didn't take them long to close the door and start telling me that they were really "worried" about a lot of the sexual information they had picked up from babysitters and the media—and which they were naturally busy exchanging with each other.

When their fears and misconceptions started to pour out, I understood why they felt so threatened by this barrage of frightening half-truths. No wonder they couldn't concentrate in class! Only one child in the group felt comfortable talking to her mother, who had always made a habit of limiting TV, watching it with her, and discussing what they saw. For these girls, a "learning" difficulty turned out to have far different roots.

Young children are even more susceptible to inappropriate content. It's a hard parental assignment, but try to be aware of potentially anxiety-producing information to which your child is exposed, and make yourself available to help put it in perspective. TV violence and even current events are hard enough for adults to comprehend, but impossible for children. They need protection, help with interpreting what they see, and lots of reassurance in dealing with the complexities of the world.

CHILDREN AT WORK
Evaluating Early Learning

Children between the ages of two and seven need intellectual challenges they can understand and pursue actively. They also need solid basic skills, but not in a "drill-and-kill" format. Some very able brains simply take a little longer or need special teaching methods in order to absorb these basics, as we shall see in the next chapter. Above all, we want them to emerge from early childhood excited and confident about learning.

Let's take a minute to return again to the classroom described at the beginning of this chapter to evaluate the "work" in progress. The children measuring cupfuls of sand are making mental patterns—putting together visual and motor learning with concepts of size, density, texture, volume, and fractions. Handling the materials brings important tactile information—and new synapses—into their brains. Because making judgments, predictions, and plans are a part of this play, they are laying groundwork for the brain's executive control function. Language develops as they discuss their project, and attention is sharpened as they ignore the other play in the room.

In the book corner, a great deal of literacy instruction is occurring, even though it just looks like story-reading and telling. As you will find in chapter 9, listening skills, comprehension, vocabulary-building, questioning techniques, and awareness of the sounds making up each word—not to mention pleasure in reading—are the important "basics" for later skill development.

The clay animals in the art corner integrate not only creativity and fine motor skills but also vocabulary and descriptive language. When a parent volunteer noticed that several children were inventing imaginary animals, she encouraged them to dictate a book of original stories, make drawings, and create a plaster-of-paris relief map based on their mythical animal world.

How about the pet rabbit? It enabled one little boy to get some badly needed tactile stimulation as well as a feeling of comfort and importance as he assumed the responsibility for its feeding.

This is the type of classroom you should seek for your young child, and the same principles hold for early primary grades even as the curriculum becomes more academic. Learning that arises from personal experience helps brains at any age receive, associate, organize, and comprehend at the appropriate neural levels. Far from marking time, well-planned programs at each level develop the hooks of meaning that underlie intelligence.

What's the Hurry?

The parents choosing a school for their son at the beginning of this chapter finally enrolled him in an "accelerated" class where children spend a lot of time sitting at desks, filling in work sheets, and "being taught." He may, of course, become a good student if he can overcome the monotony of this introduction to learning, but his chances would be far better in a school that understood young children's needs. Studies show that four-, five-, and six-year-olds in heavily "academic" classes tend to become less creative and more anxious—without gaining significant advantages over their peers. Youngsters in well-structured "play"-oriented preschools and developmentally appropriate primary grades develop more positive attitudes toward learning along with better ultimate skill development.

If tasks are too inappropriate for this child's level of development, moreover, or if patterns of meaning are neglected, he could end up as a "behavior problem" or be mistakenly labeled "learning disabled." By overlooking the developmental imperatives of childhood, these parents have deprived him of the richest possible foundation for future learning.

Give your child the gift of patience for the broad-based mental experiences that will underlie joyous learning throughout life. Pushing academic skills before the levels of sensory reception and association are in place is like trying to build a large penthouse on an apartment building before the intermediate floors are completed. It may look good for a while, but eventually you're in for a collapse. Childhood is a process, not a product, and so is learning. In a society that often respects products more than the processes of creation and thought, it is easy to fall into the trap of anxiety over measuring achievement in isolated skills. Have faith—in childhood and yourself. Children's brains generally seek what they need, and nature has given you the instincts to help them get it.

Recently I was pleased to have as houseguests a friend from Austria and her charming five-year-old daughter, a bright little girl who has lived in two countries and is fluent in both English and German. During their visit I was particularly struck by the close relationship between mother and daughter and the little girl's sunny disposition, which survived both jet lag and a hectic social schedule. In a rare quiet afternoon, we sat on my porch and talked while the child entertained herself inventing games with a few pieces of plastic packing material.

"She's so smart," I finally said to my friend, a math teacher. "Are you ever tempted to try and teach her to read or do math?"

"That's nonsense!" she replied. "I want her to be eager for it when the time comes, not spoil it for her."

Relax, parents, your children will not get behind if you allow them the time to accomplish the natural work of childhood.

If the Train Is Late, Will We Miss the Boat?: Development Timetables, Learning Disabilities, and Attention

One of our boys' favorite stories used to be the one about the little engine that was given the awesome responsibility of pulling all the children's Christmas presents to the other side of the mountain. I'm sure you remember that determined little fellow, puffing along earnestly with his heavy load. His refrain "I think I can, I think I can," and finally "I know I can!" have inspired generations of children to muster up the extra effort to go for the top—an important lesson, indeed. I wonder, though, if the shiny moral wrapping in which the gifts were delivered should carry a warning label: CAUTION! Don't expect all little engines to do the job of bigger ones, no matter how hard they try.

I firmly believe that children must learn not to give up too easily, but as a learning specialist, I see many little engines who didn't make it to the top. Their gifts come in dull wrappings—unfulfilled promise, defeat—often with cards attached that say, "If only you would try harder." They droop with the certainty that they are inadequate and, probably, even stupid. Yet they are often very bright children. Somehow they got derailed along the way.

Children run on different developmental timetables. By age six, teachers should expect a four-year span in maturation among students of the same chronological age. Moreover, each child's unique profile of strengths and weaknesses may constitute a learning difference that eventually becomes a "disability." One of the hardest things for everyone to understand is that *bright children are not necessarily on the fastest train.* Many problems of "underachievement" result from an incongruity between the child's neurological pattern and the expectations of the family and school. In this chapter I would like to explore some of these emotion-laden issues so you can be a wiser judge—and advocate—of a child's learning.

THE PUZZLE OF "READINESS"
A Slow Starter

Whenever I think of late bloomers, I remember Heather, a small wistful blond first grader. Young for her class, she appeared less mature than her classmates and uncomplainingly accepted the role of "baby" in group play. When playtime ended, however, her friends' tolerance decreased rapidly. One day, as usual, Heather arrived last at the reading circle, minus book and pencil. The others fidgeted while she was sent back to rummage through her desk, from which she finally produced a coverless book and an unsharpened pencil. While her classmates competently located the assigned page, she ruffled frantically through her book, unable to grasp the order of the page numbers, flipping forward, then backward as she struggled to match her book to her neighbor's.

By the time she found the page, the teacher had finished giving directions, and the group was once more delayed while Heather got another explanation. I could see her classmates' thinly disguised impatience giving way to eye rolling and giggles as the lesson proceeded and

Heather was called on to read aloud. Straddling her chair with determination, feet swinging with the force of mental effort, she struggled unsuccessfully to decode a simple sentence. Finally, the teacher sighed, "Mary, you try it," ending only momentarily Heather's daily battle in an endless war.

Would it surprise you to hear that Heather's overall mental ability was above average? It was, yet her genuine difficulty in dealing with most aspects of school had already convinced her that she was "stupid" and that learning was no fun at all. Like too many children, she suffered acutely from the gap between her need for success and the grinding daily experience of defeat and humiliation.

While a good start in school does not guarantee future success, a beginning such as Heather's—without skilled intervention—almost assures future trouble. A large proportion of youth who become serious discipline problems or drop out of school have had similar experiences. Yet almost all children, regardless of social class or background, enter school believing they will be successful; tragically, by the time they are seven, many have already been derailed.

Heather's parents, convinced that she was smart enough but a bit "lazy," had turned down recommendations that she be given special help and another year in kindergarten to gain in maturity. They thought all she needed was to be "pushed." Well-intentioned, they had unknowingly put Heather on the wrong train, an express going too fast for her and dangerously aimed at an educational scrap heap. Fortunately, in this case, skilled intervention got Heather back on track, but I have seen many children who aren't so lucky. Survival is their business, and learning remains a tense and joyless process. Plunged daily into the fire of inappropriate expectations, their early promise shrivels, and nonlearning becomes a habit. They may be labeled, treated, exhorted, and eventually tutored, but the basic issue remains unchanged. The school and the child are on different schedules.

Readiness for School

For many years experts told us that school "readiness" resulted from "neural ripening," which they insisted would unfold despite environmental influences. We now know that a child's life experiences interact with the developmental schedule of the nervous system in five separate areas, each of which is integral to learning.

1. Physical well-being and motor development.
2. Social and emotional growth.
3. Approaches toward learning, such as receptivity and a "can-do" attitude.
4. Language development.
5. Cognition (thinking skills) and general knowledge.

The quality of environmental experience primes these connections, but, despite parents' best efforts, there are some things we can't control. As described earlier, there are basically two ways in which brain cells grow. First, message-receiving dendrites arborize, growing larger and heavier, and synapses develop and strengthen as these circuits are exercised. Second, the long axons over which messages travel to other cells develop protective coatings of myelin, which make transmission systems more efficient.

All these processes depend on both the brain's experience and the child's own developmental timetable. In general, maturation moves from lower structures, sensory systems, and areas responsible for motor programs (e.g., reaching, walking) up to the highest centers for academic skills, abstract thought, self-control, and wise decision-making. Specific school skills such as handwriting, remembering math facts, and reading with comprehension require a certain level of neural development in addition to background understanding and practice. To make things even more complicated, children seem to mature for different skills on different schedules; some who are advanced in large-muscle co-

SPEEDING THE MESSAGES

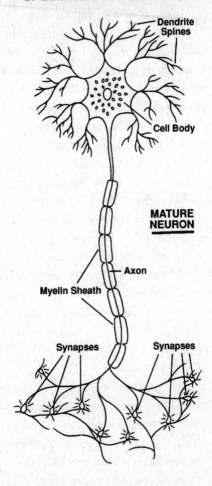

ordination may be slower in fine motor control, such as holding a pencil or knitting. A precocious artist may be a slow-developing reader, and a walking encyclopedia of facts may be severely lacking in social skills. Your child will do much better if she gets suitable support in the weaker areas even while her strong points are recognized.

Simply making demands on undeveloped or unprepared brain systems is a mistake, so our efforts must be tempered by patience and preparation until the child's mental transmission systems are equal to the task. Otherwise we risk frustration, inferior skill development, and an abiding distaste and incompetence for the activity. I have visited too many classrooms where I could painfully observe bewildered children who didn't even "get" what it was they were supposed to be able to do. Tragically, these situations are most prevalent in underfunded inner-city schools that have big classes of children, many of whom enter lacking basic school skills. Blasting them with academic expectations without taking the time to pave the way is a recipe for personal and societal disaster!

The ideal situation is to consider each child's individual pattern for learning, and plan activities in which she can experience success and progress as a result of her efforts. Yet children who need such help very often struggle on until third or fourth grade, when test scores make "diagnosis by failure" a bleak reality. By then, negative attitudes and poor learning habits have already been entrenched.

Children may fall behind because they are "late bloomers," have a learning pattern that is different, and/or are in a school that makes academic demands without adequate preliminary teaching.

Lagging Timetables

A child who is lagging slightly in development is on the same track as the others. His train simply goes at a slower pace, although it stands every chance of reaching the same destination. This type of mild delay often signals an immature nervous system. Such problems may not show up in routine medical or school testing, however. Following are some signals to watch out for. While none of these indicators alone is unusual, you would be wise to read the rest of this chapter carefully if your child shows several symptoms of delay.

1. Family patterns of slow development, "late-blooming" parents or siblings, a family history of late puberty.

2. Prematurity, which almost invariably sets back a child's developmental clock.

3. Physical or emotional problems in the early months of life.

4. Chronic diseases such as asthma, kidney disease, or ear infections. Children who spend time and energy battling such problems may not pass through stages of learning as quickly and need extra time to catch up.

5. Physical size. Developmentally immature children are often, although not always, physically small. Even large children may have a "babylike" look compared to others of the same chronological age. (Not all small children are immature, however.)

6. Lagging social development: difficulty taking turns, sharing, or communicating with peers. A child who consistently chooses younger playmates may be expressing a need for more time to grow up.

7. Immature whole-body movements and lack of control over large-muscle activities such as skipping, hopping, catching a ball, or small-muscle skills such as cutting, holding a pencil, or crayoning. Most children can go up and down stairs alternating feet by age five.

8. "Overflow movement" shows up when a child moves body parts that aren't involved in an activity—arms flap when he climbs stairs, tongue moves during coloring, feet "dance" when he sits doing a puzzle. Common in preschoolers, it is a sign of neurological immaturity in older children.

9. Delayed development of "motor timing." For example, elementary-aged children may be asked to tap their fingers first in time with a metronome and then keep up the pattern after the metronome is turned off.

10. Delayed language development, which may also be a symptom of language disability.

11. Easy distractibility and short attention span inappropriate for age. This child can't sit still and pay attention, particularly in a group, or may tend to withdraw and daydream. Remember, though, all young children have this characteristic to some degree.

12. Difficulty with impulse control inappropriate for age. Simon Says is an interesting game for diagnosis, as a child must pay attention and inhibit responses unless "Simon says" to do something. By school age, children should be able to inhibit some responses.

13. Difficulty with eye-hand coordination. One test used is copying shapes, which requires cross-modal integration of fine visual and motor skills.

14. A tendency to engage in "magical" thinking rather than confronting the realities of a situation. "If I don't notice it, it will go away" seems to be the immature child's attitude toward any demanding task (including homework later on!).

15. Chronological age, as compared with classmates. Many "problem" learners have summer or fall birthdays and are younger than others in the same class. This situation is particularly acute for boys, who may be, on average, about six months behind girls in school readiness at age six. For this reason, girls should always be evaluated in comparison with other girls, not with the boys in the class.

It is important to help all children develop good learning habits. If you want to improve your preschooler's ability to adapt to school routines, you should know that surveys of kindergarten teachers find they care much less about a child's academic skills, such as using a pencil or counting to twenty, than about the following:

- Child can verbally communicate thoughts and needs.
- Child shows enthusiasm and curiosity.
- Child can follow directions.
- Child gets along with peers.

On a Different Track

Some children don't seem so much delayed as different in development. Children do, indeed, have "styles" for thinking and processing information, differences that are either inherited or environmentally induced. In chapter 6 we will explore differences in the two sides of the brain that may help account for styles of learning, even in preschool years.

Children with "different" learning styles can have trouble because their natural talents don't conform with the school's demands. For example, I think of Sam, a seven-year-old boy who is a whiz at block-building and can fix any mechanical device he gets his hands on (after he has it for a few minutes it needs fixing, because he takes it apart). His room is a "disaster," but it contains a novel "kitten catcher" that he has rigged up with string and boxes, and his toy shelves hold several half-completed models of "my latest invention."

Sam sounds like a budding genius, but he is already in trouble in school. First of all, his language development is unsophisticated and he sometimes confuses sounds. When he tries to describe something, he splashes words all over his topic without organizing them very well or getting to the point. He would much rather show than tell you about something, and he is massively disinterested in his mother's efforts to read to him. As far as Sam is concerned, pencils are good only for drawing, and he is quite unclear about the left and right sides of the page. At school he finds reading difficult, preferring to play or build things outdoors. He has trouble following oral directions, but he can patiently figure out how to make two pieces of wood go together just right. No one can be good at everything, and the parts of his brain that control language and reading are lagging behind his other areas of advanced development.

In another culture Sam might be considered gifted, but his school expects children to spend most of their time reading, writing, listening, and doing math papers. His pattern of learning is different, not deficient, but he may always struggle in a setting that values verbal and analytical skills more than his creative, hands-on talents.

A thorough professional evaluation reveals that Sam is dyslexic even though his overall IQ is in the "gifted" range. He needs special teaching techniques in order to learn to read and spell successfully. What will happen to Sam? The things for which he is "ready" aren't in the curriculum. His father, a successful architect, remembers his own grim school experience and wants to spare Sam similar anguish. What can he do?

No Easy Answers

No easy answers exist for these dilemmas. There is no point in forcing learning on a brain that is unequipped—either through delay or difference—to handle it. But young brains are plastic; they can be changed by good teaching and family support. For example, new imaging studies show that the areas in Sam's brain needed for successful reading can be activated by systematic teaching techniques, which you will read about in chapter 7.

In an ideal world—and in well-informed schools today—several things help prevent failure. Parents and teachers work together to understand the problem, preserve the child's self-respect, and develop a coordinated plan that includes specialized help, as indicated. Since different children learn through different channels, good teachers vary instructional approaches to make learning a more successful experience for all. Sam can receive special help in language, reading, and spelling; learn math through a "hands-on" approach with manipulative materials; and get lots of positive recognition for his mechanical skills, creative ideas, and generous disposition. Standardized tests should be used diagnostically—to gain information about Sam's progress and needs, not merely to label him as inadequate.

Heather also needs some special help, and she would have a much better chance in a less rigid classroom organization that could accommodate different levels of maturation, perhaps by grouping children of multiple ages together in the early grades. If the school is hopelessly inflexible or expects children to accomplish work that is developmentally too advanced for their age, immature children sometimes have a better chance if they repeat a year—preferably in preschool or kindergarten. Repeating helps some struggling students, but it is far from a panacea and should be considered only IF:

1. The major problem is immaturity;
2. The school judges that the child can be successful with another try;

3. It is done as early as possible;
4. It is presented to the child as an opportunity rather than a failure, and her parents are sold on the idea;
5. She receives help if she continues to need it.

In Heather's case, another year in first grade, with special support from a learning specialist, seemed to be the best option. After observing her frustration in class, her parents not only helped sell Heather on the idea, but they and the school also gave her a great deal of positive emotional support throughout the transition. Above all, no one ever accused Heather of "failing," and she went on to eventually become a good student and a class leader.

Alas, not all parents have access to a school that puts children's needs at the top of the list. If you have a child like Sam or Heather, or if your child is having any kind of difficulty that lasts more than a few months, you should step in and try to discover what the problem might be. Talk with the teacher, describe your concerns in a nonjudgmental way, and try to work out an action plan for both home and school. Often this is all that is necessary. If the problem continues and appears serious, however, you will find specific steps to take later in the chapter.

One thing is clear: children do not desire to fail. From the day they are born, children are naturally motivated to learn, to master their environments, and to feel competent. Naturally, they learn best the things that are meaningful or important to them. It is our job as adults to devise tasks to harness that natural learning power, not to play the Blame Game if our demands are unfair. We can give children the desire to succeed at the things we want to teach them—by helping them feel competent and making early learning experiences interesting, successful, and understandable. Even drill on basic skills can be energizing if it is embedded in a rich curriculum that is intellectually meaningful to the child.

Promoting Learning at Home

Parents must help. Sam might sit still for stories about inventors, machines, or gadgets. He might respond with interest if someone at home offered to write large labels for his inventions or type up his descriptions of them and help him read them. A parent might help him draw plans for a new bookcase in his room, improving fine motor control and planning. He could dictate directions, in order, for making a "kitten catcher," and play games following other directions.

Heather's family can try to boost her confidence in herself while guiding her to assume more personal responsibility and praising her for acting more mature. They can make sure she has all the equipment she needs for school each day and help her practice organizing and using it. They can read interesting books to her that she is not yet ready to read herself. She might like to dictate stories or keep a journal (see chapter 10).

For children who are not lucky enough to have such supportive homes, the community and child care centers have a big role to fill. Children's initial experiences in school shape their lifelong attitudes about learning, cooperating in society, and being responsible and productive.

Formal instruction places a whole set of new demands on the child's nervous system. To be ready, children need:

1. Sufficient rest and nourishment in order to concentrate for several hours.

2. The experience of listening, following directions, and responding politely to adults.

3. Knowledge of appropriate behavioral limits.

4. The experience of socializing with other children.

5. Help in obtaining and organizing school supplies.

6. Clothing chosen because it is easy for the child to manage, not because it has a designer label or is cute.

7. Help in learning to express needs, concerns, or questions independently.

8. Practice in holding small objects and manipulating scissors, glue, crayons, paint brushes, and rulers. Practice in following a left-to-right pattern.

9. Understanding that books are interesting gateways to stories and information.

10. Physical and emotional safety.

"But She'll Be Bored"

Some parents face a totally different problem—a child who takes to learning at an unusually fast pace. If your child is stuck in a deadly-dull curriculum, you should try to change things if at all possible and supplement schoolwork with interesting learning opportunities at home to keep curiosity alive. Good curriculum doesn't necessarily mean pushing kids into more advanced learning activities simply for the sake of acceleration, however. Research shows that your child's ultimate success in life will depend more on personal characteristics like motivation, creativity, and the ability to communicate effectively with other people than on whether he reads Dickens in the fourth grade. Some parents, in fact, are overly concerned about "boredom." Young children enjoy repetition, for it gives them a feeling of control and mastery, and sometimes clever children learn to use the word "boring" to avoid difficult tasks. Their parents are so panicky about slow progress that a reaction is guaranteed.

Remember that the heady experience of daily success and mastery is not boring for a child. Remember, too, to listen. I remember one mother storming into a nursery school to complain that they weren't challenging her daughter, who had come home and announced that she was "bored at school." The teacher was surprised, since the little girl acted happy and excited about classroom activities. The impasse continued until someone decided to ask the child what "bored" meant. "Oh, it means I'm hot," she replied cheerfully. Indeed, there were some problems with the furnace, and in dance class, when she heard another child comment that he was "bored," she thought she had learned a new word! Happily, the mother apologized and the child continued to learn in a stimulating but unpressured setting. I guess the moral of that story is, listen to the child's feelings, not to your own.

Even in upper grades, when brains are primed for more advanced learning, youngsters still have a strong need to feel competent. The main challenge of good teaching is to find that golden mean combining curiosity, challenge, and possibility.

The Fast Track

What about skipping a grade? Occasionally, in cases where the child is truly precocious in overall mental, physical, and social development, acceleration may be advised, but such children are rare. A series of studies looked at such exceptional twelve-to-fourteen-year-olds who were accelerated because they scored as well as high school seniors in mathematics achievement. At age twenty-three they showed little difference in social or personal factors compared to a comparable group that had stayed with their own grade, nor were most of the precocious group significantly advanced in academic and personal achievement.

Generally speaking, it is desirable to keep the youngster with age mates when possible, working with the school to develop opportunities for appropriately challenging work. The all-important interpersonal skills are best gained from successful peer relationships. Intellectual stimulation is a valuable goal, but it takes a truly exceptional child to avoid compromising social and emotional needs by skipping grades.

In cases where a child is truly bored or has tuned out because his exceptional talents simply cannot be addressed, acceleration in one or more subjects may be advisable if:

- the student receives ongoing support from teachers and parents;
- the student has effective study habits;
- the student has access to similarly talented peers and/or an adult mentor.

Such decisions should always be made thoughtfully. Last year a friend of mine asked his son's principal for advice about the boy, who was small and physically immature for his age but academically gifted. The teacher had suggested that Paul might skip fourth grade, possibly because his parents kept pushing for extra enrichment. My friend was worried about such a major step, not only because of his son's physical immaturity but also because Paul had many good friends in his current class and seemed happy and successful in school. After hearing the whole story, the principal casually reminded Dad that when Paul got to junior high, the boys in the locker room would not be comparing IQs. Paul stayed with his class.

On a Different Track: What to Do?

If you suspect your child may be a candidate either for slow or unusually rapid maturation, or for a learning difference that will cause trouble, what should you do? First, try to be as objective as you can about the situation. Observe your child in groups of peers and strive for a candid view of all areas of development. Teachers are more objective than you, since they see your child in an age-centered context every day. Most schools have psychologists on staff who can observe children and perhaps administer diagnostic tests. They tend to be overscheduled, however, so you may choose to speed up the process by consulting an outside specialist.

Start by having a heart-to-heart talk with an understanding physician to rule out unidentified physical problems. Pediatricians are becoming much more aware of learning problems, but they still don't see the child in school every day. Inform yourself from among the many books written about learning styles and learning differences so you can ask good questions. You may wish to request a thorough evaluation from an educational psychologist who specializes in these issues, or a neurodevelopmental evaluation at a hospital or clinic. A one-shot group-administered test is a very poor index of a child's development, and parents should not accept such results as definitive. Read chapter 8 to learn more about testing. Insist on the services you need; the school is obligated to provide them but sometimes, in order to get the train on the track, you need to rock the boat!

In any case, resist that urge to panic, which may cause you to start pressuring the child. If recommendations are made, take them seriously. Analyze ways in which you can provide pleasurable experiences at home that are directed to your child's particular needs. Above all, focus on your child's special talents and emotional needs. They are particularly important for the brain's most basic assignment—paying attention.

LET'S PAY ATTENTION

Attention and its partner, self-regulation, are the foundation of learning. They are also an increasing problem in our "multitasking" society. Genetic factors, prenatal toxins, drugs, and alcohol as well as prematurity put children more at risk for attention deficits, but many other possible causes exist. In fact, difficulties with attention now comprise a large proportion of referrals and diagnosis for all childhood psychiatric disorders, and many children are taking some sort of medication—stimulant or otherwise—to help them settle down and concentrate. In this section I will summarize a huge body of research and opinion on this subject and try to offer some useful suggestions. Although these core abilities are rooted in the physiology of the brain, the home and school environments have a great deal to do with how a child learns to use his particular attention mechanisms.

The whole issue of attention disorder, which is called ADHD, or Attention Deficit (with or without Hyperactivity) Disorder, is controversial. Definitions of and testing procedures for the disorder are vague and vary greatly among different communities and professionals. Moreover, the widespread use of psychotropic medications, such as Ritalin, Concerta, or Strattera, has come under question because of potential side effects and uncertainty about long-term effects. While they clearly help some children control their behavior more effectively in the short term, they are not a "cure" and should be accompanied by behavioral treatment and careful monitoring.

Many ADHD children are very bright and creative. The increasing medicalization of attention problems as well as the term "disorder" is questioned by many specialists. A number of highly successful and productive adults might have been so labeled if this category had been around when they were growing up. Some children with attention problems show significant improvement at adolescence, but increasing numbers of attention-disordered adults are currently being diagnosed.

Attention changes with age—a normal lack of inhibition in a four-year-old becomes a serious problem in a ten-year-old. Moreover, a regular bumptious child (usually a boy) may seem very much out of place in an overly restrictive and stressful classroom. When normally active youngsters are condemned to desks and routine pencil-and-paper tasks all day, we should not be surprised if they show up with problems. Many schools are increasingly restricting children's free playtime. This is bad for everyone, but especially for children with a strong need to work off physical energy.

Attention problems are also found in many children who have language or reading problems; sometimes treating that problem makes it easier for the child to focus on learning. It is also probable that too much time with TV and video games exacerbates attention difficulties, as I have explained in *Endangered Minds*. One mom just told me that after their house was burglarized and her ADHD son's electronic game cube stolen, his behavior and attention span improved almost at once.

Different Brain?

Scans show that the brains of "attention-disordered" individuals function differently from "normals" when they are given various types of tasks. Figuring out why is not a simple issue, however. Paying attention requires maturation and use of a number of widely scattered brain areas, all the way from the brain stem up to the top level of the prefrontal cortex. Interconnecting loops pass up and down and forward and back

MAKING CONNECTIONS: THE ATTENTION LOOP

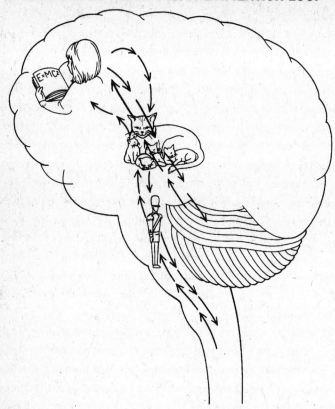

(feed-forward and feed-back systems) through structures in the limbic system, or "emotional" brain, including areas involved in memory and motivation. These connections function partially on neurotransmitters in the catecholamine system called dopamine and norepinephrine. Most drugs used to treat ADHD regulate these chemicals, although no one has agreed on exactly how they do it. We also do not know how much of one's neurotransmitter balance is determined by genetics and how much by experiences, activities, and emotions.

Research has clearly demonstrated that there is a hereditary tendency for attention difficulties, but there is also evidence that the brain's chemical balance can be changed by environmental factors. For example, chronic stress revs up fight-or-flight hormone and neurotransmitter systems and can even kill off neurons. On the other hand, numerous studies suggest that learning to keep one's brain quiet, as in reflection or meditation, has the opposite effect. So, even though your child inherits genes for an attention problem, the severity with which it expresses itself will be influenced by home and school.

The best time to intervene to build positive attention habits in the brain is as early as possible, and definitely before age seven. You should be particularly mindful of this possible "sensitive period" if anyone in the child's family suffers from distractibility, mental disorganization, or impulsivity. Nonetheless, changes are still possible at any age, especially if the individual is highly motivated.

Step One: is to aim for a positive and understanding emotional climate. Parents who are overly permissive or overly bossy are more likely to have children with problems. "Authoritative" parenting produces children most able to manage their own behavior (self-regulation), who get into less trouble in school, are better adjusted socially, and who develop more powerful attention and motivation systems. These parents are (most of the time—no one's perfect!) firm, loving, reasonably patient, empathetic, willing to listen to the child and negotiate rules, and available to give emotional support when the child needs it. Emotion, motivation, and attention are wound together so tightly in the brain that it is impossible to separate them.

Step Two: Establish reasonable expectations for behavior, set clear rules, and discuss or negotiate them with the child. Also, talk over what the consequences will be for infractions. Check the child's understanding by asking her to tell you what you just talked about. Please heed the word "reasonable." Sometimes parents tell me they insist that their five- or six-year-old sit and work on schoolwork with them each night for an hour or more. Many adults have trouble understanding the real limitations that immaturity places on the ability to stay with one task—especially one the child didn't choose. On the other hand, some parents have never learned to say "no," which is, unfortunately, part of our job. It is no kindness to either the child or the world to turn loose an individual who has never had a chance to experience and internalize a reasonable control system.

Step Three: Direct your best efforts to establishing a well-regulated household environment. If your child inherited the attention problem from you, this task is a real challenge—but your child needs it. Uncontrolled households, where routines are never made clear and that blast young brains with too many stimuli and too little structure, impose stress on the growing brain and may diminish the development of internal control systems. Even ongoing background noise stresses out adult brains, and it can be a real trial for a child's tender synapses. Conversely, rigidly structured households that place unrealistic demands on children or keep them in fear of making a mistake can be equally damaging.

You can help your child find the best stimulus level during different activities. The brain has instinctive drives to regulate the amounts of stimulation—auditory, visual, and tactile—that come in, but children can miss their own cues. Watch for signs of unusual behavior, overexcitedness, wildness, or withdrawal, which signal a need for protection from sensory bombardment. Do not expect children to realize when they have had enough excitement. The same goes for "screen time." It is much harder to turn off a TV or computer than to turn it on—even for adults.

Step Four: Teach your child to use words to plan and control behavior. We will return to this very important point later. Language is also a major route to good social relationships, which are jeopardized if the impulsive child is annoying to peers in play or cooperative learning situations.

Step Five: If you think your child has an attention deficit that is inconsistent with age and has persisted more than six months, you may decide to consult with your pediatrician or a pediatric neurologist for a clearer diagnosis. First, inform yourself by consulting several books, since there are many different points of view on this "disorder." Be aware, also, that chronically hurried physicians are noted for prescribing medications, period. Experts agree that any treatment plan—whether or not you choose to use medications—must include behavioral counseling for both parent and child. A good professional can help you understand how to manage the child and the behavior most effectively. Systems of clear, short-term rewards and consequences are often spelled out, so the child can start to take control of managing himself. The school should also be informed and involved in the treatment program, and a helpful teacher can make a big difference. Do remember that if your child has a real self-regulation problem, he is not doing this on purpose. Keep the emotional supports and conversation in place, and you will get much better outcomes.

Many parents do not wish to give medications to their child. In this case, it is doubly important to read widely and try sensible alternative approaches. Some of the general suggestions below may be helpful.

In a Nutshell: Helping the Attention Regulator

• Establish firm limits and predictable routines. Teach your child what "no" means—but not punitively.

• Insist on a regular bedtime and adequate rest. Insufficient sleep can cause attention problems. Make a routine of story time before bed.

• As the child grows, make sure she feels she has more say in setting rules and some choices in negotiating them.

• Insist on a noise level in the home that is within reasonable limits. Some parents refer to "indoor voices" and "outdoor voices" to give children a concrete cue. Moderate or eliminate background TV noise.

• Remember that you have a framework of experience that helps you screen out sounds, while the child does not. One little boy was terribly distracted until his mother finally realized he was frightened by the sound of airplanes overhead, which she hadn't even noticed. After she showed him what they were, he was able to concentrate better.

• Make sure the young child has a quiet space of his own to go to at any time—even if it is only a card table covered by a blanket.

• Keep adult-type stimulation to a minimum (e.g., inappropriate movies, TV, or adult magazines; overly exciting or alarming adult conversations). Help "mediate" your child's response by discussing content together.

• Limit TV viewing. Be tough—it's important. Until we have research to the contrary, we must consider that too much viewing may change brain patterns and make it harder for a child to concentrate in school.

• Supervise and restrict the amount of time spent on the computer. See "Mediating the Media" later in this chapter for specific guidelines.

• Insist that your child get some physical exercise every day, preferably outdoors.

• Some youngsters who have attention problems also have difficulty managing sequences of movements. For a child like this, individual sports like swimming, bowling, or hiking may be preferable to team sports. Sometimes training in tae kwon do, karate, or yoga can enhance control systems.

• Spend some time working with your child and showing him how to solve problems systematically. Play a game, start a project, take up a hobby, such as model-building or cooking together. Talk about the steps you take to attack each problem.

• Let attention span develop naturally by also allowing time for a child to become actively engaged in a task without interruption.

• Be sure there is someone in the home to whom the child can go to be hugged, held, and calmed down if necessary.

• Physical contact (hugging, rocking) is still necessary for children beyond infancy.

• An overexcited child may respond to a gentle but firm touch. Hold him gently by the shoulders or sit close to him with your arm around him.

• Get the child's attention, with eye contact, before you give a direction. Check understanding by asking him what he heard.

• You may need to help a young child shift focus from one activity to another. Pave the way in advance. ("When you finish putting the spools in the jar, I'm going to ask you to wash your hands for dinner.")

• Prepare the child for potentially alarming or upsetting situations. ("On Halloween children will come to our door dressed in funny costumes that may look scary sometimes.")

• Some children may have trouble regulating attention because of allergic responses in brain tissue to food or environmental substances; if you suspect an allergy, check with a specialist.

• Pay attention to nutrition. Try to identify substances or situations that create problems. Some parents find that excess sugar or sugar substitutes in a child's diet seem to contribute to "hyper" behavior and mood swings. Again, it is worth your effort to maintain a firm hand here. Some nutritionists are convinced of the benefits of essential fatty acids or certain vitamins in a wholesome diet.

• Avoid frenetic scheduling. Your child's brain will thrive with some downtime instead of constant activity.

• Use words along with actions when showing something to the child; language is the ultimate mediator of attention.

• Some attention problems may show up as lethargy or "spaciness." While the dimensions of this problem are not entirely clear, it too may warrant a consultation with a specialist.

The Power of Language in Regulating Attention

The effectiveness of the prefrontal cortex, which governs the attention system, may be improved by using words to guide behavior. Most adults instinctively use this brain-building "inner language" to work through problems or plans—literally talking to themselves inside their heads. Studies show that even little children perform a task better when they use "private speech" along with actions. Parents can help a toddler, for example, by describing what she is doing and encouraging her to use words. ("You are pounding the pegs into the board. Let's say 'hit' every time you pound one.") Household tasks such as cooking present many opportunities. ("Let's go over the steps before we start." "What ingredients do we need?" "Did I do it right?" "What's the next step?")

An interesting long-term study started with kindergartners and ended when they took the SAT years later. Experimenters gave each child a marshmallow with the instruction that if they could wait a cer-tain number of minutes before eating it, they would get two marsh-mallows to eat. Those who were able to control their impulses and wait had higher scores years later on the SAT than those who were unable to defer gratification and gobbled up the treat at once. The strategies that successful "waiters" used included trying to ignore the marshmal-low and, significantly, talking to themselves about how important it was to wait and how happy they would be when they received the ex-tra marshmallow. The gobblers had no such strategies to help put their brains in charge of their behavior.

Children of all ages should be encouraged to talk through situa-tions before plunging in and while they are working. I frequently ask distractible youngsters to "sit on your hands and *tell* me what you think you should do with this problem" (work sheet, drawing, sentence, math equation). They think it is funny, but it gets their brain into com-munication with itself and they do a better job.

I remember one impulsive eight-year-old who could not remem-ber to bring both book and pencil to the reading table. Every day the teacher said to her, "Tell me what you will need. Now ask yourself, 'Do I have my pencil? My book?'" She thought this was a wonderful game, and soon we had only to say, "Have you asked yourself *the question?*" Eventually, Daneesha was able to do it herself. Now a sophisticated pre-teen, she sidled up to me in the hall not long ago with a big grin on her face. "You know," she said, "I still ask myself *the question!*"

Mediating the Media

Since I wrote two books about the effects—both good and bad—of TV and computers on the growing brain, I have been traveling around the country speaking with quite a few parent groups. I invariably find some-one who tells me about successfully banning the tube completely from their home—and subsequently watching their children's attention, their grades, and their family life together begin to flourish in new and won-derful ways. I admire the grit of such folks, and I suspect that their chil-

MANAGING "SCREEN TIME":
TV, VIDEO GAMES, AND COMPUTER USE

- Guidelines from the American Academy of Pediatrics:
  1. Remove TV and computers from your child's bedroom, and keep them in a central area where you can keep an eye on the amount and type of use.
  2. Screen carefully for content. Watching violence is poisonous, especially for some children who seem to be most susceptible to its effects. Even some sports video games contain gratuitous violence. Monitor for inappropriate sexual material or overly frightening content.
  3. Enforce time limits:
     a. Ages below two years: No screen time.
     b. Above age two: Limit TV, movies, and video and computer games to one to two hours a day (or less, or even none) of educational, nonviolent content.
- If you want your child to be a good student and a motivated reader, and she is spending more than ten hours a week with TV and video, take some constructive limiting action. You may need to negotiate a new plan with the child and effect a staged withdrawal.
- Moderate amounts of well-supervised television viewing do not appear to detract from children's school achievement. Likewise, by the time children are in elementary school they can profit from working with some types of computer programs—especially if you are part of the activity. We know too little about the effects of video games; they do improve eye-hand coordination in ways appropriate for airplane pilots, but not necessarily for readers and writers. Screen time definitely detracts from reading time and from imaginative free play.
- Consider the possibility that children are better off without computer use until age seven, when their brain is better able to process this type of two-dimensional learning.
- Be especially careful to scrutinize TV programs for children under six.

(Programs that may be most suitable for preschoolers, such as *Mr. Rogers,* tend to bore many adults. Don't apply your standards; watch your child's response.) Look for:

—comprehensibility: Can the child tell you what it was about?

—slow pace of conversation and segment length

—invitations to the child to respond

—good language use

—positive attitudes conveyed about others

—good models of behavior; absence of "sassy" content or language

- Negotiate limits for all screen time and program choices with your school-age child. Help her plan what she will watch each week. Stick to it.
- Watch TV with your child when possible. *Discuss* what you see. Don't be afraid to model your own values by questioning characters' behavior or plot formats.
- If your child is allowed to watch an unsuitable program at the house of a friend, try to put it in perspective by discussing with your child why you do not allow that material in your home. Ask for the child's opinions, and listen to them. You may find he really didn't care for it, either.
- Insist that substitute caregivers follow your rules.
- Check out the National TV Turn-Off Week, held every April (see bibliography). You will get some new ideas, and your whole family will benefit.

dren will have a very good chance of becoming successful. Most families are seeking milder alternatives, however, so above are some practical tips.

In chapter 5 we will look at the new field of "media literacy," in which parents can use TV programs and even commercials as learning tools. The bottom line is that we do not know for sure what any of our electronic media do to the growing brain, but repeated exposure to any stimulus is bound to have neurological consequences. Parents who have made the hard decision to be temporarily considered ogres often receive their children's gratitude much later on. They know they were right when their grown children insist on similar guidelines for their own youngsters. Have courage—you are wiser and you own the house.

ON THE RIGHT TRACK

Many perspectives on learning converge on one point: Children must have time to do their own mental growing. Parents and teachers are the "scaffolds" for the process, but the child is the true magician, with an instinctive need to learn, to master, and to seek out the right challenges. Adults who try to take over the show run a serious risk. By imposing demands relating to their own cognitive frameworks instead of to the child's, they can distort the natural timetable. Pushing little engines up the mountain doesn't work in the long run, because there will always be higher mountains on the other side that the child must eventually tackle on his own.

As one who has watched many late and different bloomers flourish as the years passed, I can honestly tell parents, "Keep the faith." Heather is now about to receive her PhD in environmental biology, and Sam is successfully running his own construction company. It took many caring adults and many years for them to find their own routes, but patience paid off.

Both the fast and the slow starters need an opportunity to explore the schemas of childhood on their way to the top. Since we don't have a "golden screwdriver" to magically alter neural growth (if we should even want to!), we must accept and work with each child's pattern. Many "late" or "different" bloomers are children who have formidable potential. Lest their talents be lost to society and to themselves, let's do our best to keep them on the right track.

Chapter 5

Childhood into Adolescence: Furnishing the Adult Mind, Age Eight and Beyond

The growth of a child's mind toward the capacity for adult thinking is one of the most dynamic aspects of brain development. Nature builds the framework; it is up to the child, parents, and school to complete the walls and do the interior decorating. Throughout childhood, development moves upward from the basement of reflex response toward the highest levels where the frontal lobes take over. At least twenty years are needed to finish this process, and for adults with active minds the job may never be finished!

Children need time to practice with fancier mental furnishings at each stage of development. The more they use the equipment, the more comfortable they become with it—and the better their base for the next level. The middle elementary years are an important time for consolidating early foundations, because sometime around age eleven the mind's top floors start to get a new set of furnishings. New types of thinking are suddenly possible, but the view from the penthouse is often scary and confusing. Let's explore some of the perils—and wonders—of the fascinating years that mark this transition.

MENTAL GROWTH IN ACTION

One bonus of my job, working with students at all grade levels, is the opportunity to see mental growth in action. For a bird's-eye view of children's thinking, consider these responses from different ages to the question, "Why do we have laws?"

Age six:

SUZIE: "Because some people eat bubble gum and it's *not fair* if some people have it and others don't!"

PETER: "If you're driving too fast they might give you a ticket."

RICARDO: "Because you might get hurt."

These children are all delightfully concrete thinkers, but there are some interesting differences in their answers. Suzie's answer is typical of a younger child—caught by personal, very concrete experience. Peter has moved on a bit, pushing out beyond his playground to one particular law, and Ricardo manages a rudimentary generalization. Such different levels of abstraction are common at age six and seven—an important transition point in children's ability to grasp ideas that go beyond concrete physical experience.

Age ten:

GEORGE: "If we didn't have laws people would go out and steal things. Car crashes would be to often because people wouldn't stop for red lights. Other people would shoot each other."

NAOMI: "We have laws because if we didn't, then the world would go biserk. If we didn't have laws like 'DON'T LITTER' or 'DON'T FISH HERE' or 'NO HUNTING' then people won't know if their supposed to do this or that."

ANN: "Laws were made to protect us and to keep the world or our country safe."

These typical ten-year-olds wrote their answers—and their spelling is, as always, just as interesting as their ideas. Notice how this age level loves rules, law, and order—one of the hallmarks of late elementary years. Having absorbed a lot of information about the way the world works, they are still inclined to relate ideas back to concrete personal experiences. Ann is one of the few in the class who managed a more abstract statement. At this age there is usually less variability than at others. Let's see what happens in three years.

Age thirteen:

TYRONE: "We have laws to keep control of people. Laws help us to be safe. They teach us to follow directions and obey them. If you do not, you may be severely punished just as in school."

KATE: "The main reason is to keep this world under control. For example: an eleven-year-old boy could go into a bar and ask for a vodka, but since there are laws they prevent eleven-year-olds to be able to do that."

BIANCA: "Laws are very important to have in any form of group. They protect people from others. No one or group could or would survive without them. If we had no laws we would have no rights."

FRANKLIN: "We have to run by some sort of guidelines to live by and to run our society in an efficient way. If we did not have laws, we would probably be the only animals that would not have some sort of system."

Welcome to adolescence! Notice the striking contrast between two students' personal, concrete thinking (Tyrone, Kate), and near-adult perspectives on society's needs and universal principles (Bianca, Franklin). The rigid law-and-order emphasis of middle childhood (rules should be followed so you won't be punished) eventually gives way, for most teenagers, to larger perspectives (laws are necessary for the survival of a society), but timetables for this change vary dramatically. How would you like to be a teacher trying to plan a lesson to interest every student in this class? Something exciting is taking place, but it hasn't fully happened to everyone.

Everyone knows that the physical changes of adolescence are important, and neurological changes are also an important part of the process. This chapter will summarize the most current information on brain development from middle childhood through adolescence, give you a look inside some schools, and suggest ways parents and teachers can collaborate to help.

FINISHING CHILDHOOD:
THE YEARS FROM EIGHT TO ELEVEN
"School's OK, I'm OK"

Ages eight to ten are a relatively calm period for many children. As academic skills from previous years are practiced and refined, most students feel capable and in control. The brain strengthens its abilities for learning as myelination of fibers speeds associations between senses and ideas. Late elementary grades are an ideal time to apply skills already learned. Reading to learn replaces learning to read; math becomes useful in the shopping mall or on the computer. Repeating skills and rituals lays a solid base for moving on to new challenges.

Children at this age love to soak up information and facts, but they may not reflect very deeply about them unless an adult guides them. They painstakingly copy paragraphs for reports but need help in paraphrasing them. Lots of practice is needed—and instruction on organization skills. Above all, older children need plenty of time for their own brands of play. They still learn best by starting with concrete experience. The most helpful parents and the most successful teachers capture their wide-ranging curiosity in active, project-oriented learning.

Hands-On Justice

One creative teacher got wonderful results when she capitalized on a "teachable moment." Noticing that all her "sophisticated" nine-year-old girls were bringing their dolls to recess, she wisely figured they were expressing a need to be children for a little while longer. As she eavesdropped on the doll society, it was rocked by an argument over playground territory (reptilian brain?). The girls set up a "court" to mediate the dispute, and soon the boys began to take sides, although no one was too clear on the judicial process. Sensing a golden opportunity to weave together interest, concept, and skill development, the teacher expanded her plans and suggested that the class investigate firsthand how courts work, neatly supplementing the fourth grade American history curriculum objectives. In the following weeks students searched out books, newspaper articles, and Internet sources to write about and discuss in class. Children chose group or independent projects and practiced defending a point of view with oral and multimedia presentations. A lawyer father came to discuss his experiences in court and answer questions. Parent volunteers organized a visit to a real courtroom, where the judge was so impressed with these young scholars' knowledge that she let them sit in on a trial and took them on an unscheduled tour of the justice center. Finally, the dolls' own court was held, and the classroom newspaper proclaimed the result—a hung jury.

Not all teachers are this imaginative or hardworking, but all need parents' support if they try to flee now and then from the tyranny of worksheets, overly abstract curricula, and from artificial standards of "competence" that put limits on intellectual curiosity. The human brain learns and remembers best what it understands. Simply restricting students to the memorization of facts for which they have little conceptual grasp is poor preparation for grasping the complex issues of a complex world. Such "real" experiences are particularly important in late elementary years because students need help with abstract concepts such as "justice" or "law." At home, parents have an important role in seeking out opportunities to supplement the school's efforts, capitalizing on children's ready curiosity for mind-stretching conversations, family trips, and activities. The following list may give you some ideas.

STRETCHING THE BRAINS OF PRETEENS

- Help them begin challenging literal fact:
    "Why do we go to school only on weekdays? Why five days a week?"
    "Why shouldn't *people steal?"*

- Let them see that there are many points of view on issues, and probably *no one right answer* on many questions.
- Play games with open-ended questions:
    "What would happen if . . .
    every day were Monday?
    automobiles were declared illegal?
    computers needed to be fed three times a day?"

    "What would you do if . . .
    we won the lottery?
    we lost all our money?
    you woke up one morning seven feet tall?"

- Help them articulate their feelings, and don't be afraid to talk about yours. ("I really felt scared when I thought Grandma was seriously ill. I bet you did, too.")
- Play games of strategy that require weighing alternatives, planning moves ahead, or viewing a situation from the opponent's perspective (Stratego, Battleship, Uno, chess, checkers, gin rummy, hearts).
- Play Twenty Questions. Show how to ask categorical questions. ("Is it an animal?" rather than "Is it a dog?")
- Practice allowing the child to make some reasonable choices and to experience the natural consequences. ("If you use your allowance on the CD,

you won't have enough to go to the movies on Saturday.") Don't weaken and bail them out of minor consequences.

- If your child has trouble understanding a school assignment, look for a way to present it with pictures, time lines, maps, or objects that can be manipulated. Have fun acting out ideas or situations. Your child still learns best from concrete experience.
- Get a book of simple science experiments and try some at home. Talk about possibilities of what might happen. Make guesses together, without worrying about who's right or wrong.
- Have dinner together and talk with your child.
- Watch TV together and talk about what happened. *Listen* to what your child is saying. Good family conversation times produce good students, and psychologists know that parents who are good listeners tend to have better-adjusted teenagers.
- Don't stop reading aloud. Encourage memorization of fine poetry or prose. Try round-robin family reading.
- Appreciate those childlike qualities even while you help preteens stretch. Remember, they still reason differently from you.

STUMBLING BLOCKS TO LEARNING

Although brains work quite smoothly for many children of this age, untreated learning differences may finally be recognized as schoolwork places more complex demands on basic sensory systems and executive function. As described in chapter 4, parents may need to press the school for needed services or consult with outside specialists. Two common and baffling quirks are particularly likely to show up now.

A Problem of Output

Some children are fine until required to write something down presentably or get it organized and executed in some other way. They understand and reason as well as anyone else but can't "get it together" for homework or written assignments. They may score adequately on standardized tests where all they have to do is check the right answer, but if asked to produce a report or project, their output may resemble a childish-looking mess even after hours of effort. This puzzling problem often gets blamed on lack of effort or "carelessness," but more likely results from some sort of glitch in the nervous system that causes far more anguish to the child than to anyone else.

One young friend of mine, Jules, had trouble from the early grades, when he couldn't organize his fingers around a pencil. He always found writing slow and frustrating—even though he was one of the brightest children in the class. Jules managed to get by until he arrived in the middle school with serious difficulties in producing decent written work or even getting organized to do his homework. By now he had a secondary problem—avoidance of normal amounts of practice. His parents became really worried and altered their busy schedules to help him every evening. Pitched battles ensued as they pushed and Jules dug in his heels.

Luckily, Jules attended a school where special help was available. At his parents' request, he was tested by a psychologist, who confirmed a high IQ and a specific learning problem. The psychologist leveled with Jules and they developed a plan together. His teachers were asked to shorten some written assignments, but to insist that Jules keep up his end of the bargain and complete a reasonable amount. He was encouraged to shine in oral reports and class discussions. His parents were counseled in understanding his difficulty and helping him plan homework time and proofread assignments without taking over his share of the responsibility.

As the tension eased, Jules began to try harder. He practiced keyboarding so he could use a word processor and developed some basic strategies for tackling homework. He still writes the bare minimum, but when I saw him in the hall recently, he confided that he had decided it was "worth it" to keep trying.

It is not too late for such early difficulties to be overcome in the middle grades if parents and teachers work together. Like Jules, many students suffer from what Dr. Melvin Levine calls "developmental output failure," which may go unnoticed until an emphasis on "decoding"—reading words—changes to a need for "encoding," which requires organizing, remembering, and restating information. Neural systems for input are working just fine, but immaturity at the output level causes trouble. Such youngsters also have trouble organizing their thoughts. Pulling together information from many sources, managing time and materials, and handling heavy demands on memory may be too much for them. "Mind-mapping," as described in chapter 11, can be a big help.

Calling such a child "lazy" makes the problem worse, as Levine's book, *The Myth of Laziness,* asserts. I have seen many boys and girls like Jules, and I believe this problem is one of the most pervasive—and difficult—of the middle childhood years and is a hidden component of underachievement, attention deficits, and problem behavior later on. Not all schools are as enlightened as the one Jules attends. Many teachers and even some psychologists are not informed about this type of learning problem, so parents must become the first line of defense. Help from an expert tutor may be required. Meanwhile, don't let a child like this develop habits of "lost" homework and deception. ("The dog ate it." "It blew out of the school bus.") Understanding children's problems does not mean we stop expecting anything from them. Here are some points to keep in mind:

• Some neurological differences, particularly in later-developing parts of the brain, may not show up until those areas are called upon for new kinds of school learning; when children run into trouble in middle years, do not rush to blame the teacher or the child.

• Be alert for a negative change in attitude toward school, or avoidance of homework or classroom assignments.

• Make yourself available (or, if necessary, inescapable) to help with assignments that are genuinely difficult for your child.

• Keep in close contact with the school and ask for the teacher's advice about helping at home. You may need to help organize study times, assignment books, and long-range projects.

- If problems persist, get an evaluation from the school psychologist or a learning disability specialist.

- Ask the school to provide special support services, or modify demands for written output. Keep the child's ego intact so he can compensate for his difficulty.

- The word processor and spell checker are life rafts for this child, along with good instruction in keyboarding skills. Some computer software also helps organize thoughts for writing, although it does not substitute for good educational therapy to teach basic organization skills and strategies.

- Your hardest job will be to let the child suffer the natural consequences if he falls down on his end of the bargain. Refuse to "own" his school responsibilities if they are reasonable.

- Be patient! If a task is genuinely hard, your child suffers enough from feelings of "stupidity" when he yearns to be competent. Remind him and yourself that, even in very smart people, all parts of the brain do not grow equally fast, and some need time and extra practice to do their job.

- If you cannot work with your child without damaging self-esteem (even the best parents get into "scenes"), find someone who can. Look for a tutor who understands this type of problem.

- Remind yourself that children are not by nature lazy!

The Homework Issue

Supervising schoolwork at home puts parents on a tightrope over two fearsome chasms. On one side lies the danger of making a child overly dependent, negative, or downright defiant; on the other—school failure. What a choice! While perfect solutions are, as always, only dreams, here are some suggestions that have helped other parents.

HELPING WITH HOMEWORK

Rule No. 1: Wait to be asked.

If your child is succeeding in school and neither he nor his teachers ask for your help, it probably is not needed. Trying to force a child to work with you may short-circuit his desire to come to you in the future. If you sense trouble, make an appointment with the school for advice. Remember that schoolwork is the territory of the child, who needs to feel responsible and in control.

Rule No. 2: Be available and supportive when help is requested.

Your attitude toward the importance of homework will shape your child's. If a TV program is more important to you than his need to practice multiplication tables, don't be surprised if he agrees.

Rule No. 3: Focus on process, not product.

Often the ultimate product (the answer, the perfect paragraph, one day's assignment) is secondary to the process of learning. Think about the learning you are encouraging:

a. "If I whine enough, I can get someone else to do my work for me."

b. "Every time I ask for help, we wind up in a fight because the whole thing isn't perfect enough."

c. "It was sort of fun figuring out the answers, even though neither Dad nor I really understood the questions at first."

Rule No. 4: The final product must represent the pupil's work.

Don't deprive your child of valuable learning because you're afraid of a bad grade. The college student who is still relying on Mom to write her papers by e-mail (yes, this happens!) is a poor candidate for future success in any job. Don't let this happen to you! If your child isn't up to the work, it is everyone's job to figure out why and get something done—not to enable her to sink deeper into a situation she can't handle.

Rule No. 5: Children are often hardier than they would like us to believe.

If assignments seem unreasonably long, check the following: Can she organize time effectively? Are study times at school used productively? Are job, telephone conversations, or I-messaging interfering? If the child is truly overloaded, a conference at school should be scheduled with you, your child, and the teacher present to discuss the problem and develop a plan. As more and more schools lay on more and more academic demands, parents need to talk together, organize, and raise a major fuss if exaggerated expectations— or too many extracurricular commitments—are grinding the youth out of their young.

Rule No. 6: Let him fight his own battles whenever possible.

Your moral support is essential, but it is the student's job to learn to get along with people in the world—including teachers!

Rule No. 7: Provide the tools necessary for success.

Your child needs a quiet, well-lit place to study, a regular routine, and a moratorium on weeknight TV, video games, and nonschool computer use until homework is satisfactorily completed. Be tough; this is important. Older students also may need a tape recorder, a good dictionary and thesaurus, a word processor with a spell-checker, Internet access for research, and transportation to libraries (if they give you advance notice).

Rule No. 8: You don't have to know everything.

Parents feel uncomfortable when they don't know everything, but admitting your confusion and working problems through with your child may be the best teaching you can do. Even if you don't get the answer, you have both experienced "cognitive dissonance"—the basis for the most lasting learning.

The Enigma of Automaticity

Another sticky wicket for some children during these middle years is getting "automatic" on basic learning skills. Automaticity is at the heart of most daily behavior, helping us tend to routine matters so our brain's working memory can deal with more challenging problems. For example, most people can wash dishes or pull weeds at the same time they carry on a conversation. When driving a car along an uncrowded freeway, they may plan a dinner menu or listen to a talk show. If a truck roars into view, however, neural control instantly moves to conscious attention, pushing aside everything else until the danger is past.

Most adults can listen to a lecture and take notes without using much of their brains to spell words or form letters, but if they must write an unfamiliar word with several syllables, they may temporarily lose the speaker's message as working memory is redirected to the mechanics of the task. When talking, most people give their conscious effort to the ideas they want to get across. Some children have difficulty forming or using well-worn neural pathways for such "easy" tasks.

Infant brains are busy starting a base of automatic connections as they absorb knowledge about the frequency of normal events, how to use their bodies, and what can be expected in everyday situations. With practice, most learning probably becomes condensed and reallocated to different areas, leaving the rest of the brain free to work on more complicated problems. If you had to devote conscious awareness to how this book feels in your hands, you would miss a lot of the content!

Automaticity is essential in school. Instant recall of phonics and a core of "sight words" underlie rapid reading and good comprehension; if higher thinking centers are cluttered up sounding out words, fluency and understanding suffer. A youngster who needs to stop and worry about spelling or letter formation when writing a word will have trouble writing originally or taking notes in class. In math, addition must be automatic before multiplication becomes easy. Middle childhood and early adolescence are the most critical times to firm up automatic skills before the child is besieged with higher-level processing demands.

"Multitasking," which requires a certain degree of automaticity, is not new, but it is newly trendy in a culture buzzed on technology. Many parents ask me if I really believe their child can instant-message to several friends, listen to music, and do homework all at the same time. Maybe, but when attention is divided in this manner, none of the tasks get done very well or with any degree of depth. Combining two tasks from the same modality (as in doing two language tasks—talking on the phone and writing messages at the same time) is most difficult. Even if your child is a quick multitasker, do make sure she can also "task," as doing one job thoroughly and thoughtfully is a far more important ability in the long run.

Making Learning Automatic

• Children differ in the ease with which they master routine skills.

• Different types of automaticity are learned at different ages. Babies and young children must get an automatic feel for their bodies and space and for taking in and understanding sensory information. School years are the time to practice academic and other skills, since adults must work harder to get new learning effortlessly embedded (e.g., your golf swing, a new foreign language).

• Remember that a child who is using cortical energy on poorly automatized "basics" will have little left for reasoning or comprehension of the task.

• Repeated practice seems to be the key to automaticity; children learn to become fluent readers and writers by reading and writing.

• Drill and practice are more effective if they are varied, because the brain responds to novelty. Sensitivity to the child's response helps balance these competing needs.

• Synapses may get "tired" with repeated use over a long period of time. They need a short rest before becoming effective again. Changing activities for a while unblocks the pathways.

• If movement, emotional content, or personal interest is combined with practice, memory should improve. Long periods of boring repetition may cause daydreaming as higher centers seek stimulation.

• Positive feelings improve neurotransmitter conduction for efficient learning. Middle grade children love any concrete evidence of their own progress (e.g., keeping individual progress charts or portfolios of a year's work).

• Sufficient sleep and physical exercise enhance connectivity in the brain. It is shortsighted for schools to limit or eliminate physical education, especially in the middle years. Competitive team sports are not as important as having everyone participate in some sort of exercise on a regular basis. Being outside in a natural, relaxing setting can enhance one's mental state.

• Stress, such as tension over exams, can reduce automaticity. Recent studies also suggest, by the way, that excessive stress connected with exams can temporarily impair the immune system. Youngsters who are taught thoroughly, who learn to prepare systematically, and who take exams that are fair tests of what they have actually been taught should not be at risk for these problems. The milder stress of a manageable challenge actually improves brain functioning.

• Computer drill and practice may help promote automaticity. This type of learning should not replace original problem-solving, however, because there is a difference between automatic and conceptual responses. *All children should be encouraged to develop proficiency with original thinking and reasoning as well as with memorized skills.*

• Some people are better than others at "incidental learning." Even when concentrating on one task, they pick up and remember extraneous details. A child who is encouraged to investigate, be actively curious, and notice details may get in the habit of picking up more information than a frightened, passive child who is stifled by fears of being "wrong."

Beyond Automaticity: Parents at School

Children who achieve automaticity easily are not necessarily smarter, but it is ridiculous for them to spend time drilling on material they have already mastered. Late elementary years are a prime time for everyone to enlarge vocabulary, investigate scientific and mathematical challenges, and participate in creative activities. Because of myelination that links different cortical areas, activities connecting language with the arts may be especially appropriate here. If your child is stuck in a classroom where drill and boredom replace intellectual stimulation, you should consider carefully whether you ought to become involved—tactfully, of course.

Children older than age eight are mortified if their parents hang around school, and you should beware of fighting their battles for them. Nevertheless, a teacher with a large class will sometimes welcome specific offers of help. In one school, volunteer parents developed a reading club and led small book-discussion groups. Field trips and theater and museum visits can be initiated by parents, as can career talks by adults in different vocations. You might explore possibilities of creative drama, puppetry, debate, or a videotaped production.

The issue of parent involvement in schools is a sensitive one; the child's need for autonomy is just as important as his need for intellectual stimulation. Some families prefer to concentrate on developing a home environment that encourages intellectual excitement and creativity. These years are a good time for refining artistic skills, and experiences in the arts or sports provide a base for future achievements. There's another trap, though—the insidious danger of overprogramming and getting hung up on "child as product."

Perfecting the Product

Several years ago I was leaving school one afternoon when I saw a forlorn little nine-year-old shape hunched on the curb near my car.

"What's the matter, Celia?" I asked, wondering what had reduced one of our most promising students to such a pile of misery.

"I missed my ride, and no one's home, and I'm going to be late for ballet," she snuffled.

Naturally, I drove her home so that she could change clothes in time for her next carpool. "You must like ballet," I ventured.

"No, I really hate it, but my mom wants me to be good."

Deciding to change the subject, I asked, "What do you like to do best?"

"I don't know. I have ballet on Monday, French on Tuesday, gymnastics on Wednesday, art on Thursday, and piano on Friday. Sometimes I wish I could just not do anything."

Celia's parents had fallen into the trap. Like many couples, they were both successful in business, accustomed to setting goals and measuring achievements. Trying to give their daughter the best chance, the most competitive edge, they arranged an "enriched" environment that ultimately convinced her that she was loved mainly for her measurable accomplishments.

These attitudes carried over into schoolwork. Celia's teachers worried about her compulsive concern over grades and her lack of time for relaxation. One of them said, "What that child needs most is to forget about her 'schedule' and go sit under a tree for a while. I don't think she has any idea what a wonderful little kid she is—she thinks her parents love her only because she's good at adult sorts of things. I keep telling her it's okay to be a child, but she doesn't know how!"

When Celia was a straight-A student in high school, she wrote a theme about "The Price of Perfection"—her obsessive inner pressure to perform "not well but brilliantly." She felt "special" only because of her academic success and would "stay up all night studying if it means the difference between an A minus and an A." Her worst fear was that one day she will lose "whatever I have that makes me special and capable of achieving that which others cannot." She confided, "I am not sure I will ever be satisfied, and that is, perhaps, the most terrifying thought I have ever had. The panic caused by the idea of failure is overwhelming. I only hope that one day I will be free of it."

Externally, Celia is a perfect product. What a tragedy that she has never learned to feel "special" inside herself. Her story is a good reminder that the most central—and most elusive—element of finishing childhood may be simply for parents to appreciate it while it lasts.

UNDERSTANDING THE ADOLESCENT BRAIN
Furnishing the Frontal Lobes

By age nine, most youngsters have basic processing skills in place, and somewhere around age eleven, dramatic new mental events begin to unfold. Having mastered the world of objects, the early teenager must move on to manipulating abstract ideas—a transition from the security of concrete skills and rules to a world of infinite possibilities and points of view. As with adolescent physical development, the timing of these changes varies widely among individuals and can be troublesome and confusing. Some believe that only about two-thirds of adults ever reach the stage of abstract thinking that Piaget labeled formal operational thought. Probably very few reach the ultimate stage, termed "problem finding," generating creative solutions for abstract issues, which may not appear until age twenty or thirty. Our society needs more people with these capabilities. How can they be developed?

Intellectual growth during adolescence depends on several factors: (1) inherited potential and timetable; (2) the quality of previous brain development in reception and association areas; (3) cultural expectations; (4) the amount and type of stimulation given by school and home; (5) a balance of support and challenge at home; (6) the child's own emotional strength and motivation to make sense out of new information and practice skills. Do these sound familiar? The principles remain the same, whether we're building the foundation or furnishing the penthouse.

The "Brain's Brain"

From preadolescence to adulthood, the prefrontal cortex of the frontal lobes, often called the "brain's brain," is a major focus of growth. The diagram in chapter 2 illustrates its location. While the earlier-maturing areas in the back of the brain are a vast storehouse of information, the front is a control center for selecting and acting on accumulated knowledge. Adult patients with frontal lobe disease act a lot like impulsive children.

They have trouble with initiative, with analyzing the steps of a problem, thinking ahead, and planning actions; they act unrestrained and socially tactless and have a childish sense of humor. They get some kinds of memory all mixed up and lose the ability to guide actions with words. Doctors observe frontal lobe patients who talk about what they want to do but are unable to do it.

If you look back to the diagram, you can see the prefrontal cortex is right next door to the frontal motor strip, which gets a growth spurt right after birth and develops quickly during the early months. No wonder many believe that adult learning is based on early physical experiences!

In the normally developing brain, prefrontal areas become active soon after birth, undergo spurts of development during the first few years, and experience a major explosion of synapses sometime around ages eleven to twelve. Other fiber tracts are late-maturing as well; some studies have shown peaks in brain electrical activity at around twelve, fifteen, and eighteen to nineteen years. Once the development occurs, the brain must refine and prune the systems as the youngster learns to use these impressive new connections. As at younger ages, the quality of the individual's experience can make a difference in what gets connected and what gets sloughed off.

Unlike the other cortical lobes, the frontal lobes do not have a direct "window onto the world" for sensory reception, so their development builds on sensory connections formed in earlier years and on the child's inner thoughts, language, curiosity, emotional experience, reasoning, and attempts to make mental connections.

Along with all this new possibility comes confusion. Because the more-developed brain can now reason in new and different ways, a child may appear to regress on skills while he re-sorts his thinking processes and tunes up the new systems.

Climbing into Grown-Up Thought

Early adolescent thinking reminds me of a little child parading around in grown-up clothes, stumbling a bit but acting very grandiose. Unlike the child, however, the teenager experiences unrelenting selfconsciousness. New possibilities for neural connections enable him to glimpse all kinds of new possibilities in any situation, but it also makes him step outside and view himself for the first time. How embarrassing! One of our sons fussed for two hours about which shirt he would wear to a concert with three thousand spectators because he was sure "everyone" would notice him. Yet, even as the young teen is mortified by his own imperfection, he finds himself so special that normal rules may not apply, and a cavalier attitude toward homework or school rules sometimes follows. Parents get buffeted by sudden outbursts and inconsistencies. Remember that teenagers' confusion is greater than yours, even if they don't admit it.

Enlarged mental perspectives create a sudden awareness of "ideals," and the adolescent may ruthlessly criticize his own family. David Elkind says, "In early adolescence not only is the grass greener in the other person's yard, but the house is bigger and more comfortable and the parents are nicer." Yet difficult as they are, these youngsters are covering necessary ground, learning to build with abstract ideas just as they once manipulated their blocks.

It is not surprising, given the angst of an adolescent's struggle with social relationships, worries about self, and grinding self-consciousness, that some youngsters, usually boys, find it easier to retreat into the virtual, self-gratifying worlds of video or Internet gaming. So many, in fact, that video and Internet "addiction" are now recognized psychiatric specialties. Not only can such behavior lead to depression, school failure, social withdrawal, and health concerns, but it also may result in youngsters skipping over valuable developmental stages, depriving the brain of necessary challenges to developing an adult personality and mature cognitive skills. Clearly, reasonable amounts of any activity, particularly if pursued in a healthy social context, are not going to turn your child into a mental case. Some kids are more susceptible than others; your job is to know what is going on and intercede if you see increasing hours spent with electronic diversions at the expense of schoolwork, social activities, acceptable family interactions, or health needs such as sleep. While a reasonable amount of gaming is natural, be aware that it can slide from "normal" into pathological with a vulnerable child. If this is happening in your home, I would suggest you seek a consultation with a specialist who understands such problems.

PARENTS AND THE ADOLESCENT BRAIN

- Understand that your child needs more rest than at any time since infancy and that it is normal for boundless energy to suddenly give way to lassitude.
- Good nutrition, while difficult to enforce at this age, is important for optimal brain functioning. Present your adolescent with breakfast and dinner, and hope for the best. "Fast food" is not complete brain food, either nutritionally or intellectually. Urge the school to pay attention, too.
- Have dinner together regularly, even if it requires rearranging schedules, and give your teen an opportunity to enter into the conversation without being put on the spot. Watch TV (but not at mealtimes) and read newspapers or magazines together. Talk about what is happening. It is important to deal with abstract concepts, values, and moral issues. If your child disagrees with you, remain calm. Say, "That's interesting [original; what many believe]. Tell me about your reasons." If she shares her thoughts with you, respect them! You don't have to agree.
- New neural circuitry may slow down normal patterns of conversation and make it hard for a teenager to communicate ideas; give her time to respond in conversation.
- Expect your child to have rapidly changing perceptions of himself. It is normal to try on different selves; it takes practice to integrate varying personality traits into a cohesive self-image.
- Your child needs more privacy than ever before; he also needs to have you available.
- One school administrator begs parents to value their children for their "decency or personality," not for their grades or competitiveness.

- Keep up with what your child is reading in school. Read it yourself. You may be able to get a conversation going.
- Encourage deductive reasoning: "If x is true, what are the implications in situation y?"
- Expose your child to adult views of the real world: work, politics, social issues. Encourage thinking about real problems—but be ready to listen to some idealistic solutions.
- Encourage constructive involvement in the community, such as volunteer work.
- Help your youngster express anger verbally, and encourage talking through problems.
- Expect criticism of school, of teachers, and of you. Don't undermine the school by criticizing teachers in front of your child, but be supportive if she needs to confront a teacher with a valid concern. Kids needs to learn to fight their own battles, but within reason.
- Take courage from studies finding that moderate parent-child conflict promotes mental growth and moral development, and that only 5 to 10 percent of families experience a major deterioration of relationships during these years.
- Remember that adolescents need to exercise their frontal lobes by playing tug-of-war with authority. Don't be afraid to set standards and stick to them. One adolescent girl admitted, "The best excuse is still, 'My mother won't let me.'"

Juggling the Abstract

With mental juggling of abstract alternatives, scientific reasoning becomes possible. Whereas younger children can form rudimentary hypotheses, they tend to get caught on the first possible solution to a problem. The classic game of "Twenty Questions" is a good example. When asked, "What am I thinking of?" the young child quickly gives a specific association. ("Is it a dog?") Older children learn to deal with categories ("Is it an animal?"), whereas an adult can evaluate and plan a strategy of broad to narrow categories. ("Is it alive? Is it an animal?") The section that follows illustrates some examples of learning situations that require adult-style reasoning and often cause trouble for students who haven't quite gotten there yet.

Tools of Abstract Thought

Deductive reasoning: The human brain is programmed to look for rules and order in experience. Young children learn to look at many different pieces of information and put them together into a broad rule or category (all of these insects seem to have eight legs; therefore, a rule for being an insect must be having eight legs); this is inductive reasoning. Only later does deductive reasoning develop—taking a general principle and applying it to unfamiliar instances, for example:

   a. "The square of a right triangle's hypotenuse is equal to the sum of the squares of the other two sides." Is this a right triangle? (If this seems confusing, you know how the student feels!)
   b. "All Latin adjectives agree with the noun in both gender and case. Add the appropriate endings to these words."

Hypothesis testing: Generating possible solutions to a problem and testing them systematically until finding one that works is the basis of scientific reasoning. For example, a classic chemistry problem involves five bottles of colorless liquid that can be combined in only one special way to produce a yellow color. Young children make combinations randomly. Older adolescents are able to make systematic combinations, holding different alternatives in mind until they solve the problem. Middle schoolers need help from adults who can show them how to go about considering a number of possible solutions instead of getting one idea and trying to force the facts to fit it. Open-minded approaches to everyday problems are one obvious channel toward this important growth.

Propositional logic: "If Mary is taller than Sally and Sally is taller than Marge, who is the tallest?" A child who has mastered concrete operations may be able to figure this one out. It is harder, though, to understand other kinds of propositions, such as "If it is raining, it must be summer. It is summer. Is it raining?" or "If *a* or *b,* then *c.*" A good example is a direction that gives preadolescents trouble: "If it is on your assignment sheet *or* I write it on the board, you must do it for homework."

Proportion: "For every six students there are two teachers. There are fifty-four students. How many teachers?" Problems like this require concrete materials (counters, pictures, diagrams) or a formula until students can mentally juggle the relationships.

Second-order symbol systems: Algebra and grammar are both examples of symbol systems that stand for other symbol systems. In algebra, numerals stand for ideas of number; algebraic terms (e.g., *x*) are arbitrarily chosen to stand for the numerals. Grammatical terms (e.g., a pronoun) represent classes of words that in turn stand for things or ideas. This is pretty complicated stuff if you aren't too clear on the original symbol system! Younger children can learn specific principles of grammar (noun, verb) from their own language experience but should not be expected to apply rules abstractly.

The "abstract attitude": This is the name given to the ability to stand outside a situation and connect ideas that don't go together in any kind of literal way. Examples are metaphor, drawing inferences that are not directly stated in a text, some forms of humor, analogies, nonliteral opposites, and a realistic appraisal of oneself. A sensitive adult can pull children toward this type of reasoning by asking the right questions, but these abilities don't develop overnight. Youngsters poised on the brink of adult logic still need the safety of something concrete to fall back on when confronted with new ideas. George, a twelve-year-old studying the novel *To Kill a Mockingbird,* was enthralled by the plot but couldn't understand the metaphor in the title. When he came to his father for help, Dad suggested they work up a literal word-by-word translation: "To Destroy Innocence." "Now I get it!" George cried.

Some quality computer simulations may help with abstract concepts like proportion or hypothesis testing. Good teaching at this—or any—age starts with some sort of concrete demonstration, and teenagers particularly need this kind of support. Another type of help they need is learning to use their executive systems to control and plan behavior.

The Importance of Inhibition for Motivation and Attention

One of the most important functions of the prefrontal cortex is that of being a wet blanket—an inhibitor of excitement. Although we admire an active brain, one that is overly aroused can be a problem as it responds to too many stimuli at once and jumps from idea to idea. As the frontal lobes mature, they team up with subcortical structures that direct arousal and alertness, emotion, and memory, forming loops that work as a "gating system" to select and direct attention, as described in chapter 4.

Another important function is regulating the ability to use "feedback," which simply means an ongoing check on one's own behavior. Feedback systems help us catch our own errors and remember what we're supposed to be doing and how. They should become more automatic during late childhood and adolescence. Students with poor feedback systems don't seem to notice when they've made a mistake; they may behave like younger children, habitually forgetting to bring the right materials to class, or getting distracted while doing a job at home such as setting the table. This is a frustrating situation, but there are a few positive steps that seem to help:

Helping the Brain Regulate Behavior

Verbal feedback: We have already seen how important "inner language" is for paying attention. Students who are able to talk through a problem mentally before springing into impulsive action do better in school and gain higher-level thinking skills sooner. By the way, parents are the child's most important models for regulating behavior. If you act before you think, your child may adopt the same tactics. If you discipline physically instead of talking problems through, if you tend to express emotion bodily instead of with words, be aware of the pattern you are demonstrating.

Natural consequences: A parent who continually picks up the pieces becomes a feedback system that prevents a youngster from developing one of her own. Unfortunately, it is sometimes necessary to grit your teeth and let a child feel the effects of her own carelessness. If the expectations were reasonable and she messed up, she needs to bear at least minor consequences. This is without a doubt the hardest task of parenthood. Have courage. We all learn best from our errors, not from our successes. Try saying, "I'm proud of you. You made a mistake and you *learned* something from it!"

Structure: Particularly during the early years of adolescence, when these control systems are being refined, the youngster may need help organizing his life, his responsibilities, and his possessions. Without taking over, you can firmly insist on certain parameters of neatness, schedule, health routines, and household tasks. Reasonable expectations, consistently enforced, can help a child get a comfortable "feel" for internal control. Young teens tend to experiment with their new mental powers by pushing and testing the limits. It is your job to give them something to push against. I know it isn't easy; my psyche is still bruised from angry adolescent outbursts—but now our three young men admit that the rules were really very reassuring.

Motivation: The "attention loop" includes motivational centers of the limbic system. More about motivation in chapter 8.

Decisions—Good and Bad

New mental perspectives give youngsters a whole new framework for personal decision-making. As they practice using it, they alternate between wanting to be dependent and wanting to argue. Incidentally, because they can now see some of your point of view, they become better arguers!

One logical way to practice decision-making is in making summer plans. A high school student came to his parents last spring for "advice." He knew that he should take a summer-school reading course recommended by his English teacher, but he really wanted a job as a lifeguard. His parents started to talk him into the reading course, but soon realized they would accomplish more by asking questions instead of giving opinions. Their son argued himself in and out of all possible situations while they tried to be interested but neutral. He finally decided to take the course, and he worked hard because he "owned" his decision. A friend whose parents "made" him take the course acted up in class and was dismissed after the first week.

Allowing kids to take responsibility is agonizing for everyone, but this is one more mountain they must learn to climb. What if this boy had made the "wrong" choice? He would still have learned a lot—including the fact that inadequate reading skills make English class a drag, and that the course might be a good idea next summer. Let teenagers make choices you can live with, but be ready to take a hard line on dangerous alternatives.

Avoiding Dangerous Decisions: Drugs and Alcohol

Teenage substance abuse can alter, perhaps permanently, brain centers for higher-level thinking, attention, and motivation, affecting long-term intellectual and personal growth. Effects seem to vary among individuals, so the safest course is to avoid them completely.

Parents' attitudes help shape teenagers' choices. Many studies have shown that parents whose children avoid dangerous practices tend to be:

• Described as "warm"—available to help without being overly judgmental.
• "Close to children."
• "Traditional in orientation," not afraid to set limits or discuss their own values, but also willing to listen to the youngester's point of view and bend on less important issues.
• Non–drug users themselves.
• Negative about use of medications to "make you feel better."
• Able to help keep the child's ego strength firm; teens with poor

self-concepts, anxiety, or difficulty with social relationships are more likely to engage in antisocial behavior of all types.

• Those who pay attention and are interested in their child's activities—without being intrusive.

• Those who have expected the child to take responsibility for the consequences of his own behavior.

• Interested in the teens' choice of friends. Young people's behavior is strongly influenced by peer group standards. An adolescent in a school with less alcohol, drug, and tobacco use among students is less likely to get involved himself.

Mediating the Media

In the last chapter you found general guidelines for managing "screen time," but because electronic media—especially television—are so prevalent in our culture, it is important for youngsters to learn to understand the influences it may have on them. A recent movement for "media literacy" teaches how to "deconstruct" (analyze) not only the content of media information, plots, and ads, but also the subtle messages they convey. For example, Bob McCannon of the New Mexico Media Literacy Project points out that advertisements strive for "emotional transfer," such as linking cigarette smoking to images of success or manliness, transferring "love" from a cute friend or furry animal to a sugary candy, or conveying the message that various products will make you happier or more popular. Many programs reinforce gender or other stereotypes, and the way news is presented tends to influence the way naive viewers interpret events. Instead of letting TV put your family into a passive, reactive state, here are some tips on how to make viewing an intellectual and reflective experience. Even bad content can be used to teach critical thinking. I have distilled some sample ideas from the work of McCannon and of Gloria de Gaetano, director of the Parent Coaching Institute, and I suggest you seek out more complete information on this important topic, which is now also taught in some schools.

HELPING YOUR CHILD ANALYZE MEDIA MESSAGES

1. Set up firm rules for media use, as previously described, and reserve plenty of time for family conversations. Ban television at the dinner table.

2. Place home screens in a place where you can keep your eye on them.

3. Watch TV together. Taping programs enables you to stop them and discuss things as they happen. Skip commercials or "mute" them.

4. Help your child ask critical questions about the content of shows or news. (Children under age eight should probably not watch the news.) Analyze together the values conveyed and whether you agree with them or not. Discuss the issues that come up. Are women, men, races, or age groups stereotyped? Did the writer have a point of view? What is someone trying to sell us—a product, an idea, an attitude? Is this solution realistic or simplistic? Is this really how we want to see our lives? How does this commercial subtly link a soft drink with sex appeal?

5. Analyze together what your physiological reactions are to viewing. Do you feel more depressed afterward? Is it hard to tear yourself away even if you're not particularly interested in the program? These are common reactions. Is this program worth the time we are spending on it? What else might we be doing with this time?

6. Confront violence directly. Your children will doubtless be exposed, hopefully not until they are old enough to gain some perspective. Don't be afraid to convey your own value judgments, even if the child disagrees (she is taking in your ideas, even if she won't admit it). Discuss together whether things like this should be seen by children.

7. Use TV and video creatively. Put a sheet over the screen and listen to a favorite show. How is this experience different? How do the characters look in our minds? Rent classic films or travel videos to learn about a country or a national park; have a picnic or an ethnic dinner as an accompaniment.

WORKING WITH THE SCHOOL
The Middle School Muddle

Research suggests that many schools are not very healthy places for young brains. In fact, some of the negative psychological changes we tend to associate with adolescence may result from a mismatch between teenagers' needs and the opportunities offered them. Young people want to learn and to feel competent, and they need environments in which they are carefully guided in assuming more responsibility and control over their own lives. They need a middle or high school small enough to offer close and supportive relationships with respected adult mentors: teachers or other community members. Unfortunately, these needs have not generally been considered in planning either school buildings, curricula, or class groupings.

Middle schools and junior highs in particular have too often been regarded as the trenches of academia where teachers complain about students' lack of motivation and await a "promotion" to high school teaching. Programs that keep early adolescents even more powerless than elementary school children yet expect them to learn by teaching methods used in high school can turn off capable minds.

Fortunately, many schools are now considering the unique needs of the young adolescent brain. If you visit your child's school and find students dramatizing history lessons, drawing diagrams of reading assignments, or "playing" with math games, don't dismiss the curriculum as "frivolous." It may be based on the latest and best research. Since it has been estimated that only about 12 percent of twelve- and thirteen-year-olds have achieved the ability to reason abstractly, most still need to "do" in addition to sitting in lecture-style classes. This does *not* mean we need to water down the curriculum—rather to present it by methods that can tie abstract concepts to something in students' real experience. In fact, many high school teachers find these methods work for them, too. Likewise, kids at any age need a school attuned to personal development, often through supportive relationships with teachers, coaches, or counselors.

The Power of Parents

It is the school's job to understand teaching methods and curricula, but administrators listen to parents whether they admit it or not. Parents should hold schools accountable both for imparting skills and keeping intellectual curiosity alive, but some inadvertently encourage inappropriate policies. With the best of intentions, they worry that a school which doesn't appear to have their child on the "fast track" may impair her future chances. One typical issue illustrates this point.

It has become fashionable to take algebra in early adolescence, and schools feel strong parental pressure to offer this option. While a few children are conceptually ready for traditional algebra courses at this age, many more are not. Experienced teachers find, even for good math students, they must overly simplify the course in order to get middle schoolers through. Moreover, in one school district where high-achieving thirteen-year-olds were encouraged to take algebra, 70 percent of these potentially gifted mathematicians did not go on to study higher math in high school. Why? Because they were "turned off" by algebra.

Students whose brains are not yet equipped to understand material conceptually can pass such a course—but mainly by memorizing. Any subject can be memorized up to a point, but without underlying comprehension of the ideas and relationships, learning eventually bogs down.

Tests may be the first evidence of trouble. "I studied and studied, but when I got in there I just couldn't answer the questions," wails the student. What happened? Despite hours of work, a child who lacks the underlying cognitive development never quite gets the idea. Test-taking becomes a desperate attempt to plug in isolated facts from memory, but if problems are stated differently or information must be applied, watch out! Teachers may not realize that the basic problem is a mismatch between the developmental level of the pupil and the demands of the material. They blame the student for lack of effort, or decide that he "isn't really that smart after all." The student is clear on only one thing: math is not for him. Yet another year or two of development—or a different teaching method—might have produced a love match instead of a divorce.

New instructional approaches have demonstrated that even elementary-age students can master complex mathematical concepts *if* they are taught in a manner appropriate for their developing brains, with real-life examples coming before abstract rules. Contrary to what many believe, the young adolescent does love to learn, but only if we accept and accommodate those special needs.

WHAT TO LOOK FOR IN A MIDDLE SCHOOL: BRAIN-BUILDING MIDDLE SCHOOLS

- Have a clear sense of purpose in meeting the needs of this age group.
- Have teachers who understand the cognitive development of adolescents and enjoy working with them.
- Encourage high academic standards that are age-appropriate, not falsely accelerated classes.
- Allow students to work together in pairs or teams for some projects.
- Realize that few middle schoolers are conceptually ready for traditional high school subjects taught in lecture-style classes.
- Resist parental efforts to push students into inappropriate courses.
- Use sophisticated manipulative (hands-on) materials, computer simulations, and real-life applications to teach math and science concepts in addition to memorization and written exercises.
- Provide individual support for students having difficulty.
- Encourage mastery rather than covering a large volume of material inadequately.
- Take time to review material from earlier levels.
- Try to meet social, emotional, and physical development needs.

- Emphasize study skills and learning about how to learn.
- Allow students physical movement as part of classes.
- Demonstrate the use of both inductive and deductive reasoning.
- Insist on students' original writing and speaking before a group rather than having them simply absorb material.
- Capitalize on the real interests and concerns of students, and allow individuals or groups of students to pursue well-planned projects of their own.
- Encourage structured collaborative learning in small peer groups.
- Use computers and other interactive video technology for exciting conceptual learning, not just "skill and drill."
- Allow for interaction with the larger community and nature outside the school, and encourage volunteer involvement.
- Challenge each child to move into more abstract levels of understanding by integrating courses in different subject areas.
- Have a well-planned program for prevention of drug, tobacco, and alcohol use, and incorporate media literacy into the curriculum.
- Give equal classroom attention to boys and girls.
- Regard music and visual and performing arts as integral parts of the curriculum.
- Downplay highly competitive sports and encourage individual challenge for each student. Allow some time and space for free play, quiet reflection, or just plain being a kid for a little while longer.

REMARKS FROM THE TRENCHES

The more I am around adolescents, the more fascinating I find them. Every day my students amuse and delight me—and at the same time they irritate, challenge, and exhaust me. I must continually remind myself that these young adult bodies contain brains far from "finished" by adult standards. Teachers are perpetually amazed at the way kids "get it together" sometime around age sixteen. Many late-maturing thinkers are extremely bright children, but parents and schools must hold on to their patience and good humor to refrain from pushing such youngsters into defeat or alienation. The late bloomers *can* make it—unless adults have convinced them they are failures by age sixteen. Many psychologists believe the alarming increase in teenage suicide is partially attributable to adults' urging teens to make choices too soon, coupled with unreasonable expectations and being pressured into adults' ideas of the right decisions.

High academic standards are an important national priority, but they must be brain-appropriate for each child's level of development. As one who teaches the same students at several points during their school years, I know that for months I can beat my head (and theirs) against the wall of an inappropriate objective, only to find that, two years later, they learn it in an hour. This latter way is a lot more efficient and fun for everyone.

As at earlier ages, emotion may be the ultimate catalyst for mental growth. While you are trying to understand your teenagers' brains, don't forget to love, respect, and honestly compliment them. Their struggle for individuality is worth admiring. Become a partner in the furnishing of a new adult mind and you are guaranteed a front-row seat for nature's most exciting developmental drama.

Part Two

Foundations

of

Learning

"A Path to the Future": Hemispheres, Learning Styles, Handedness, and Gender Differences

A guidance counselor once recommended that a ninth grade boy who was having academic difficulty be given only ten minutes of homework each night. The reason? She claimed the boy was "right-brained" and couldn't be expected to concentrate normally. His parents sensibly refused to go along with this idea, which, unfortunately, is not the only peculiar one that emerged when research about the two hemispheres became a popular topic.

Most parents have heard about differences between the two sides of the brain, but they share professionals' confusion about their practical implications. Is there a battle going on inside children's heads as these two halves fight for control? Are some children "right-brained" learners destined to experience failure in a "left-brained" curriculum? Can a child's "learning style" be changed? What is a learning style anyway?

Despite what you may have heard, two facts are clear. Children are whole-brained learners, and the brain prefers cooperation to conflict. Moreover, anyone who claims to have answers or "cures" based on hemispheric research is undoubtedly guilty of oversimplification. While the terms "right-" and "left-brained" may provide an interesting metaphor, they are neither a scientific fact nor an unchanging aspect of brain function. In this chapter I will try to explain what is understood scientifically and how it can sensibly be applied to help children link both hemispheres into an efficient and flexible system for learning.

Partners in Thinking

If you looked down at the top of the head and could peer through the skull, you would see that the cortex is not one solid mass, but it consists of two distinct halves—the cerebral hemispheres. These hardworking teammates contain two sets of cortical lobes and the associated subcortical structures that work together for all mental activity.

In a mature brain, a thick bridge of fibers called the *corpus callosum* carries messages in a constant flow between the hemispheres. With the exception of a few surgical cases, which you will learn about shortly, it isn't possible to be "left-brained" or "right-brained." Even after surgery the brain fights for normalcy. Likewise, a curriculum could not be developed for only one side, since *any activity automatically engages both of a child's hemispheres.* There are, however, many individual variations in the way the brain distributes the load, and experience does help "sculpt" their balance.

Carl Sagan termed the corpus callosum a "path to the future" because he believed that only dynamic cooperation between the hemispheres can achieve mankind's highest objectives.

LUMPERS AND SPLITTERS
"Careless" or Too Careful?

As he stood to leave my office, Mr. Jarvis turned to his wife. "Well, we have our work cut out for us, but at least we know he isn't lazy or stupid. Now that I understand Tim a little better, I'll try to be more patient and appreciate the things he's good at."

Although there is no such thing as a "typical" child, Tim Jarvis has a lot in common with many youngsters who strain the patience of parents. In fact, twelve-year-old Tim was baffling all the adults in his life because he was so good at some things and, as he admitted, so poor at others. A star soccer player and vice president of his class, he excelled in art and showed a real talent for Web design, but he was running into trouble with math and English. He astonished his father with his intuitive ability to figure out the relationship between wind, waves, and the speed of their sailboat, but he couldn't remember the order of the multiplication tables. He was popular with his teachers, but his report card reflected their frustration:

"Writing and spelling need attention. Tim should take more time on sentence structure."

"Tim seems to get the ideas in math, but is careless with written work. He often forgets assignments given in class."

"Tim can understand stories very well, but he makes many careless errors when he reads out loud. I wish he would participate more in class discussions, as he always has good ideas."

I spent several hours talking to Tim and administering some tests, on which he scored, overall, somewhat above average. The extremely uneven profile of his abilities, however, suggested a neurological basis for his apparent "carelessness." His style of thinking was weighted toward processes usually associated with the right hemisphere—even when he was performing tasks more appropriately managed by the left.

Tim's classmate, Carl, on the other hand, was a whiz with the kind of details that really "bugged" Tim. His English compositions were meticulously written, although his teacher lamented that he should "use more imagination." A flawless oral reader, he sometimes missed the point of a story even when he could recall all the details. In math, he loved computation but avoided story problems, just as he tried to avoid graphs, charts, and maps. Carl preferred writing linear computer programs to athletics, admitting that he had a hard time getting the "feel" of positions and plays in team sports. Carl didn't have a lot of problems in school, but his parents wondered why he wasn't very popular.

These boys' differences reflect the "styles" with which their brains balance various types of learning. For purposes of illustration, let's call Tim a "lumper" and Carl a "splitter." These terms characterize the hemispheric modes of handling information.

Dividing Brains

Scientists first learned about hemispheric differences from adult patients who needed surgery to stop epileptic seizures. These sudden electrical storms flood the brain with uncontrolled activity; sometimes the only way to stop them is by cutting through the corpus callosum. Such "split-brain" patients, whose hemispheres are deprived of a chance to communicate with each other, have cooperated in research to discover how each hemisphere functions. Because cortical areas are primarily connected with sensory organs on the opposite (contralateral) side of the body, scientists are able to "feed" information into one side or the other depending on where they present it. These studies have shown that each hemisphere has its own unique style of processing information. For most people the right hemisphere learns by getting the whole intuitive "feel" of a situation, while the left tends to analyze systematically and sequentially. The right sees outlines and wholes ("Gestalts"), while the left arranges the details in order. The right is a *simultaneous* "lumper," the left a *sequential* "splitter."

The left hemisphere "splitter" is a natural for the analytic, sequential requirements of spoken language. It can deal with rapidly changing sound patterns such as phonics or words in sentences and fast-moving fine-motor patterns such as writing or rapid, repeating finger movements.

While the left hemisphere thinks in words, the right relies more on emotional and sensory images. Its primary jobs are important ones—maintaining control of visual space and enabling us to understand situations. It can form mental maps, organize physical exploration, mentally "look at" or conceptualize an idea, or know how to rotate suitcases in order to make them all fit into the trunk of a car. Artistic talent and ability to "see" others' perspectives also seems to spring from this side of the brain. It has stronger fiber connections to the emotional

HOW THE HEMISPHERES SHARE THE LOAD

LEFT: THE "SPLITTER"	RIGHT: THE "LUMPER"
Analytic-sequential	*Wholistic-simultaneous-"hands-on"*
Provides details	Sees wholes
Reasons logically	Reasons intuitively
Analyzes, understands time	Designs, understands three-dimensional space
Language: speech, letter sounds, grammar	Language: pitch, gesture, prosody (melody), social interaction
Rapidly changing motor patterns (writing, repeated finger movements)	Manipulospatial abilities: changing environment with hands
Likes automatic routines	Likes novelty
Verbal short-term memory	Memory for sensory images
Processing rapidly changing auditory patterns (understanding speech)	Generating mental maps, conceptualizing mentally
Putting things in order	Understanding intuitively
Emotion: approach	Emotion: withdraw

centers in the limbic system than does the left, and limbic emotional centers are also larger on the right.

What are the implications for children's learning? First, both hemispheres are important! One major job of childhood is to develop an efficient system that utilizes a combination of "lumper" and "splitter" skills. On the following page is a summary of some important strengths and weaknesses of Tim and Carl at age twelve.

Clearly these boys illustrate only two of the innumerable ways in which learning abilities are mixed and matched in each individual's brain. No such thing exists as a "one-size-fits-all" diagnosis or

TIM: A "LUMPER"

STRENGTHS	WEAKNESSES
Large-muscle (global) sports (soccer, swimming)	Small, patterned motor sequences (writing)
Spatial relationships (sailing, mechanical drawing): scores at high school level	Auditory short-term memory for words: scores like an eight-year-old
Visual creativity (excels at art and design)	Following sequential directions, being neat and punctual
Learning by doing (carpentry, mechanical gadgets)	Language expression, grammar, accurate oral reading, spelling
Doing puzzles without small internal details (seeing "wholes")	Getting math equations in order (analyzing and sequencing)
Getting along with peers	Hearing and remembering homework assignments, taking notes in class

CARL: A "SPLITTER"

STRENGTHS	WEAKNESSES
Linear-sequential computer programming	Large-muscle sports, sense of field positions
Phonics, grammar, story details	Comprehension of "big picture" (reading comprehension, relationships)
Math "facts"	Math concepts; unfamiliar story problems
Algebra (formulae)	Geometry, maps, charts, graphs
Punctuality	Imagination, creativity
Auditory memory for words or digits	Social awareness, understanding others' points of view

teaching plan, and even the usual labels can't capture an individual mind.

How do all these differences come about? As with almost every aspect of brain development, each child comes into the world with a special pattern, but environmental influences affect its realization.

WERE THEY BORN THIS WAY?
Infant Specialists

When a baby is born, the brain is waiting for experience to turn on the switches. The right and left hemispheres, although clearly defined, are not yet functionally connected, since the bridge between them is one of the last membranes to be "finished" with coatings of myelin, at age twelve or later. The two hemispheres are primed, even before birth, for different types of work. Sequential noises, such as a series of clicks, pro-

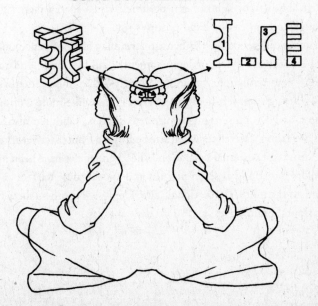

USING BOTH HEMISPHERES

voke greater brain wave activity in newborns' left hemispheres, whereas visual flashes of light arouse the right side, which also responds to non-verbal musical notes or the sound of the washing machine.

Scientists are finding that maturation seems to move in waves, first toward the right, and then toward the left side at around eighteen months when language comprehension and speech are actively developing. This right-left alternation continues even through adolescence and may differ between boys and girls. While we can't yet draw much in the way of implications from these findings, they certainly point to a need for adults to be patient and supportive while a youngster's brain takes on new challenges with new mental equipment.

One way to track hemispheric development is by observing the skills exhibited by the two hands, since the right hand usually reflects left-hemisphere use and vice versa—at least with most right-handed people. For example, one study evaluated whether three-, four-, and five-year-olds were better at using their right or left hands for different kinds of activities. The right hand (left hemisphere) was better at sequential motor actions, such as finger tapping or peg moving, whereas the left hand (right hemisphere) preferred visual-spatial tasks such as copying another person's hand postures.

Innate differences in the hemispheres may also influence our habitual emotional "style," or temperament. Children who tend to approach new situations more positively—the more extroverted ones—show greater left-hemisphere activation, while more withdrawn children activate more right-hemisphere circuits. Children also show brain activation differences when stressed; right-frontal activators show more distress at maternal separation. These tendencies have been found in children as young as seven months and appear to be related, at least in part, to the mother's emotional state. Depressed mothers show more right frontal brain waves, and so do their infants.

One Side Instead of Two

Several dramatic cases prove that hemispheric organization can be altered to some degree. Imagine yourself as a parent who has a terrible decision to make: Your child has been afflicted since birth by a rare convulsive disorder that does not respond to medication. Neurologists find that one side of the brain is seriously injured, causing continual, violent reactions throughout the brain. The remedy is drastic: removing the entire hemisphere that is the source of the trouble.

A number of children who have undergone this surgery, called "hemidecortication," have demonstrated brain plasticity in action. As they grew up, the children have astonished doctors by their apparent normalcy, as the opposite hemisphere and subcortical structures assumed many of the duties of the missing hemisphere. Children without a left hemisphere developed language and learned to read, while right hemidecorticates could perform visual-spatial tasks.

Long-term studies have shown that overall ability is somewhat lower than might be expected if the child's brain had been able to develop normally. The younger the brain at the time of surgery, the greater its potential for redistributing assignments, but any such compensation has its cost.

Some children are born with agenesis of the corpus callosum, lacking part or all of the fiber bridge, much like the "split-brain" patients. These youngsters often have problems with language and social skills, but sometimes they show up without debilitating learning disabilities. I have talked to mothers who discovered that their child had this condition only when the child's brain had to be scanned for some other reason—showing once again how adaptive the human brain is. Moreover, their language difficulties often respond well to skilled intervention.

Thinking Styles

As we consider the implications of all this information, it becomes clear that, while no normal environment will make a child "left-" or "right-brained," experience does influence how we deploy different types of thinking skills. In chapter 9, I will describe how specific aspects of a child's brain function for reading can be switched from one hemisphere to the other by particular instructional techniques, as just one example.

Here's a summary of some major points about the hemispheres:

1. *Hemispheric specialization* is present from birth, but development is shaped by input to the brain. Heavy auditory-verbal stimulation may increase left-hemisphere capabilities and vice versa. Deaf children, for example, show a pattern of hemispheric organization that is different from that of hearing children. In *Endangered Minds*, I suggest that diminished language use and less time for reflection in the lives of children today may be eroding left-hemisphere language areas.

2. *Lateralization* means the pattern by which abilities such as language are distributed between the two sides.

3. *Hemispheric dominance* is one side's tendency to determine the style of processing to be used for a job. In our highly verbal society, the

EXERCISING BOTH HEMISPHERES
SAMPLE ACTIVITIES

SPLITTING	LUMPING
Sequential: Analytic	*Simultaneous: Visual-Spatial*
Fine-motor activities: cutting out small items, coloring inside lines, detailed needlework,	Large-muscle play: team sports, gymnastics, climbing, free play (tag, etc.)

finger games with sequenced movements	
Listening to language, verbal analogies	Free-form drawing, painting
Talking about events	Looking at pictures
Putting things in order, making lists	Working with shapes, block-building, inventing
Understanding time sequences	Doing three-dimensional puzzles
Music: the words	Music: the melody
Writing sentences	Manipulating mechanical devices
Describing objects systematically	Dramatizing, creative movement
Using pig Latin, rhyming words	Finding hidden pictures
Repeating directions in order	Seeing or creating patterns
Listing steps in an activity	Easels, paints, fingerpaints, clay, craft activities

HELPING THEM WORK TOGETHER

- Games that combine visual and verbal cues (e.g., Simon Says).
- Visualizing pictures from listening or reading (make a "mental movie").
- Large block play with a story attached.
- Describing actions with words.
- Talking about manipulating toys or mechanical gadgets.
- Verbalizing intuitive discoveries. ("How did you know that? What clues did you use? What came into your mind first?")
- Describing problem-solving experiences. ("Can you tell me how you did that puzzle?")
- Memorizing math facts to music.
- Spelling words backward, remembering number sequences backward.
- Keeping the score of the game in your head.

- Doing proofs in geometry (proving an intuitive process with sequential logic).
- Writing up science experiments.
- Cooking by following recipes.
- Watching TV and then retelling the story in order. ("First they found the treasure, and then . . .")
- Doing electrical wiring from a sequential plan.
- Building models from directions.
- Reading music.
- Telling time from a nondigital clock.

side with language in it, usually the left, is more often dominant; but for visual, holistic thinking, the right may need to be the leader.

4. Individuals vary in their ability to communicate between hemispheres. Such flexibility may be a major factor in intellectual ability as well as in differences between male and female brains.

5. *Hemispheric style* is a term suggesting an individual's preferred way of processing information. For example, in putting a puzzle together, you can use a predominantly analytic strategy by naming each piece and assembling them in a logical order, or you can work from the whole outline, using mainly visual clues. Although both hemispheres are working, one may set the tone.

6. Younger children may tend to use a right-hemisphere style, acting on situations globally without analyzing them; as verbal demands increase, the left side takes over more often. An activity such as reading may be handled in different ways at different ages.

7. Hormones, particularly sex hormones such as testosterone and estrogen, influence hemisphericity. They appear to be powerful factors before birth and again at adolescence. One unproven hypothesis suggests that the reason some early-developing teenage girls fall behind in math is that estrogen suppresses development of right hemisphere visual-spatial skills.

Age Guidelines

The hemispheres communicate by way of the corpus callosum, the thickest network of connections in the entire body. It holds one key to mental efficiency by activating and suppressing hemispheric control. For example, in reading, areas in both sides are used, but if the language centers of the left hemisphere aren't dominant, accuracy, fluency, and comprehension may suffer.

Parents who want to help their children build this pathway to the future can follow three major guidelines:

1. Encourage a wide variety of activities to engage all parts of the brain.
2. Let the child's interest direct learning. Connections develop in response to demands from the child's brain, not from an adult's.
3. Don't expect full hemispheric integration until after puberty.

Here are suggestions for each age level:

Birth to three years: The baby and toddler may still be using primitive brain areas for many tasks that the cortex has not yet taken over. During this period the child essentially has a "split brain," because the corpus callosum is immature. You may have noticed a young child transfer a crayon from one hand to the other when crossing the center of the paper. This inability to cross the body's midline is a sign that the hemispheres are still working independently. We can't expect a child of this age to put complex things together—either physically or mentally. She can't effortlessly coordinate two sides of the body or link words and images for reasoning. She can't picture the characters in a story in her mind, remember complicated directions, understand her own reasoning process, or solve problems that she must "see" in her head. ("Sally walks behind Suzie. Who walks first?") These years are important foundations for expanded use of both hemispheres (see "Exercising Both Hemispheres").

Four to six years: Did you ever wonder why so many people have trouble remembering much from their lives before age four? At around that time the corpus callosum undergoes major development, so children can become much more aware of what is happening and even begin to reflect on some of their own learning. Thus they begin to form conscious memories—a talent that will expand through the school years. You can observe increases in connectivity when children instinctively start to talk to themselves while doing puzzles or planning the use of art materials, and they make progress in activities, like riding a tricycle, that involve coordinating two sides of the body. By age six, mental activities combining right- and left-hemisphere skills become even more important for schoolwork. Real-life challenges build connections—especially when the child has a *real* reason to solve them. Tying shoes, for example, combines two hands using sequential motor movements in a visual-spatial task, and handwriting requires motor sequences as well as a global concept of where you are on the paper and where the spaces should be between words.

Wise parents use these years to link language with creativity and hands-on manipulative skills, which build bridges to abstract reasoning. They pass up rote-level memorization tasks designed to make the child (or the parent) look impressive.

A nursery school teacher told me one story about a mother who was anxious to make her little girl appear intelligent by teaching her some important facts. When the teacher reported that Susie had succeeded in tying her shoes for the first time, Mother brushed off the news.

"Tell us whose picture is on the one-dollar bill, Susie," she demanded.

Agreeably, the child replied, "Washington Redskins!"

To build hemispheric bridges, stick with things that have meaning for the child.

Six to ten years: Hemispheric allocation of labor may be affected by school demands for reading, writing, spelling, and computation. Children who tend to be "lumpers" often experience difficulty and begin to think they are "stupid" because their individual style seems out of place.

They require extra practice with language (seasoned with recognition of their visual or creative talents) and specialized help with the skills of reading, personal organization, and solving math equations. Conversely, "splitters" adept in linear detail (sounding out words, computation) may risk becoming one-dimensional if their school fails to emphasize comprehension and original thinking. Visual-spatial skills, like verbal skills, are very responsive to environmental stimulation. Because they underlie many types of conceptual reasoning, they're worth working on. Wise parents try to understand their child's preferred style and provide supplementary experiences for balance, especially encouragement of creativity and the arts. Go together to museums, children's concerts, plays; try sculpture, creative movement, or drama. If these activities are not your favorites, give them a try anyhow. You are a wonderful example of "parent as learner," and you may even build a few bridges of your own!

Eleven years and up: This is the age for the final maturation of the "path to the future." By now your child has a distinct learning style, which adult expectations should take into account. Children who still "march to a different drummer" probably have strong creative talents. Help each child respect his own style, but don't give up on making connections. For many children this is a time when new myelin and synapse growth or changing hormone balances eventually help things fit together, if the emotional climate permits. Let the youngster know that his brain is gaining wonderful new powers—it's worth the effort to try again on some old problem areas. Visualizing stories or "seeing" and turning ideas around mentally should become easier, but some young teens, especially girls, may need verbal strategies for talking through maps, geometric problems, or complex visual displays. Some types of visual-spatial skills can be improved by appropriate computer activities that require mental manipulation of objects on the screen.

During this period of rapid change, parents take on more of a spectator role. Don't forget to applaud! In addition, keep providing supplementary cultural experiences and lots of conversation about thoughts and ideas.

Construction Delays

In a recent parent conference, the father, a neurologist, was sympathizing with his second grade son's spelling difficulties.

"I realize now," he explained, "that I am still hopelessly confused about all the words I learned before I was in sixth grade. Then, suddenly, spelling just came together."

Fortunately, he hadn't already been pressured into believing he was a failure. If your child has trouble making connections of any kind, I would suggest that you focus hard on keeping the road open with emotional support and good teaching while the bridges have a chance to develop.

BUILDING BRIDGES BETWEEN THE HEMISPHERES: PRACTICAL TIPS

- Using two parts of the brain at the same time develops with age and practice. The farther apart two areas are, the easier it is to use them together. (It is easier to carry on a conversation while drawing a picture than while writing a letter.)
- A positive emotional state improves connectivity for messages crossing between hemispheres, while excess pressure or anxiety may interfere.
- Food allergies may slow down transfer time across the corpus callosum. Since traditional skin tests are not always a reliable detector of food sensitivities, you should keep track of any substances that seem to make your child tired, grouchy, listless, less mentally alert, or "hyper."
- When transfer time is impaired, the most complicated thinking goes first.
- Some parents inadvertently give different signals to each hemisphere. If your words say "That's okay" but your body signals are negative, your child's brain will be understandably confused.
- Your own hemispheric style influences the activities you choose for your child. Be aware of it and don't limit varieties of adventure. If you hate puz-

zles or word games, for example, let your child know that you are approaching a challenge together.

- Help your child learn to estimate in math. Seeing the big picture before starting gives a framework for understanding. Young children find this very hard.
- Visualization—also hard for young children—is important for learning and memory. At first, read stories out loud while you show pictures; then have children draw pictures of their own. Eventually, suggest that they close their eyes and make a "mental movie" while you read a short passage. Ask, "What color was the queen's dress in your imagination? What did the house look like?" Don't be surprised if it takes a lot of practice. You can start gently around age four. Audiotaped stories are useful and fun.

Not Enough Bridges?

Recently I received a cry for help from a prekindergarten teacher. Charles, she reported, "is very bright and has wonderful language comprehension but is miserable in school. He is exceptionally awkward with crayons and scissors, frustrated because he can't write his name, and he resists clay and fingerpaints because they are 'messy.' He is socially inept, can't seem to imagine or pretend, and always waits for a teacher to tell him how to use new materials. He is so clumsy in gym class that the other children are starting to make fun of him. I found him crying in the hall yesterday."

After observing Charles in the classroom, I understood the teacher's concern. The only joy this handsome little boy showed was when his turn came at the computer. He kept to himself despite the teachers' tactful efforts to get him involved.

When we voiced our concerns to his mother, she was surprised. She recognized that Charles was verbally advanced and was proud of the fact that he spent a lot of time at home playing with educational computer alphabet and number games. He disliked puzzles, however, and they didn't have an easel, paints, crayons, clay, or fingerpaints in the house. Charles loved books and stories, but he had never liked pretend play and had little contact with other children. Since they lived in an apartment, he got outside only for supervised walks to the park. His parents thought they had provided their son with the latest and best tools for learning. What happened?

A child's basic learning profile is innate, but Charles's parents had unwittingly created an environment that augmented some of his potential problems. His family didn't realize how important feeling, touching, manipulating, seeing, hearing, expressing, imagining, socializing, and three-dimensional reasoning are as forerunners to learning. The difficulty was complicated by the fact that Charles didn't seek out these activities for himself. He lived in an environment enriched in one sense but deprived in others. When Charles got to preschool age, he qualified for a diagnosis of mild developmental disorder.

It is hard to write a prescription for mud pie making and tree climbing, especially for a child who tends to avoid them. For Charles, we settled for an occupational therapist who began sensory integration therapy and urged the parents to limit his obsessive use of the computer. We encouraged them to slowly initiate activities to balance his skill development: finger games, painting, sewing cards, bead stringing, large motor games such as rolling and kicking a ball, tactile and movement activities—and some free play outdoors. Since Charles also needed a lot of help in making connections with other children, a teacher worked with him on social interaction skills, and his parents were encouraged to invite classmates for short, well-structured play dates.

Charles will always have his own set of abilities and quirks, but the least we can do, while his brain is still able to learn new things so easily, is to give him the fullest possible shot at a complete adjustment to school, other people, and life.

THE QUESTION OF HANDEDNESS
Whose Responsibility?

One interesting question related to hemispheric interaction is that of right-, left-, or mixed (ambidextrous) handedness. Handedness is in part genetically determined. Approximately 90 percent of all people are right-handed, but up to 30 percent may carry genes for left-handedness. To determine handedness, several tests should be used: for example, eating with a spoon, writing, throwing, hammering, and threading a needle. If a child does any of these with the left hand, he is classified as "not right-handed" or "mixed."

Since each hand is connected to the opposite cerebral hemisphere, it was once assumed that a right-hander inevitably has left-hemisphere language lateralization, and vice versa. While it is true that almost all right-handers have speech housed in the left hemisphere, so do 60 to 70 percent of nonright-handers. Some nonright-handers have speech in the right hemisphere, and some in both sides.

Handedness does not tell us anything definite about a person's learning style, although it can offer clues. Many left or mixed-handers end up in professions that require visual, holistic, nonverbal, and creative thinking—but so do some right-handers. We do have some evidence that nonright-handers' brains are different. They may have language more evenly distributed between the two hemispheres, giving them a "reserve" in case of damage to either side. Lefties with left-handed relatives may have different patterns of brain organization than those without. Some believe that nonfamilial left-handers were meant to be right-handed but suffered some subtle early damage that changed things around.

Handedness can also be influenced by less dramatic environmental factors. Recent studies have shown that even the way a primate fetus is carried in the womb, or which side the mother cradles the infant on, may affect handedness. In humans, this finding might also apply to a mother's habitually handing her infant a spoon in one hand or the other. In turn, an infant's handedness seems to influence the hemispheres' *functional specialization,* or the way they apportion different tasks. Most newborns show right-sided preferences by lying on their backs facing right with their right arms outstretched, and most infants use their right hand more than the left by age nine months. About half of infants have established a dominant hand for most things by the end of the first year; those that do are more skilled in manipulating objects. Most children have clear hand preference by age four, but sometimes as late as age seven.

The Hand and the Brain

Research in anthropology and neurology have converged on the importance of hand and tool use as promoting higher forms of human intelligence. With growing numbers of "mouse pushers," sedentary viewers, and children with learning and behavior problems, renewed interest is being focused on the critical interaction between motor patterning (coordinated use of the body) and development of cognitive skills. Lifestyles that limit either a child's manual play or her two-sided body coordination may have longer-range effects than anyone has imagined. Read Frank Wilson's interesting book *The Hand* to learn more about how tool use has influenced the development of human intelligence.

"Exceptional" Brains

An unusually high percentage of nonright-handers is found among children who have developmental disabilities, including reading problems—and also among the ranks of unusually gifted math students, chess players, and musicians. Individuals and families who have reading problems often excel in right-hemisphere skills: visual-spatial abilities or creative fields (e.g., engineers, artists, architects, surgeons, carpenters, interior designers). After eight dyslexic adults who had lifelong reading and spelling problems donated their brains for postmortem study at Harvard Medical School, scientists discovered that their left-hemisphere language areas had some unusual cell formations, and that right-hemisphere areas were bigger than they are in most people. Why these tendencies seem to occur in certain families is being looked at very carefully. We do know that people who have atypical lateralization often prove to be extremely talented if they can get by the verbal/analytical priorities of our education system!

Should We Change Handedness?

Some parents feel they should insist a child use the right hand, but forcing the issue may create a new set of problems. Such pressure has also been suspected of causing stuttering by confusing innate brain organization or, more likely, by creating emotional conflict. Given current information, the best advice seems to be to let your child be the guide about which will be the preferred hand.

I once knew a four-year-old girl whose father, a physician, insisted she use her right hand instead of her preferred left because he thought he could force her left hemisphere to become dominant. He was convinced that this switch would counteract a family tendency toward reading problems. When he asked my opinion, I reminded him that even top neurologists are hesitant about tampering with the developing brain. More important, the child was clearly a nervous wreck. Undeterred, he persisted, and I lost track of the case until two years later when a tutor called me. She had been hired to work with the little girl, who had just been diagnosed as having a learning disability—accompanied by emotional problems. Would she have had it anyway? I don't know.

HANDEDNESS IN A NUTSHELL

- We do not yet know enough to fool around with children's development in any way that violates common sense.
- If members of your family are nonright-handed, you may transmit the tendency even if you are right-handed.

- If your child is not right-handed, it does not mean that he will automatically be either reading disabled or a visual-spatial genius, but he may have a better statistical chance for both.
- Ambidexterity may suggest incomplete language lateralization, putting a child more at risk for delay in language or reading. If your child does not have a hand preference by age five, shows signs of language delay described in chapter 7, and has difficulty with school readiness, you might consider a professional evaluation. Please try to shield the child from your anxiety, however. You don't want to *create* a "problem"!
- At this time there is no solid evidence that "mixed dominance" of hand, foot, or eye is of any diagnostic importance.

"THE OTHER DIFFERENCE" BETWEEN BOYS AND GIRLS
Alike but Different

After a recent parents' meeting, one mother asked a question that was obviously troubling her.

"I don't know what to do about my five-year-old twins," she confessed. "I'm doing my best to raise them in a 'nonsexist' environment, but Shauna spends a lot of time playing 'house' with her friends, and Buddy only wants to build things and run around the neighborhood. No matter how much I encourage them toward other activities, they seem to be stereotyping themselves!"

The topic of gender differences has been hotly debated in professional circles. First of all, there are many more differences among children of the same sex than between the sexes. If we lined up all boys and then all girls on the basis of almost any characteristic, there would be lots more overlap than difference attributable only to gender. Nevertheless, two important strands of research are confirming what parents have known all along: Overall, boys and girls prefer different activities and excel at different skills. They may even think differently. Much of this variation is clearly due to environmental factors, but some of it reflects biological variation in brain organization.

Females score better on tests of some verbal skills. Female infants are more sensitive to voices, particularly their mother's, respond more readily to face-to-face contact, and are more easily startled by loud noises. The majority of girls talk earlier than boys. They score better on tests of verbal abilities throughout the elementary years, tending to master reading and writing sooner and to excel in grammar and spelling. They are more verbally fluent and do better on tests of naming objects quickly. Females, overall, rely more on talking and have fewer language disorders and better hearing throughout life. Generally they are superior to males in fine motor coordination, such as placing pegs in pegboards or using a pencil, and in perceptual speed at matching items. They surpass males in mathematical calculation and in tests of "ideational fluency," such as quickly thinking of things that are a certain color. Socially they are more sensitive to others' facial expressions; girls (but not boys) recognize photographs of their mother as early as four months. They tend to prefer one-on-one play with a friend, while boys tend to play more in groups. Girls pick up "clues" from the environment more subtly; this ability for incidental learning may account for the phenomenon of "woman's intuition."

Males on the other hand excel overall in tests of visual-spatial skills such as moving three-dimensional objects around in their minds, finding shapes hidden in a picture, understanding relationships in the physical world, and in throwing things at a target or catching projectiles. Studies in different cultures have shown that they are better at solving mazes—a task that many women find irritating. Boys consistently do better in mathematical reasoning; in one study they outpaced girls at age thirteen in the "highly gifted" math category by thirteen to one. By tenth grade the majority of boys of normal intelligence have passed most girls up in math. This differential could be related to their tendency to solve problems by touching and looking instead of "talking" them through, since higher math requires a type of abstract reasoning based on relationships in the physical world.

Many boys shine at activities requiring large body movement and show more aggressive behavior. They are less dependent on others' reactions for their own judgments, being more influenced by the objective characteristics of a situation.

Before we conclude that these differences are all rooted in biology, however, it is important to remember some important facts: Many children of both sexes don't fit the pattern, and it has often been shown that adults tend to treat boys and girls differently—even when they think they do not. Both parents and teachers tend to expect more of boys in problem-solving, and some teachers inadvertently give boys more feedback and call on them more often than they do on girls. Moreover, TV, ads, and video games continually reinforce gender stereotypes, as do toys advertised to children and products directed at teens. Perhaps as a result, peer pressure starts very early for gender-role conformity. No one can measure how these subtle pressures have contributed to the differences between the sexes that show up on school tests.

Sex and the Hemispheres

Most scientists now agree that there are genuine differences between the average female and male brain. When your daughter is learning how to walk to school, she is more likely to find her way by observing landmarks; your son may be more inclined to map out the route in his mind. The same gender differences are also found in rats—unless an experiment has altered the balance of their sex hormones during a critical period of brain development, in which case females can be made to behave more like males and vice versa. Spatial abilities may be affected by "masculinizing" hormones, and hormone balances may be influenced by either genetic or environmental factors. One hypothesis holds that stress in the pregnant mother may tend to masculinize the fetal brain, which might cause an increase in such male-linked characteristics as visual-spatial skills and assertiveness in a girl.

Many girls (and some boys) have earlier left-hemisphere language lateralization, but overall abilities are more widely distributed. A section in the back of the corpus callosum called the *splenium* is thicker in females, enabling them to use both hemispheres interchangeably, which may account for their skill at picking up nuances of a situation or doing several things at once. How many husbands wonder how their wives can talk on the phone, cook dinner, and discipline the children all at the same time? Some males, on the other hand, seem to have stronger connections between the front and the back parts of the brain, perhaps accounting for a greater interest in the sensory properties of objects rather than the nuances of human relationships.

Boys (and some girls) may also have more assertive right hemispheres, particularly when they are young. Their interest in large-motor and visual-spatial play activities (climbing, building, manipulating) precedes later maturation of left-hemisphere language centers—and puts many little boys at a disadvantage in school, although this early object play may make them better at math later on. By the time language is fully lateralized, it is shoved firmly into the male left hemisphere; consequently, when information comes in, more of an either-or choice of strategies must be made. Boys may miss information because they are concentrating on another kind of input. Yet they score higher in tests of abstract thinking because they are not as dependent on outside cues.

What Can Parents Do?

We are only beginning to understand the influence of gender and learning style differences in our society. Perhaps you wonder, "What's wrong with differences, anyway?" Clearly, they make us more interesting, but if a child is going to be penalized at any stage in the learning process because of lagging development, parents will want to take some action.

• Certain individual differences seem to come with the package. Each child's basic pattern of brain organization is valuable. Parents are often the main cheering section for one whose pattern is slightly divergent from school expectations. I think the term "nontraditional learner" is a helpful one for describing such youngsters, whether male or female.

• Studies show that parents unconsciously increase reinforcement of traditional gender-linked play and social roles when children are about one year old, a time when the brain is very malleable.

• Young boys (and some girls) suffer needlessly in early school years if they lack verbal and fine motor skills. Likewise, your daughter (or son) may bog down in mathematical and some types of abstract reasoning if she lacks visual-spatial ability. We don't know how much you can shape these abilities, but it makes sense to plan activities with an eye to balance. Consult the suggestions listed under "Expanding Learning for Boys and Girls."

• Encourage your school to appreciate each child's talents. When I go into an elementary classroom and see that all the spelling papers with smiley faces have girls' names on them, I understand why boys sometimes grow up resenting the female of the species.

• You and the school may be orchestrating gender differences by projecting subtle attitudes that you are not aware of.

• Boys' later-blooming verbal abilities put them more at risk for early learning problems. If your son has a late birthday, consider his learning pattern carefully before you enter him in school. A professional evaluation may be helpful.

EXPANDING LEARNING FOR BOYS AND GIRLS
Attitudes

• Be aware of subtle pressures you exert. Parental models may be one of the most important factors in creating sex differences. Mom telling her daughter "It's okay. I was terrible in math, too" is clearly a no-no, but more subtle messages are also powerful.

• Fathers seem more likely to perpetuate sex stereotypes with children than do mothers.

• Boys may be placed "at risk" for educational problems by a lack of responsiveness in their mothers; girls are more "at risk" if they lack exposure to challenges.

• Praise girls for achievements just as you would praise boys. Don't lower your expectations for either sex on the basis of anticipated differences.

• Don't assume that girls won't take to blocks and other building toys, engineering, or math, or that boys won't be interested in reading or cooking. Your assumptions may become self-fulfilling prophecies.

• Be alert to your child's "style" of responding and its influence on your interactions. For example, a child who is very context-sensitive will sense your moods and say things to make you feel positive toward him, and vice versa. You may need to help some boys be more sensitive in their personal relationships. Show them how to respond. ("It really made me feel uncomfortable when you didn't say anything after I told you about my new project. If you made a comment, I would know you were interested.")

• Be sympathetic to some inevitable but unfair pressures in school. Whereas expectations in primary schools are sometimes more appropriate for little girls, some college entrance exams may favor males.

• Help all children learn to rely on their own judgment. Girls in science class tend to look to adults or peers, while boys are better at judging their own work.

• Don't provide too much assistance as children confront unfamiliar equipment or activities. They will gain skill and confidence if you stay in the background as a support rather than a director.

Activities

• Provide all children with varied toys and experiences.

• Providing variety in toys and activities isn't enough. You may have to sit down and *play* together. Show your child how to play in a variety of ways, avoiding sex stereotypes. Mother may be surprised how much fun she can have with an electric train or a set of blocks; Dad can read to his son in addition to playing baseball with him. Boys can enjoy needlework and girls love carpentry.

• Encourage children to use mechanical and scientific equipment: telescopes, microscopes, cameras, radio kits, and science kits. Let them take things apart. Some children need to *talk* their way through, while others should also be encouraged to use words describing what they are doing and seeing.

• You may need to help some children broaden their contexts and help others focus theirs. Broadening means calling attention to elements in a situation that they have missed. ("While you were kicking the ball, did you notice that Dad was having a conversation with your school bus driver?") Focusing calls for specific suggestions. ("While you're watching that TV program for social studies, why not save your talk with Sue until later?")

• Some children may need help relating ideas to their own experiences ("When the characters in the story couldn't achieve their ambition, did it remind you of the time you didn't make the first team?"), whereas others may profit from a push toward more abstract, less personal thinking. ("You noticed that it is harder to squeeze the icing out of the narrower tube; can you figure out a rule about how force and the size of a tube are related?")

• Remember that many children—even into their teen years—must manipulate the environment in order to learn; they don't get information well by only listening.

• You can help both sexes develop lagging spatial skills by play that involves manipulating and exploring three-dimensional space and objects.

• More verbal children may need to talk through problems in math, chemistry, and physics. Others profit from diagrams, pictures, and demonstrations.

• Hands-on computer programs, such as LEGO/Logo, offer interesting possibilities for combining analytic and spatial skills.

• Appropriate computer games (e.g., Tetris) that promote manip-

SEEING THE FOREST OR THE TREES

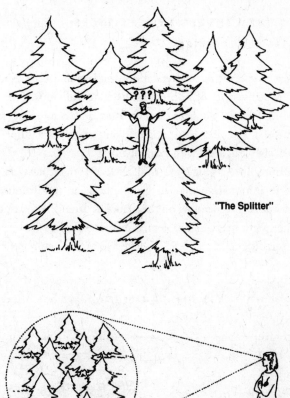

"The Splitter"

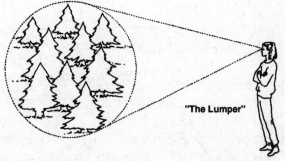

"The Lumper"

ulation of spatial concepts can improve these abilities in children for whom they are weak. Players already adept in these areas do not seem to gain much in skill level through extra practice.

BACK TO THE LUMPERS AND SPLITTERS
Strategies for Learning

Let's return to specific recommendations for Tim and Carl. Although there are as many styles of learning as there are individuals, flexibility in presenting material can help most children understand and remember more easily. The idea is to capitalize on the child's natural "style" while boosting weak areas with extra help.

Carl, our splitter, is big on facts, details, and "right" answers. More interested in information than in people, he is an industrious, well-organized student. Depending on the school he attends, his lack of creativity and insight may be a problem, but youngsters like Carl generally do well in traditional classrooms. They thrive with a lecture method of

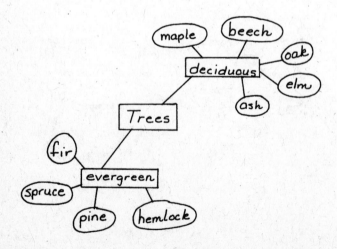

A Visual Outline

instruction, memorization, and objective, short-answer tests. Their weaknesses show up when they must stand back and view the whole forest instead of concentrating on the individual trees. Often a child like this becomes mentally lost unless someone reminds him where he is supposed to be going.

Carl had a habit of getting caught up with details and missing the main point of class discussions. I gave him a drawing of the forest and the trees and suggested his teacher take him aside when he started to get enmeshed in splitting and ask, "Carl, can you stand back and look for the forest, or are you bumping into the trees?" One day he looked up in pure frustration and said, "I haven't even gotten to the trees. I'm stuck in the bushes!"

Carl benefited from being encouraged to look for the big picture before he started anything. We tried to help him see connections and understand how details fit together to make wholes. One tactic that helped him pull ideas together was summarizing a paragraph or a story in only ten words or one sentence. He learned to think about his main

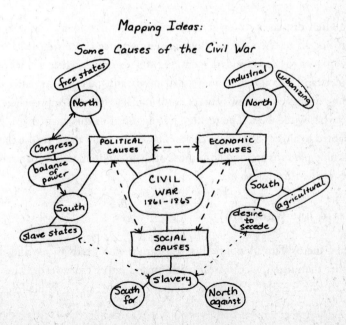

Mapping Ideas:
Some Causes of the Civil War

idea before he tried to make a point in a discussion. His teachers tried to provide Carl with a framework before he started to plug in isolated facts. They discovered that most students like a verbal outline and a blackboard diagram of the general ideas to be covered at the beginning of a lesson. ("Today we're going to talk about the causes of the American Revolution. You will need to think about what we have learned about life in the colonies before you can understand them.") They also used timelines and other devices to put facts into perspective.

Drawing diagrams, or "mind maps," of ideas is a way to put verbal material into visual form; it seems to help both lumpers and splitters. It is initially hard for many people, but since using this technique with students, I am a convert. They don't care how inept I am; they love the way it helps them "see" the main points. Other teachers and I improvised the ones in this chapter. Try it with your child, remembering that there is no "right" way, as long as it expands understanding.

The Parents' Role

Children display learning style differences as early as nursery school, but not all teachers know about the importance of varying teaching techniques to accommodate them. Parents may have to help the school understand a youngster's individual needs and take the initiative at home in suggesting new ways of studying. Try different approaches to see what works best. The techniques suggested in this chapter can be adapted to almost any age level. Parents often remark that because their learning patterns are similar to those of their children, they have strategies of their own to share.

Weird but Wonderful

Then there's Tim. A nontraditional learner who needs to see and do rather than listen, who reasons with images rather than words, Tim is on the other end of the splitter-lumper scale. He can see whole forests easily, but usually lacks the patience to go in and analyze the trees. He jumps into the middle of situations and may intuitively come up with the right solution—or one that is way off base. He can't organize himself—or his strategies for schoolwork.

"How can he read so carelessly and still get the idea?" his English teacher asks. "Tim gets the answer but can't write out the equation," complains his math teacher. Sometimes, if people are willing to listen as Tim struggles to describe it, his idea is "weird but wonderful." The Tims of this world usually have a harder time in school than the Carls, but not because they lack ability. If they get out of school with their self-esteem still intact, they are often very successful in the "real world." If your child is like Tim, your work is cut out for you, but the first step must be to get rid of the words "lazy" and "stupid."

Evaluating Tim's strengths and weaknesses helped me and his parents understand some of his inconsistencies. For example, he liked math in elementary school but now found himself unable to "get it." He didn't realize that earlier math classes had involved a lot of *doing*—writing on the board, and manipulating objects and shapes. Now he was in a class where the teacher taught by talking. Considering Tim's difficulty with remembering even one sentence at a time, it is no surprise he was in trouble. I explained to Tim that he needs to ask the teacher to *show* examples in addition to telling him, and that he needs to write problems in his notebook as well as sit and listen (or fail to!). Fortunately, his teachers were all willing to cooperate because they recognized that he really wanted to improve.

Tim was missing homework assignments that, teachers being only human, were often given quickly at the end of class: "Oh, by the way, tomorrow's homework is to do all the odd-numbered examples on pages seventeen and twenty and write a short paragraph about the effects of climatic conditions on fossil formation." Forget it! (That's what Tim usually did.) Tim's parents went to the school to explain that he needed to have directions *written down* or given more slowly. He may eventually need to use a tape recorder, as some students do, in high school lecture classes and use some type of electronic device to speed up note-taking and help with organization. Simultaneously, he can practice trying to remember longer and longer chunks by repeating them back and working on improving his summarizing skills. Understanding his style does not mean lowering our ultimate expectations for him.

Tim's quick intelligence had succeeded in masking the serious deficits in his reading skills, but he finally admitted they were causing him a great deal of trouble. He began to work with a special tutor who focused on the basics he had missed out on earlier, and he soon showed rapid improvement in both reading and spelling. She also helped him with study skills and note-taking.

At home, in addition to reassuring him that all this work is worth the effort, Tim's parents can help him organize longer reading assignments in a visual form. Tim took readily to mapping ideas to help him remember what he has studied. It is also never too late to work on language development and expression of ideas at the dinner table; these habits may carry over into increased classroom participation. Parents can help with auditory memory by practicing a limited number of directions at a time. ("Please go upstairs, close your bedroom window, and bring down the newspaper.") They will undoubtedly have to help him organize his homework time and be available to proofread reports. A computer helps him be more fluent and accurate in his writing. Students like Tim often like to study to music; if it works, let him.

The bad news for Tim is that he will have to work harder in school than some of his friends. The good news is that he can succeed—both in school and, more importantly, when real life exerts a different set of demands. The ultimate success of many "nontraditional" learners confirms this pattern as *different, not inferior.*

Does accepting divergent learning styles mean lowering academic standards? *No!* Helping children achieve and enjoy learning can only improve the intellectual climate. Parents and teachers must take the time and effort to meet individual needs without caving in on expectations. Truly, we all have our work cut out for us!

Different Drummers

This chapter has been about making connections—between the hemispheres, between the sexes, between individuals. We are just beginning to explore the neural variations that underlie the colorful mosaic of human talent. Differences make us interesting and provide society with a broad pool of abilities. Underlying the history of human accomplishment are myriad combinations of left and right, male and female, lumpers and splitters. The most effective thinkers are those who can link their mental talents in varying combinations—who can see ideas and plan their implementation, grasp a total problem and analyze its elements, create and communicate.

We're not yet sure where people get their unique styles of taking on the world, or how much we can—or should—change them. The suggestions in this book are for expanding, not altering. I hope you will apply them with the love and common sense that are your parental gifts. By broadening bridges, you can ease your child's intellectual passage, for differences often cause children pain. Adults are privileged because they are respected and even acclaimed for uniqueness. They choose the arenas in which they wish to appear and avoid those where they are inept. Children are not so lucky. If their skills are unbalanced, if the school fails to appreciate their gifts, there is little respite from inadequacy. Parents, frustrated by their child's defeats, can easily lose sight of talents that reach beyond the classroom walls.

One little girl, a fourth grader whose main strengths are creative and intuitive, came up with an important thought one day as we were discussing a story about prejudice. Face clenched in concentration, she struggled mightily to find words for her idea. Here they are:

Feelings about Others

Some people are nicer
Because their brains
Are differently attached to their hearts
Than other people's.

No matter how your child's brain is attached, I hope you can respect that singular pattern even as you help to integrate its design. Society needs pathways to the future built by effective, flexible, and interesting minds.

Chapter 7

"Do Pigs Have Wishbones?":
Unfolding Language

One evening a number of years ago, when our youngest son was about four, I was preparing dinner and studying for an exam on children's language development while he pursued his favorite hobby of rearranging the kitchen cupboards. Suddenly he gazed up, regarded the pork chops in my hand, and asked, "Do pigs have wishbones?" I remember laughing at this "cute" comment and jotting it down on a scrap of paper, but I don't recall how I responded; quick explanations were the rule in those days of return to graduate study and part-time work. No doubt Doug was left to contemplate the mysteries of wishbones on his own.

Not long ago, with student days and exams far behind me, I came upon that scrap of paper stuck in a dusty cookbook. After years of studying other children's language development, I was struck by the irony of having overlooked the importance of my own son's words. With those four simple words, Doug, like most children of his age, showed that in a few short years he had mastered the most complex rule system of the human intellect—with no formal instruction. I didn't pay much attention at the time, but that funny question, with all the learning that lay behind it, presaged well for his future with reading, writing, organizing solutions to problems, reasoning about abstract ideas, and even leadership ability. Moreover, by using language, Doug was building his own brain.

I have learned a great deal since that day in the kitchen, and I would like to help you appreciate, better than I did, your own children's language development. To understand how you can take the most constructive role in helping it unfold, we should first consider the four things that a child must learn: its purposes, its mechanics, its meanings, and its rules.

THE PURPOSES OF LANGUAGE
Nature's Mysterious Device

Where does language come from? Experts have waged intellectual fisticuffs about whether it is preprogrammed or determined by input into specialized areas of the brain. As usual, the answer lies somewhere in between. Both "language," a general term for the use of verbal symbols, and "speech," its means of expression, are an instinctive reflection of humans' need to communicate. Did you know that a two-month-old reaching out with one finger pointed is practicing a form of language? Have you noticed how, by the age of six to nine months, *without knowing a single word*, a child can participate in a "conversation" and even control it? (If you doubt this, watch baby and Grandma sometime.) Nature has built the basics of language into most infants' brains.

A deaf child starts to babble at the same age as do hearing children, so we know that auditory stimulation is not necessary for prelanguage development. One of the most intriguing theories proposed a "language acquisition device" somewhere in the brain that makes it inevitable. No one has yet located this mysterious machine (which I whimsically picture as a small square box with lots of wires sticking out), but it is true that infants around the world, exposed to different languages and dialects, all babble remarkably similar sounds. They produce vowels before consonants and are instinctively sensitive to sound differences. Infants' left hemispheres can already sort out human speech from noises in the environment. You might say that children are biologically programmed to talk. By eight months, however, the brain is already pruning away sounds not in the child's environment, so that babies from Japan or the United States are now babbling in Japanese or English. By adolescence, and perhaps even earlier, it is almost impossible for most people to capture a perfect native accent in a foreign language, even when they become otherwise fluent.

Most of our language abilities are housed in widely separated parts of the left hemisphere, although this pattern may differ in a small percentage of people. For example, *Wernecke's area*, responsible for understanding words and constructing grammatical sentences, is a long way from *Broca's area*, where they get ready to be pronounced. Effortless communication depends on development of each area as well as the thick fiber connections between them. Some teachers have difficulty understanding how a child can do one language task very well, such as getting the meaning of a story, but another quite poorly, such as retelling it clearly. Understanding the complexity of the system helps us target each skill more effectively.

Some parts of the right hemisphere contribute as well, especially when it comes to understanding and interpreting language messages. Clearly, not everything matures at once. Language development proceeds throughout childhood; while the process becomes less dramatic as plasticity declines at puberty, most language skills can still be refined even in college and adulthood.

Because the right hemisphere is more active during the first couple of years, some authorities have suggested teaching babies sign language, which doesn't require maturation of special left hemisphere systems or articulation ability. Some parents seem to think this helps them communicate with the infant, and vice versa. The jury is still out on whether this system has any permanent effect—positive or negative—on the child's development.

One young mother takes great delight in reporting her infant daughter's progress—without sign language—to me. "Only two months old, and I swear she's imitating me. I say 'Hi,' and she says 'I-i-i-i.' My husband says it isn't possible." Her husband has underestimated the power of the language acquisition device—and also the verbal inclinations of many females of the species, who usually operate on a slightly faster speech timetable than their male peers. Yet despite the brain's predilection, it takes coaching from the environment to build the staggering number of neural connections required for further development.

The deaf children who start to babble do not develop speech without special intervention, although they show their predisposition to communicate in sign language. The better the language environment, the better any child's outcome. Parents have a bigger role in this critical area of learning than in almost any other. Fortunately, nature has also programmed parents instinctively to become their child's best teachers. The first lesson they present is about loving communication.

Primitive Purposes

An infant's first communication usually takes the form of a piercing wail, which sounds as if it arises from a primitive part of the brain. It does. As the child begins to coo, babble, and receive verbal messages, new networks are forming in language centers of the cortex. By six to nine months the higher centers assert some control. Language is closely linked with emotion, and it is important to remember that children who get enough cuddling and unconditional love have a better chance at learning language—and everything else.

Specialized brain centers need to be stimulated for listening, speaking, and understanding. Most children invite your assistance, and the adult's positive response is instinctive—and important. If Mother, for example, acts "different," seeming aloof or upset, the infant responds with body language signaling distress. During the first six months, a strong bond with a parent or caregiver is also important to model appropriate pronunciation and grammar as well as to teach the rules of the game of conversation.

PRAGMATICS: LEARNING THE GAME OF CONVERSATION

Did you know that playing peekaboo is a language game? It teaches turn-taking, the first lesson. Between four and nine months this concept is practiced over and over as children imitate adult words and learn that "talk" involves waiting your turn. There are other rules to be learned: Gestures go along with sounds and help everyone understand what is meant; you can get people to do things for you by making noises of various kinds; people respond when you "talk" to them. Sometimes they even know what you mean: "Well, how did that taste, Janeel?" Janeel wiggles eloquently and emits a loud burp. "Oh, you liked it, didn't you!"

All of these reasons and conventions for using language come under one heading—*pragmatics*. Children who lack them are at a serious disadvantage because they have trouble using language as a tool. Much "social maladjustment" stems from such poor understanding—not of the words themselves, but of the game of conversation. Such children can't "read" gestures or facial expressions of emotion, size up where the other person is "coming from," or understand how to incorporate others' points of view into their behavior. They may verbally barge into situations or withdraw, wondering why no one seems to like them.

Sensitive periods for pragmatics occur early in life, so it is unwise to expect overtaxed caregivers or electronic appliances to teach these important lessons. They require a real person, face-to-face, responding directly to whatever the child says or does.

Helping Children Understand Purposes for Language

Look at this list of seven reasons for using language, and notice how many are based on interaction with others.

1. **Instrumental:** To satisfy needs and wants.
   > *"Lou, if you would like a cookie, please use words to ask me instead of whining and pounding on the shopping cart."*

2. **Regulatory:** To control the behavior of others and of self.

> *"Let's talk about a fair way to decide who plays with the truck now. Then we'll talk about how you'd like to take turns."*
>
> *"Let's say 'hit' each time we pound the peg."*

3. **Interactional:** To establish and maintain contact with others.

> *"While I'm getting dinner, I love it when you stay near and tell me about your day."*
>
> *"Girls, I want you to use words instead of hitting each other."*

4. **Personal:** To express choices, assert the self, and take responsibility.

> *"Don't be afraid to tell me which one you want; I'll let you know if I don't have enough money."*
>
> *"If you feel sad, it might help to talk about it."*
>
> *"Why don't you talk to Ms. Smith before school tomorrow. I would be proud if you could try to solve this problem without asking me to call the teacher."*

5. **Learning:** To ask questions and get information.

> *"I don't know if pigs have wishbones, but that surely is an interesting question. I'll help you ask the butcher when we go to the store tomorrow."*
>
> *"I like to have you ask questions about things you're interested in—it lets me know you're building your brain for thinking."*

6. **Imaginative:** To pretend, to create images and patterns.

> *"Let's take turns making up stories about a pretend trip we would like to take."*
>
> *"Let's think of all the things that would happen if our street turned to chocolate pudding. Can you make a picture in your mind of what it would look like?"*

7. **Representational:** To inform others, to tell about ideas.

> *"Please tell me your ideas about whether we should go to the library this morning or wait until after dinner."*

"Your report for science sounds so interesting; can you explain to me how a battery works?"

"Would you like me to help you and Mark organize a debate about that?"

Full maturation of language pathways is not completed until at least adolescence, and possibly later. Parents can demonstrate all these purposes and patiently help a child experiment with them. Endless "Why?" questions are wearing, but they are the foundation of language as a tool for thinking, a major implement for intellectual growth.

CHARACTERISTICS OF LANGUAGE-BUILDING HOMES

- Children find adults' voices pleasant to listen to (at least usually!).
- Children see parents using language to communicate and solve problems. Adults encourage "talking through" situations before taking action.
- Parents or caregivers share activities and talk about them with each child, and give frequent praise.
- Adults respond positively to children's attempts to communicate. They listen when the child talks, refrain from interrupting, and show pleasure in the child's use of language.
- The family does not emphasize silence or submission as signs of being "good." Children are encouraged to "play" with words and express feelings verbally.
- Adults create "slots" for children's participation in family conversations.
- The child is encouraged to talk about what is happening during play with puzzles, blocks, etc., and to describe what she is doing or thinking. ("Tell me what your block house looks like." "How is that shape different from this one?")
- Children must use language in order to have needs met. Whining, crying, or gesturing does not get children what they want.

- Adults modify their own talk to the child according to his ability to understand. They also rephrase and expand the child's speech to teach more advanced forms. (Child:"I dooed it." Adult:"Yes, you did the whole puzzle, didn't you? Now would you like to do this one?")
- Video viewing is limited, and children are encouraged to talk about what they have seen.
- Tapes, "talking" picture books, and other toys that encourage listening skills are used, but not in place of real human voices. Incidentally, noisy electronic toys or voices that don't sound human are poor models because they lack prosody and the normal rhythm and intonation of language. Surprising or funny noises attract a child's attention, but they do *not* encourage good listening habits.
- Television does not substitute for conversation. Children must learn to formulate sentences and not just soak up input. Even good discrimination of sounds—the basis of "phonics"—comes from talking, not from TV, which is mainly a visual experience for children.*

Mother or "Mother Figure"?

Studies of early language strongly emphasize the mother's role. What if she is not the primary caregiver? This question is a hard one to answer, for it is clear that there is a biological base for mother-child interactions that lay the foundations for communication. Yet warm and loving physical care is not enough. A normal child who had been well cared for and loved by deaf and mute parents had abnormal language when he began to receive regular therapy after he was three years old. Fortunately he was young enough to make up much lost ground, but the message is clear: Exposure to language is necessary. If you must choose a substitute caregiver for your child, or even a frequent babysitter, insist on a real concern for good language development. Check out grammar, vocabulary, and

* More about this important topic in my book *Endangered Minds*.

voice quality as carefully as you check on health and reliability. Don't hire someone who will encourage your child to "be quiet" for convenience, or give her poor models of speech, or cheat her out of a rich vocabulary. Find someone who enjoys conversation and reading, who will discipline with words rather than physical action. Likewise, when choosing day-care settings, put good language near the top of your list of "musts."

Body Linguistics

Who would ever believe that language, like so many other cognitive skills, is rooted in nonverbal bodily actions? Neurolinguists assert that language (and human intelligence, too, by the way) develops directly from gesture, and also from the process of manipulating tools (toys, in the child's world) and physical objects. If you try to make a point with-out moving your hands, you may get the idea. When children are asked to name tools, they activate the same areas in their brains that are active when they are physically using the tools. When asked to name animals, the child activates entirely different areas. If you want to help your child build a keen brain for vocabulary, make sure plenty of physical play is on the program.

Here are a few suggestions for you—or your child's caregiver—to build the pragmatic base for language learning:

Building Language Basics: Practical Tips

• Associate talking with warm, personal interactions. Young children understand loving physical contact better than long strings of words.

• Initiate games of sharing and turn-taking. Take turns banging a spoon on a tray. Build a tower and let the child knock it down. Take turns "talking," even if half of the conversation sounds like gibberish.

• "Where's your tummy? Where's your toe?" is a good example of an instinctive parent-child game that teaches both communication and vocabulary. "What does the kitty say?" is another favorite.

• Show your child from the earliest months how to look into some-one's eyes when talking to them. This comes naturally to most children. If your child habitually avoids eye contact, stop, gently turn his chin, say, "Look at my eyes," and wait for eye contact before you go on talking. Consistent problems with eye contact warrant professional evaluation.

• Use attention-getting phrases such as "Look here" or "See?" to make sure the child is "with" you.

• When a child is old enough to start conveying meaning, let her know when she has not made herself clear, and why. ("When you said you didn't want to go and then got your coat, I wondered what you meant.") Young children using the telephone may need to be reminded that the party on the other end cannot see gestures or understand terms like "this one."

• Help your child develop tact. ("I liked it when you said, 'Daddy, please help me when you're ready.' It made me feel as if you cared about what I was doing, too.")

• Don't confuse a child with "body talk" that is different from your words. If you are irritated or upset, express it in a reasonable and honest way.

• Adults and older children instinctively "pare down" their language to the child's level. Trust your instincts when you find yourself simplify-ing.

• If the child has older siblings, encourage them to talk to the baby. You will be astonished at what good teachers they are, and they will bask in the praise and warm feeling that their help elicits.

• Children learn better at first if there are only two speakers, but family conversation is important, too. The child should not always be the center of the conversation, as observing "grown-up" talk teaches the rules.

• Dramatic play, dolls, and puppets help children put themselves in another person's place. Practice exchanging roles. ("You be the mommy now and I'll be the little boy.")

• Let young children be important message-bearers. ("Please tell Daddy we will be ready to go in ten minutes.") Teach children to take responsibility for remembering things they hear.

• Encourage contacts with peers. Children learn about language from social play. You may need to bite your tongue as they work out minor differences.

• Let your child teach you how to do something or give directions for an everyday action. Follow the directions exactly to show the effect of her words. A classic example is describing how to make a peanut butter sandwich. You may get some mutual laughs trying to spread the peanut butter before picking up the knife or opening the jar! Such direction-giving skills are rarely perfected before middle school years.

• Young children gradually learn to handle indirect messages. If you say, "Would you like to help me clean the dog's pen?" don't be offended if your child responds, "No," and goes on playing. One mother was looking at pictures with her little girl and asked, "Do you see what the animals are doing?" "Uh-huh," agreed the child. Until "indirection" is mastered, you may need to be more specific if you expect a response.

• Your sensitivity also provides a lesson in inferring information. If your son comes in and announces, "The swing is broken," and there is no swing in your yard, you might answer, "Oh, you must have been playing at Jimmy's house." Inference takes a long time to develop because it goes beyond the concrete facts presented.

• Above all, make language input pleasant for your child. Children who have learned to "tune out" adult voices because they were loud, bossy, or hurtful may start school with poor listening habits.

Missed Lessons

I once tested a little boy who was labeled a "misfit" in second grade. His teacher thought he might have a learning disability because he was unable to remember the simplest directions. He had difficulty answering questions and often "said the wrong thing" to other children. After testing Paul, I knew exactly what she meant. He looked terrified when asked a question; tears actually appeared in his eyes several times when he had to express an idea. He needed to have most questions repeated, and he couldn't say back more than three numbers in a row, but he was good at block puzzles and making sense out of pictures. This profile is, indeed, typical of children who have language disabilities, and I was quite confident of my diagnosis until Paul's father came to pick him up and asked to see me privately.

"I don't want to blame my wife for Paul's problem," he confided, "but she doesn't have much patience. Actually, she yells at the kids all the time—sometimes she even swears and puts them down in a real nasty way. Our other ones fight back, but Paul just acts like he doesn't hear it at all. I feel terrible telling you this, but I thought you should know."

So much for my clear-cut diagnosis! How much did Paul's negative experiences with listening and conversation have to do with his language disability? The "problem" was a real one at the time I saw him, but its source remains open to speculation. Learning to "tune out" had enabled him to survive at home, but it wasn't helping at school! We tried to help his mother understand Paul's needs, and a specialist worked with him on the skills of listening and expressing himself. Now a teenager, he is still a "loner" who has trouble relating socially to his classmates. I often wonder what would have happened if his first language teacher had taken the time to give him all the lessons.

MILESTONES IN COMMUNICATION

Ages for each stage are approximate:

Before birth: Receives intonation patterns from Mother's voice.

By two months (possibly even at birth): Responds to Mother's speech.

Birth to nine months: Cries, smiles, vocalizes, laughs, reaches out, makes gestures of giving, pointing, showing. May copy an adult sticking out tongue.

By two to three years: Can cooperate in communication; understands how to ask and answer, take turns in talking.

Can use language for different purposes (to get something, to tell about something, to relate to others).

Responds to simple commands if phrased positively (say "Stop!"—not "*Don't* eat the spider").

By three years: Gives related response to question. Changes topics rapidly when talking.

By four years: Pretends to have conversation on toy telephone, waits for "answer."

By three to five years: Talks to self to help control behavior or solve problems.

By five years: Beginning to learn what is appropriate to say to different types of listeners.

Five to six years: Still blames listener when he's not understood.

By ten years: Can stick to a topic.

Varies conversation according to listener.

Can use language to give "hints."

Understands social "rules" for language use.

There is no question that some children pick up the forms and uses of language more easily than others, and Paul might have had difficulty despite the most loving attention. Infants who show more active brain waves in response to sounds tend to be more verbally advanced at age three and better readers in school, suggesting that some children are more linguistically oriented from birth. Sociable children also tend to develop language more rapidly.

Children also have different styles of language learning. *Referential* children use words and sentences sooner, speak more clearly, and experiment earlier with grammatical forms. They tend to use more names of people and physical objects. *Expressive*-style children are somewhat slower to talk; when they do they're more likely to start by echoing the conversation of adults or using words like "please." Their speech may be somewhat unclear, they acquire vocabulary more gradually, and their conversations focus on social interaction as well as objects. These styles are probably partially innate, but they also reflect the type and amount of speech in the home. Both are considered "normal."

How do you know if your child is learning language on schedule? Some of the earliest signs concern how accurately it is received and pronounced.

PHONOLOGY: MASTERING THE MECHANICS
Taking in Language

Like any production system, language has two main parts: input and output. Without good raw material going in, the quality of the output inevitably suffers—in auto factories and in the language production system. The name given to the ability to use sounds is *phonology*. Phonological development starts when sounds of speech activate waiting neural networks.

First of all, the child must be able to pay attention. Ability to focus on important sounds and differentiate them from background noise originates far down in the brain. You can help by providing an environment where noise is reasonably controlled. "Talking" with just one person at a time also helps.

Second, the child must be able to discriminate one sound from another. Is Mom saying "shine" or "chime"? If the brain doesn't get good quality input and interactive practice with real people during these years, the child may have later difficulty with reading, spelling, and speaking clearly. For this reason, pediatricians are on the lookout to prevent and treat ear infections that cause intermittent hearing loss.

Getting Out the Words: Practical Tips

One of our neighbor's children said "pasketti" for spaghetti so often that the whole family renamed this staple. Such confusion of sounds shows that the left hemisphere hasn't perfected its analyzing job. First, sounds in the word must be received clearly, in the proper order, and held in "short-term memory" long enough for the brain to register them. Then the order must be recaptured and forwarded to the speech

BUILDING LANGUAGE: REPETITION WITHOUT MEANING

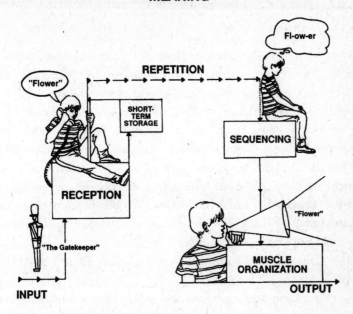

apparatus for production. A diagram of this part of the input-output system might look like the above.

During the first year the brain needs lots of practice hearing and imitating sounds, but most children are not ready to produce real words until after their first birthday. Like many other skills, this development cannot be forced, for it depends on the maturation of multiple connections. Simplified consonant-vowel combinations and mispronunciations are typical of first words: "poo" or "poon" for "spoon," "ga-ga" or "goggy" for "doggy." Articulation and memory improve with increased practice and longer words. Here are some suggestions for encouraging development of the mechanics of speech:

• When talking to children, adults tend to speak more clearly, in a higher voice, and pause longer between sounds than in adult speech. Experts call this "Motherese." Fast, rapidly changing sound patterns (such as those on TV) are confusing for children. Being sensitive to the child's response prevents your shutting down the system by overloading it.

• It's okay to exaggerate the contours of your voice to help the child get the message. Scaling down words is good for babies ("mama," "nana"), but don't use baby talk that models incorrect pronunciation.

• Early games of imitating tongue movements help build the speech apparatus. Practice imitating different pitches and volume.

• Get a book of childhood games to find possibilities for language-building. Games of syllable repetition are excellent practice. When the child can repeat one syllable ("ba"), try two ("ba-da"), and three ("ba-da-ba"; "ba-ga-da"). Later, try words. Keep it easy enough to be fun. Preschoolers and even older children benefit from games like "Grandmother's Trunk" and "Telephone," etc., where the goal is to remember and repeat words in order.

• Games that have rhyming words help later listening and reading.

• "Pig Latin" and similar games help older children remember and sequence sounds.

• Children differ widely in their tendency to imitate adult speech. It is common for children to understand more than they say.

• Children need time to think of the right words and pronounce them; don't steal their chance to learn by doing it for them.

• If your child mispronounces a word, gently repeat it correctly. Do not expect accurate articulation of all sounds until after age seven.

• You can help maintain a child's attention by touching or holding her gently (on the chin or shoulder) while you are talking. Ask, "Can you say it back?" You may need to rephrase and simplify. Don't ignore a child's habit of "tuning out."

• Some children have unusual difficulty sorting out important talk from background noise. They need a limited noise environment.

• Excess emphasis on perfection spoils the game. If you find your anxiety level building, pull back. Language that is tangled up with unpleasant feelings is hard to unravel.

MECHANICAL MILESTONES

Because of individual differences among children, these ages are only approximate.

First four months: Can distinguish between different sounds (one to two months), cooing.
Four to eight months: Babbling (may use sounds not in English language).
Nine to twelve months: First syllables (consonant-vowel:"ma,""mama").
    First consonants, usually *p, m, t,* and *k.*
    First vowels, usually *a, i, u.*
    Babbling may continue even after child acquires words.
By three years: Speech can be understood.
Four to five years: Can pronounce consonant clusters (e.g., *sm, sp, tr, cl*).
Six years: Can pronounce and distinguish between all vowel sounds.
Eight years: Can pronounce and distinguish between all consonant sounds.
Nine years: Can remember and repeat four to five numbers in a row.

• Your enthusiastic response is the trigger for your child's continued language development. Don't fall into the trap of trying to "drill" language skills; good speech develops in a context of everyday events and play.

Mechanical Problems

Sometimes this finely tuned phonological system misfires. The most commonly diagnosed language problem is with clear articulation. If your child is very slow in developing commonly acquired sounds or does not have intelligible speech by age three, you should first have a doctor rule out any primary physical problem. Then you should seek an evaluation from a speech and language clinic or private therapist.

Although often self-correcting, articulation disorders can be a harbinger of other language and school problems. Severe articulation problems causing "slushy" speech may be associated with poor control over mouth and tongue movements. This *oral dyspraxia* is often related to similar incoordination of hands or other motor dyspraxias and requires professional treatment.

All children repeat TV commercials and other familiar messages; it is normal when accompanying other efforts to communicate spontaneously. A few children with a language disorder called "echolalia" don't learn to express themselves in their own words. They repeat slogans inappropriately *in place of original speech*, sounding strangely "flat," without the normal contours of the human voice. Such children usually have several signs of developmental difference and need early professional attention.

Approximately 4 to 10 percent of all children—mainly boys—stutter at some time during their early years. Most cases clear up spontaneously within one year, and only 1 percent of adults are stutterers. Stuttering tends to run in families. If your child starts to stutter, ignore it for a while and keep the atmosphere as unpressured as possible, since perfectionism and anxiety worsen the condition. If it persists, get a professional evaluation. The same advice applies to stammering ("The . . . uh . . . uh . . . uh . . . uh . . . dog"), which may simply signal that the child's excess of rapidly firing synapses are temporarily outstripping his articulatory capability.

Some experimenters are trying to help the brain gain language abilities by directing special tapes of music or voices into left or right hemispheres. This notion is still very controversial. Be skeptical of anyone who promises dramatic "cures" or claims that one type of treatment can cure many different problems. Above all, steer away from any system in which language training is made unpleasant for children.

Computerized training programs to enhance phonological processing for school-age children are promising, but still controversial. No guarantees exist that they will improve reading skill.

Multilingual Brains

Research suggests that the brains of people who speak more than one language allocate more neural real estate to the language cortex, and each language occupies a slightly separate location. Moreover, if you learned French in high school, it probably occupies a different area than it would have if you had learned it before puberty. Which brings us to a question very much on parents' minds: how, when, and whether children should receive instruction in a second or third language.

Like any prescription based on current brain research, this one is complex and still depends on incomplete information. Absolutely no research suggests that playing foreign language tapes to your baby will make her a genius—especially a baby Einstein, who was actually something of a klutz with early language development himself! On the other hand, if you want your child to acquire a good accent in several languages later on, it might not be a bad idea to expose her to the sounds of the words in some enjoyable way, because phonology is the hardest of the language skills to recapture if you don't get it early on.

Although babies of all cultures begin by babbling similar sounds, once they drop those to which they are not exposed it becomes increasingly difficult to recover them. The grammar of a language also becomes harder to learn after puberty, although it is still possible, and older students have better strategies for mastering the rules of a new grammar.

Vocabulary can be learned anytime, but it takes longer as we age. Curiously, even fluent second-language speakers say they have trouble with one particular element of social usage (*pragmatics*)—subtle jokes and a sense of humor. So, clearly, it is preferable to get some of the basics under your belt (or hat, in this case) early on, if possible. Whether or not it works depends on both the reason and the method for the "teaching."

Most children who grow up in bilingual homes readily master both languages. For a while their overall development is a little slower, but they eventually catch up and become fluent in both. Their learning is based on the best reason—communication—and the "method" is everyday interaction with family members. This is true for *most* children. A brain with inefficient circuits for language, however, has real trouble grappling with even one set of sounds, meanings, and grammar.

Expose a young child to a foreign language *if* (1) the child does not have an incipient language problem; (2) the child is interested and learning is nonstressful; (3) the language is presented *orally* in the same way children master their natural language; (4) the speaker has a true native accent; (5) understanding of rules of grammar is not demanded. It is helpful for children in bilingual homes to be able to sort out the languages by speaker—that is, Mommy's language, Daddy's language, Dora's language. For other children, songs, rhymes, and games embed the linguistic patterns enjoyably. If the child is encouraged to formulate (speak) as well, all the better.

For children with a language disability, it pays to work hard on embedding one language before introducing formal instruction in another one.

GRAMMAR (SYNTAX): LEARNING THE RULES
The Wug that Flimmed

Four-year-old Molly listens intently. "Show me," her teacher says, "the horse kicked the cow."

Molly happily seizes the toy horse in front of her and delivers the cow a satisfying clout.

"Now listen and do this," says the teacher, "the horse is kicked by the cow."

Molly hesitates. "He just did that," she protests.

By the age of four, most children have mastered an astonishing number of rules for word order, which make up the grammar, or *syntax* of a language. Like Molly, they show sophisticated comprehension until they hit the toughest grammatical structures. How do they learn these rules? By listening, listening, listening and practicing, practicing,

practicing. Growing brains sop up language and magically wring out grammatical principles without even being aware that they're doing it.

"All right, Molly, here's another toy. Pretend this is a strange animal called a 'wug.' You try to finish what I say about the wug, okay?"

"Okay!" Molly is thoroughly enjoying this game.

"This is one wug. Now there are two of them. There are two . . . ?"

"Wugs!"

"Terrific! Now listen. This wug likes to flim. Now he is . . . ?"

"Flimming!" Molly chortles and makes the toy do a little dance on the table.

"Good. Yesterday he . . . ?"

"Flimmed."

What is the purpose of this nonsense talk? It certainly isn't a vocabulary lesson. The teacher has just demonstrated that Molly can apply rules by adding appropriate endings to words she has never heard before. It almost seems like magic that young children generalize all of these rules in a standard order; even children who are delayed in their language development usually follow the same pattern, only more slowly. When a new rule is first learned, it is usually overapplied, explaining why Molly says "I runned" instead of "I ran," and why a three-year-old asked for "a chee" when she wanted one piece of cheese. Most children have mastered almost all language rules by age four. Later-developing structures are the passive voice ("The horse was kicked by the cow"), time sequences that have the words reversed ("Before you mix in the flour, please beat the eggs"), comparative forms (big, bigger, biggest; some, more, most), and irregular plurals (mice, women).

Rule Problems

Some children have trouble latching on to these rules. Problems may result from poor models of grammar at home, from ear problems during their early years, or possibly from some delay in the brain's circuits that cause a language disability. A child who has trouble remembering word sequences will have difficulty producing them. For some, repeated exposure just doesn't seem to "take." Here are examples from the speech of children who need some help:

Patsy, age six: "Once upon a time there was a boy, and he said, 'At this store is too big.' 'I want the one with not the hat.' "
Ben, age nine: "On a big field there is two boys in the early morning because they didn't sleep all night."
Carol, age ten: "A index is a thing and in the back of the book and it's all arranged."

These children all have an adequate command of vocabulary and a clear idea of what they mean. The problem lies with how they string words together to express their ideas. Their subtle variations from standard form show that they are having problems with the nuances of oral language. When they hear their phrases repeated, they may not be aware anything is wrong. Could an enriched language environment have helped? We really don't know, since syntactic problems are among the most difficult even for professionals to treat. The confusion may lie at a more basic neural level where the brain picks up, recognizes, and remembers patterns of all kinds. Thus, play experiences that help the brain learn to organize incoming information and learn about rules and relationships are probably important in developing grammar! There are also many ways for adults to involve children in the patterns and rules of language:

• Because a critical period for acquiring the grammar of at least one language occurs in the early years, make sure good models are available. Once the grammar of one language is mastered, it is easier to learn others. The grammatical level of the mother's speech correlates with a child's reading skill even years later. Caregivers' modeling is also important.
• Children demand and need lots of pattern repetition. Repetitive patterns such as nursery rhymes are one of the best ways to organize young brains around language.

- Expose your child to good language from the beginning. In addition to talking, start reading aloud. Avoid books with "pop" language and slanglike expressions. I remember how tired I used to be at the end of the day, but now I wish I'd taken even more time for story reading.
- Don't stop reading out loud when the child learns to read. Families traveling by car have a special opportunity for round-robin reading; we found it settled irritations and postponed the inevitable "How much longer?" Although more labor-intensive than video, it will do a lot more for your child's brain circuits.
- Children love to go to plays and puppet shows. Be wary of taxing little brains with too much excitement, and keep such events infrequent and special.
- Children learn syntactic rules from helpful adults. Parents tend to correct meaning more often than grammar, but you can tactfully *reshape and expand* a child's talk. If Molly says, "I runned," Dad might say, "Yes, you ran" (reshaping), then add, "You ran to get the little box, didn't you?" (expanding).
- Linking all language learning to everyday happenings helps understanding and memory. Use concrete objects to show what you mean whenever possible. ("Before you brush your teeth, let's wash your face.")
- When looking at pictures together, show your child different ways to talk about one event. "See, the man is going shopping. He wants to shop for food because his children are hungry. What a big bag he has! It is bigger than the other one, but this one is the biggest of all."
- Children need to hear many questions in order to pick up the interrogative form. Practice asking Who? What? When? Where? How? and Why? questions and show your child how to answer them. Then reverse roles to encourage your child to ask questions using these words.
- Follow your natural tendency to increase the complexity of your sentences as your child gets older. Check her level of understanding by asking her to restate what she thinks you said. Some children act as if they understand when they really don't.
- Studies show that children do not pick up the use of articles *(a, the, an)*, connectives *(and, but, or)*, or prepositions without adult in-

teraction. You can devise games using prepositions. Hiding objects and giving clues is one example. ("It is *under* something." "Look *inside* something green.") Demonstrate how you use prepositions in everyday talk. "See, I'm putting the tomatoes *beside* the pears.")

• Be patient. These rules are incredibly complicated. Often, too, the child's idea and desire to tell you about it is more important than his exact wording.

MILESTONES IN LANGUAGE RULE LEARNING

These are only a few of the many grammatical structures children master. There is wide individual variation in this aspect of language development.

Six to twelve months: Repeats syllables ("pa-pa-pa").

Eighteen to twenty-four months: Combines two or more words in sentences.

By three years: Constructs sentences of three or four words. Uses noun and verb phrases ("Dat big doggie," "Him want cookie").

Two to four years: Uses verb tense markers (walked, walking, runned).

Three to four years: Uses auxiliary verbs, negatives ("I won't can do").

By four to five years: No overgeneralizations ("I runned").

Eight years: Uses irregular plurals (women, mice).

SEMANTICS: MOVING INTO MEANING
A Question of Semantics

The patterns of a child's personal experience are the template for language understanding and expression. Attempts to teach children language by drill don't work very well because meaning is missing. When children learn language in their natural setting, meaning comes with the package because there are all kinds of props in the situation. While Mother talks about a toy, she holds it out for the child to touch. When

Dad says, "Let's go for a walk," he gets his jacket out of the closet. Parents have an instinctive tendency to label objects and provide an ongoing commentary about daily activities. Language linked to everyday events ultimately expands to descriptions, story plots, and abstract ideas. It is a long but direct route from "See baby" to the implications of "Strike while the iron is hot."

The term "semantics" is used for language meaning, from single words to long texts. While specific areas of the left hemisphere probably control sounds, grammar, and some aspects of meaning, overall semantic abilities are more widely distributed. They also go hand in hand with mental development. A typical child repeated the above proverb perfectly, but wondered, "Didn't they get burned when they hit the hot irons?" Although he understood each word, his thinking was simply not sophisticated enough to get beyond the literal meaning. It is impossible to build language (or reading) comprehension unless basic thinking skills are part of the program.

Learning words and their meanings is all tied up with concept development because words are symbols. Exactly how do you know what a "dog" is? There are some pretty odd-looking dogs walking around, yet an adult can almost always say with certainty, "That's a dog." How do you know that something is a chair—and not a bench, or a stool? Somewhere inside your brain you have mental pictures of your typical dog and chair, which you compare with each new animal or "object to sit on." If the new one is close enough to your prototype, you feel confident about using that label. Knowledge of word meanings is stored in the brain in "semantic networks" that connect millions of prototypes for things, events, and even abstract ideas such as "freedom" or "mercy."

How do children develop semantic networks? From firsthand experiences with objects in the real world, and from hearing words associated with those objects and then with other words. "Go car-car," shouts a toddler as a bus passes by. "That's a bus," explains her mother. "You ride in a car, and you ride in a bus, but a bus is bigger. A car is smaller than a bus." A semantic network for "vehicles" has just been born. Patiently, slowly, adults help children braid the strands of experience, language, and thought.

Patterns of Relationship

Comprehending language is basically a question of understanding relationships. One early relationship problem is learning about pronouns. "You give it to me" means different things depending on who says it. Most children, however, master "I-you" and "my-your" confusions by about age three—a remarkable feat of abstraction. Continued trouble with pronouns may signal underlying difficulty that should be investigated.

Prepositions are another way to express relationships. What is "above" anyway? It might mean where an airplane is flying, or on top of a printed line on a page. "In" and "out" mean different things if you're talking about the cereal's relationship to the cupboard or Bill's membership in the club. Other parts of speech can also be confusing. What is "little"? Molly is little compared to Dad, but she is not little compared to a goldfish. "Here" and "there" change depending on where you are. Fortunately the human brain seems well adapted for this kind of work—if the child has good foundations for understanding physical relationships. As we will see in chapter 11, such language concepts are also critical for learning math!

At this point we need to add a whole new layer to our input-output system. In the previous diagram, input was simply repeated without any understanding, as when you read aloud in front of a crowd of people and then have no idea what you read about. You can also repeat mathematical formulae or words in a foreign language, but unless you have some associations to plug them into, they fall right out of your brain at the same time they fall out of your mouth! The accompanying illustration shows what happens when we move up to a level where incoming words get associated with familiar information from semantic networks.

BUILDING LANGUAGE: CONNECTING WITH THOUGHT

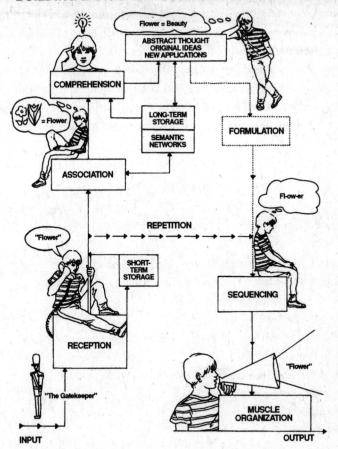

Expressing Meaning

Did you notice that there's still a gap in the system? What happens to all the good ideas churning around in the topmost layer? Take a pencil and draw in the line to connect comprehension and sequencing words. Label it "formulation"—expressing an original message. Children these days may not get enough practice formulating sentences and conversations as they watch TV, play video games, or press buttons on a computer. Good language output takes lots of practice, and schools that encourage predominantly the "input" side—reading and listening without having to express or write down ideas—deprive students of the most critical tools for using their knowledge.

For your child's future success in conveying ideas, writing, and thinking, please don't accept spaghetti talk that winds around without going anywhere. "Oh, like, well, you know, well like he could, you know, but . . ." Formulating ideas into sentences refines knowledge circuits,

---

MILESTONES IN MEANING

All ages are approximate.

Before one year: Understands words spoken by others.
Nine to eighteen months: First words; usually names or action words.
Eighteen to twenty-four months: Two-word combinations.
  Possessives, negatives, questions.
  Uses objects symbolically in pretend play (stick = horse).
  Beginning use of "and."
Three to four years: Can get an entire idea into one sentence.
  Comparative terms: big, little.
  Pronouns I-you, my-your.
  Past tense.
  "Why" questions; use of "because."
Four to five years: Can follow three simple commands.
  "If . . . , then . . ." concepts.
By six: Some use of passive voice. ("He was bumped.")
  Simple opposites (big-little, tall-short, hot-cold).
Terms: because, so, then, but, well, just, again, still, already, not yet, too, over, under, on top of, into, up, down.

---

sharpens logical thinking, and avoids "fuzzy" understandings.* A society that cannot communicate its ideas verbally may be in for trouble.

Unfolding Meaning: Practical Tips

• Always use language in a real context if you want to promote the best semantic growth. Talk about what the child is experiencing.

• Work on attaching meaning to words by "showing" what you are talking about. ("See, now I'm putting the button into the buttonhole— like this." "Look, this is the way I peel the orange.")

• Help your child build a good base of understanding by putting "talk" with age-appropriate play experiences. Get down on the floor and show how to talk about what's happening (be sure the child "gets the floor" so he can talk, too).

• Imitating words and phrases is a first step, but the ability to repeat something does not signify understanding. If you wonder whether your child has understood, ask him to *show* you what he thinks it means.

• A mother's style of conversation influences her child's. Some mothers tend to use talk as a practical tool for interaction ("I can tell you're enjoying that applesauce; would you like some more?"), and others tend to convey information. ("Applesauce is made from apples. They are fruits, like bananas.") It is probably a good idea to mix these two styles.

• Asking Socratic questions ("How do you think we can change the block tower so the blocks won't keep falling down?") stretches minds.

• Repetition is the key to children's understanding. Children looking at books repeat to themselves what adults have said about the pictures. Even if you think you will start to scream if you read *The Gingerbread Man* one more time, hang in there!

• As the child gets older, encourage her to retell stories in her own words. Retell the plots of TV shows in the order of events.

* See my book *Endangered Minds* for a full account of this issue.

- Vocabulary-building goes on all the time. Here are a few possibilities:
  - —Use the names of household objects.
  - —Point out and name things while you are walking or driving.
  - —Name things in pictures as you look at magazines together.
  - —Think of as many kinds of houses as you can (igloo, hut, mansion); ways of doing something (fast, slowly, deliberately, joyously).
  - —Act out words whenever possible to show meaning. ("See, my face is joyous now.")
  - —Teach verbs by examples: "See, that boy is running. That one is climbing a tree. The girl is jumping rope."
  - —Demonstrate prepositions. ("I'm putting the egg into the cup." "I'll hide the pencil behind the bookcase.")
  - —Expand modifiers. ("How many words can we think of to tell about how the princess looks? About how the monster is walking?")
  - —Play games with opposites. ("I say dark, you say . . ." "The knife is sharp, the eraser is . . .")
- Help your child generalize meanings. "The knife is sharp. (Can you say a word sharply? Can you find anything sharp about someone's face?)"
- It is all right to use some words that the child doesn't yet know or understand provided the situation is familiar. Children make the best progress after infancy with adults who gently stretch their understanding. Studies show that fathers may tend instinctively to challenge the child, while mothers are more sensitive to their current level of comprehension.
- When using an unfamiliar term, you might call attention to it. ("Here's a special word for that kind of dog—it's called a 'collie.' ")
- Children remember a thing better if they are asked to tell about it themselves. ("Now that I've explained where to go after school today, why don't you tell me again so I know you understand.")
- When choosing a day-care setting, look for one that emphasizes

language understanding. Children must have verbal interactions with adults, not just with other children.

- Teach relative terms by demonstrating them. ("This orange is bigger than the lemon. Which is bigger, the orange or the grapefruit?")
- If the child asks an illogical question, try to rephrase what you think she wants to know.

CHILD: Why is the airplane?
PARENT: Do you mean, "Where is the airplane? It just went behind the clouds."

- If a young child hasn't responded to a question in about five seconds, you might repeat or rephrase it.
- Family meals are a wonderful chance for children to develop both understanding and expression. Try some conversation starters to get everyone involved: "The nicest thing that happened to me today was . . . What about everyone else?") Help younger children be a part of the conversation.

Being head language coach can be tiring, but some parents take their responsibilities so seriously that they wear out the child instead. Incessant stimulation can cause young circuits to overload and shut down. The child's brain also needs quiet times in which to put together the new connections.

Faltering Formulation

"I don't know how Bea can have a language problem. She talks all the time!" This mother is right about her daughter in one respect. Bea, age seven, does indeed chatter like a magpie, but when you stop to listen, it is hard to figure out what she is talking about. Here is the way she retold a story about a boy who went on an imaginary space mission and discovered a new planet.

"Well, there were all these . . . uh . . . things he was, well, real scared and they came at him and he was, and then he got back in the—you know—in the space thingey, and they went fast he pushed the . . . pushed the button and he was scared when the things came but at the end they got back and he went in his . . . um . . . bed and that's the end."

While this child isn't exactly at a loss for words, the words she uses don't do a very good job. I call this "peanut butter" talk: If the child spreads enough of it around, she may succeed in covering the subject. This particular example illustrates a rather severe problem of "cluttering" with extra words and repetitions. Other children with milder problems are just off center when they try to answer questions or impart information. If you find your child tossing too much talk that misses the topic, try to encourage more thought and fewer words. "See if you can pick just three important ideas from the story (perhaps boy, space trip, new planet). Now let's start with telling who the main character is. When did the story happen? Where? What did he do? How did it end?"

Another problem this child shows is in "word-finding." Instead of being able to think of a word—usually a noun—she uses fillers or roundabout talk. Common examples are: "The . . . uh . . . uh . . . uh . . . you know . . ." "Thingey." "Stuff." One eight-year-old couldn't think of "doorknob" and said "doorpuller." Another called the coatrack the "hanging-up thing." A six-year-old defined a nail like this: "You put it down with a hammer in wood." Fuzzy talk like this is common (and cute) among younger children, but if it is chronic or persists into a child's school years, you should give it some attention. Reading and writing skills are based on the ability to call up familiar words, and such word retrieval difficulties (dysnomia) may signal future problems.

Here are a few things you can do at home. First, give the child time to think of what to say. Pressure makes things worse. Second, don't accept "you know," "stuff," or other empty substitutions. Gently probe for a meaningful word or help by supplying one. One helpful game is trying to name a series of common objects or pictures as fast as possible. Fast color naming is also good practice. Remember, though, keep it fun. If language difficulties are causing tension in your home, get professional help. The "window of recovery" for severe language problems is widest between ages one and six, but remedial work at any age can be effective.

WARNING SIGNALS

All children show some problems with acquiring and using language as they grow. If you notice several of these signs, however, you should obtain a professional evaluation of your child's language development. (Premature infants may be expected to show some delay because of immaturity.)

- Absence of cooing or babbling during first six months.
- Repeated failure to make eye contact with caregivers.
- Persistent difficulty with turn-taking games.
- Trouble with sucking, chewing, or swallowing.
- Excessive drooling.
- Persistent difficulty imitating tongue movements.
- "Strange-sounding" voice (may result from physical causes).
- Acquiring single words and phrases and then stopping all speech.
- No single words by eighteen months.
- "Echolalia": repeating set phrases, such as TV commercials, instead of speaking spontaneously; inappropriate repetition without intentional communication.
- Stuttering that is severe or that persists more than one year.
- No two-word combinations by thirty months or three-word sentences by age three.
- Persistent pronoun confusion after age three.
- Delayed or absent asking of questions.
- Use of language only to label or request things rather than to comment on activities or events in the environment after age three.
- Frequent articulation or grammatical errors persisting after school age.
- Frequent word substitutions; difficulty retrieving familiar words.
- Frequent irrelevant responses ("What do you like to do at school?" "Sally goes to my school but we have different teachers.").
- Persistent inability to come to the point.

- Difficulty with abstract meanings of words or "getting" age-appropriate humor.
- Purposeful withholding of speech.

Unblocking the System

I once had a student whose mother was ready to give up on her. "I can't understand how Marie can be *so* slow. Every time anyone says anything to her, she gets this vague look on her face and says, 'Huh?' She's been doing that ever since she was little, and now she's about to flunk eighth grade. There's nothing wrong with her hearing, but I can't believe she's really that dumb!"

Marie was actually much brighter than anyone realized—including Marie. While she was indeed a slow language processor, she had superior abilities to reason and possessed an extensive vocabulary, if anyone gave her time to use it. Yet she had learned to play the "dumb" game very effectively. It took a combination of language therapy, help in school, and much encouragement to convince both mother and daughter that she really was okay. Everyone's hard work evidently gave Marie the steam she needed, for her mother later called me to report that she is now getting good grades in high school. Marie still has to concentrate hard when people talk quickly to her, and it takes her a long time to read assignments, but she is a hard worker. I credit her mother's support for giving her the self-confidence to bypass some blocks in the system.

THE MAGIC OF INNER SPEECH
Language Builds Brains

Can the use of language increase the brain's ability to think? Neuropsychologists now believe that "inner speech"—the silent conversation that most of us carry on with ourselves—creates physical connections in several important parts of the brain. If you want your child to be a success in school, this ability may be the most important one of all. The best way to teach it is by example.

Let's say your toddler is trying to sort different-colored plastic chips into piles. If you demonstrate by saying "blue, green, or yellow" as each chip is sorted, your child should be able to sort them faster and learn a valuable lesson about the power of words in guiding actions. From the age of about four, you can show a child the magic words: "First I will . . . and then I will . . ." Ask a school-age child who has difficulty with a math problem, "What is the question that you're supposed to answer? What steps could you take to get it?" Very often this simple process results in, "Oh, I get it now!" Private speech also helps us delay gratification, get ourselves motivated, and regulate our emotions.

The ability to use words to manage one's brain is age-related. The more practice children get, the better the connections. This growth can usually be observed between three and five years—when you can hear children talking out loud to themselves when doing a puzzle, for example—and it should be internalized sometime between ages nine and twelve. Six-year-olds think it's lots of fun to "teach" parents by giving directions. Older children can try more complex activities. For example, have two players sit on either side of a "wall" where they can't see each other. One child arranges colored blocks or other objects in some sort of pattern and then tries to get the other player (you, perhaps) to duplicate his design by describing what to do. ("Pick up the purple triangle and put it at the top. Then take a red square and make it touch the triangle right underneath.") You can also help older children plan ahead with words—writing out time schedules for major assignments, listing parts of an assignment in order, and so on. Any activity that mediates actions with words can be regarded as brain-building material.

One language technique that is effective with impulsive children involves five steps that put higher brain centers in charge of actions:

1. What do you have to do? (Identify the problem.)
2. How do you think you should go about doing it? (Evaluate the method for attacking the problem.)
3. What will you need to do first? (Plan the attack.)
4. Are you following your plan? (Check the progress.)
5. Did you finish what you had to do? (Check the outcome.)

Working on these five steps takes a particular brand of patience, but all children will benefit from the time you spend teaching them to build their own brains with inner speech.

THE PIG'S WISHBONE

I hope you can now share my excitement as I look back at a four-year-old's seemingly simple question. It is one of the marvels of the human mind that children master the purposes, mechanics, rules, and meanings of language without explicit teaching. Adults' participation in the process of developing language is an instinctive gift to the intellects of the next generation. Be gentle and trust yourself to help unfold each layer. If I really had a pig's wishbone, I would wish you and your child a joyous journey together.

Chapter 8

Tools for Learning:
Intelligence, Memory,
and Motivation

In the not-so-good old days when I started teaching, we had a semifatalistic idea about differences in people's learning abilities. Some brains, we smugly believed, were just born to be better, to store information quickly and effortlessly, and to be eager, work hard, and succeed. Not surprisingly, we viewed IQ scores as scientific crystal balls, virtually capable of predicting a child's future on the basis of a one-hour test. If motivation problems arose, they were likely to be blamed on some character flaw. We felt deep sympathy for those of our students who just "couldn't get it," but it never occurred to us that the rigid system of which we were a part might be contributing to the problem. Frequently we neglected to observe that some of our "problem" students were enormously successful in other arenas—at least the kids who still had some fight left by the time we finished rubbing their noses in their inadequacies.

All teachers have horror stories about mistakes they have made, and I particularly remember one youngster in my first English class. Steven could not remember the grammatical rules I was relentlessly reiterating and sometimes did not even recall how to spell a simple word like "said." I thought he was unmotivated. So did his parents, and we all threatened and exhorted him to try harder. Although he seemed bright enough, he had not scored well on the standardized IQ test, which marked his school file like a disfiguring scar. In those days I believed the test-makers knew more than a mere teacher did, so I never challenged the numbers. (I later discovered that, on his IQ test, he had skipped one problem by mistake and filled in all the "bubbles" out of sequence—therefore most answers were marked wrong whether he knew them or not.)

I fear I taught Steven much more about failure than about learning. I desperately wanted to help him, but I was too schooled in absolutes and didn't know there was more than one way to learn. I have since discovered how to see potential talent and use different approaches for such youngsters, but I often wonder what became of Steven.

Fortunately things are changing. While we still want to give children every chance to succeed in traditional learning environments, we now appreciate that learning may happen in many ways, through varied channels. Moreover, what has been so important in schools—a facility to memorize rules and large amounts of data—is becoming increasingly obsolete as computers do these tasks better and faster. Students still need basic academic skills, of course, but in a dynamic, fast-changing technological world, different forms of intelligence are assuming new importance. For today's kids the ability to solve all kinds of problems, get motivated, think reflectively and flexibly, synthesize data, and actively pursue learning throughout life will be important hallmarks of success.

In this chapter I would like to explore some old and some newer views of intelligence along with three of the most important basics for lifelong learning: meaningful memory, motivation, and something called metacognition—the ability to think about our own thinking.

WHAT IS INTELLIGENCE?

The Mystery of "g"

What makes some people smarter than others? In any society we find a range of abilities for dealing with life's demands. Individuals who are considered "superior" may be more clever at solving everyday problems, more adaptable when confronted with new challenges, or quicker to learn the skills of the prevailing culture. The criteria for "intelligence" might be quite different in societies of hunters or farmers than in those of computer programmers or dancers. Nevertheless, psychologists and neuroscientists have spent decades searching for one general factor, nicknamed "g," that underlies all learning ability. They started by measuring brain size, but since the richness of connections within a brain doesn't show up in external measurements, no one has found proof that bigger is better. One current theory has it that some people have more gray matter in a small area called the lateral prefrontal cortex, which mediates problem-solving in novel situations. Other studies, seeking a genetic explanation for intelligence, have looked for particular genes associated with such measures as higher SAT scores, but results are thus far inconclusive.

Brain wave studies of infants' reaction times to various types of stimuli have also provided interesting but inconclusive results. We already know that their brain wave patterns in response to rapidly changing sounds correlate with later measures of language and reading ability; whether similar studies can predict overall mental ability is still unknown. Moreover, the presence or absence of a rich early environment can significantly change the outcomes.

Infants display variations in their responses to unfamiliar stimuli. By measuring natural reactions such as looking, sucking, kicking, or heart rate, researchers can determine children's levels of interest and the speed with which they become habituated to new sights or sounds. For example, when a baby is shown an unusual toy, he tends to look at it for long periods of time. As soon as the novelty wears off he quickly turns his attention elsewhere, showing that he remembers his previous exposures to the toy so that it no longer intrigues him. Infants who learn to recognize (remember) toys more quickly tend to score better on standardized IQ tests even as late as eight years later. Whether these early clues involve superior memory, accuracy of perception, attention, speed of understanding, or other factors is not entirely clear.

Even if brain science eventually clarifies some of the mysteries of each individual's inborn facility for learning, no one has yet shown that quicker is always better. Moreover, "intelligence" is defined differently in different cultures. In some Asian countries, conceptions of intelligence focus much more on understanding and relating to others than on the verbal-analytical skills more valued in the West. Personal and motivational factors determine how we utilize our innate abilities, and current studies also suggest that "smarter" people everywhere tend to *use* their brains more actively—perhaps the most crucial variable of all.

Putting Children in Boxes

Ever since 1908, when psychologist Alfred Binet invented the IQ test, scientists have worked to develop reliable standardized tests to measure children's intelligence by observing how they answer questions or solve various sorts of problems. Binet was initially commissioned by the French government to categorize children's intelligence, thus weeding out those who were too "slow" to profit from the educational system. Rather than searching for just one factor, Binet saw intelligence as an aggregate of abilities, which he tested with a battery of about a dozen subtests. Although the tests have been considerably refined since then, this approach is still the most prevalent one today. By administering tests to thousands of children, test-makers develop norms that enable them to compare any child's score against the average for children of the same age. Thus they obtain an IQ (intelligence quotient) that shows how a child stands, overall, on the skills tested. On the most commonly used tests, an IQ of 100 is average, with the average range 85 to 115. The accompanying figure shows the percentage of children at each level; for example, if my friend's daughter Rima tests with an IQ of 135,

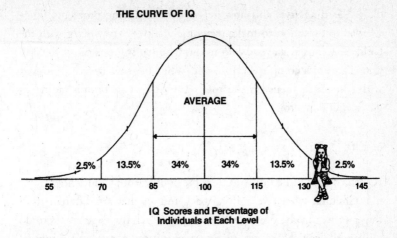

THE CURVE OF IQ

AVERAGE

| 2.5% | 13.5% | 34% | 34% | 13.5% | 2.5% |

55   70   85   100   115   130   145

IQ Scores and Percentage of
Individuals at Each Level

she scores in the top 2.5 percent of children her age *on that particular test*. Unfortunately, a few professionals have not gotten past the original intent of this approach—to label children as more or less teachable.

The best—and perhaps the only useful—IQ tests are those administered individually to children by well-trained examiners. Both verbal and performance skills are tapped in such typical subtests as:

- Defining vocabulary words.
- Remembering patterns of colored beads.
- Copying patterns of cubes.
- Telling what is "silly" about a picture (e.g., someone ice-skating on the sidewalk).
- Giving opposites of words.
- Answering questions about everyday situations. ("Where do we buy clothes?")
- Remembering a series of digits or sentences.
- Copying geometric designs.
- Answering oral arithmetic problems.
- Assembling puzzles or solving mazes.

Good psychologists are much less interested in the final IQ score than the profile of the subtests, which gives information about the child's learning style and how he goes about solving problems. They use this information to make recommendations for working with the child. When used *diagnostically* in this manner, IQ tests can be helpful as one part of a complete assessment. When used incorrectly, however, with too much focus on the total score, they can be misleading or downright dangerous.

Are IQ Tests Fair?

IQ scores tend to be influenced by previous learning and school training. Children who have cultural backgrounds that are different from those on whom the norms were based may lack the experiences to do well on the test. Moreover, such tests encourage convergent thinking: the child must come up with one of the answers the test creator had in mind instead of getting credit for novel or creative answers. A child who is imaginative may even be penalized for giving answers that are "too clever." One psychologist I know is still chuckling about a response produced by a very precocious seven-year-old. When asked, "What does 'diamond' mean?" the child replied, "Oh, a diamond is just like a dog."

Baffled, my friend asked, "Can you tell me some more about that?" "Well," said the child, "a dog is *man's* best friend." She got full credit, even though this answer wasn't in the manual. With a less patient or experienced tester, her answer would have been marked wrong.

On a group test in which a whole classroom of children answer multiple-choice questions that are scored by machine, a child like this may be penalized for thinking too deeply.

Thoughtful educators also worry that a test score may become a self-fulfilling prophecy. They point to studies of the "Pygmalion effect," in which teachers were given falsely high or low IQ scores for their students at the beginning of the school year. By the end of the year in some classrooms, the children's level of achievement had begun to correspond to the incorrect scores. What we expect of children is a powerful force indeed!

Should Your Child Be Tested?

You should never authorize any important educational decisions about a child on the basis of a single IQ test; children don't come in tidy little boxes, so a complete psychoeducational and/or neurodevelopmental evaluation is recommended. Most parents will never confront the need for this type of assessment. A few schools use individual IQ tests for admissions decisions or to diagnose learning styles, strengths, and weaknesses, but it is important that this information be interpreted by a qualified professional. Children should never be subjected to testing unless someone intends to use the results constructively to produce concrete recommendations that will help the child.

Such testing can be done by a licensed school psychologist, but they are often too overbooked to schedule complete individual evaluations except in the most severe cases. Private testing is, naturally, expensive because of the time involved. If it is indicated, a private psychologist, hospital, or clinic may be used.

PARENT GUIDELINES FOR TESTING

You should consider an individual evaluation if:

- Your child's achievement in school is persistently lower than might be expected, or if there are other reasons to suspect a learning or attention problem.
- Your child is chronically unhappy in school, and other efforts to discover the reasons have been unsuccessful.
- You have good cause to believe that an underachieving child is intellectually superior and becoming bored or turned off for lack of challenge.
- Your child is unusually slow to master appropriate skills in the early grades.

- The school asks for your help in discovering how to teach your child more effectively.

The tester should provide a complete, understandable written report and hold personal conferences with you and your child's teachers to make recommendations and provide follow-up if necessary.

The skills you might expect to learn about in an evaluation include your child's:

- Attitude and motivation during testing.
- Ability to sustain attention, think problems through, control impulsive answers, plan, and organize. Sometimes this is called "freedom from distractibility" or "executive functioning."
- Ability to follow directions.
- Auditory and visual processing strengths and weaknesses.
- Fine and gross motor development.
- Language production and comprehension.
- Ability to think creatively and solve unusual problems.
- Neurological maturation.
- Style of reasoning and problem-solving.

Preschool Testing

Intelligence tests for young children have been notoriously unreliable. I have worked with plenty of four-year-olds, and I can guarantee that their answers don't always reflect their abilities. "I don't know" may mean she doesn't have the information, but it may also mean:

"I'm tired of this silly game and I want to play by myself," or

"I have to go to the bathroom but I'm embarrassed," or

"Why should I answer these questions, anyhow? Mom told me not to talk to strangers and you look pretty strange to me!"

In my opinion, the only reason you should request preschool intelligence testing is if you suspect a dramatic difference from the average range that might call for intervention or a special educational plan. Handicapped, language delayed, or unusually late-blooming youngsters all fall into this category.

In the United States, some highly selective preschools use IQ tests to screen applicants, and some districts test four-year-olds who have borderline birthdays for early entrance. Responsible educators do not judge young children only on the basis of testing, however, and wise parents ask for an honest assessment of a child's social and emotional maturity before making important decisions. Most experts now recommend that a skilled evaluator observe the child in a natural setting and assess behavior in addition to scores.

BEYOND THE IQ: NEW DEFINITIONS OF INTELLIGENCE

Overall, IQ scores given to older children tend to correlate quite closely with school grades and grades on other standardized tests (which may tell us more about the limitations of the schools than about the success of the tests). Yet they are poor predictors of success in life. Our society may lose some of its most creative minds by defining intelligence too narrowly and penalizing those who don't fit the mold. Newer views of intelligence give us far broader contexts for guiding our youngsters' growth.

Modifying Minds

Reuven Feuerstein, an Israeli psychologist, refuses to accept the notion that IQ is a fixed commodity and insists that mental ability can be dramatically improved at all ages. When we test it, we should not look at how much the child knows, but at his ability to learn something new. To test "learning potential," Feuerstein teaches each child for several hours. He then recommends an individual program of "cognitive modification."

This approach was tried with two hundred low-achieving Israeli teenagers who had IQs between 55 and 85. Half received three hundred hours of instruction in reading, writing, and arithmetic, while the other half got the same time in a program of mental exercises called Instrumental Enrichment. Two years later there were dramatic differences in test scores between the two groups. The Instrumental Enrichment group had gained in measured intelligence while the others had not.

Using these techniques requires special training, but several of their principles provide practical guidelines for parents. According to Feuerstein, the roots of intelligence are developed by adults who help children make sense out of the world. They *do not teach directly*, but "mediate" experience for the child. For example, a mother could simply tell a child to go to the store and buy a can of tomatoes—or she might also explain that she needed three cans to make spaghetti sauce and had only two on the shelf. Such simple ways of interpreting everyday events make the child a partner in the adult's thinking process.

Feuerstein states emphatically that the main problem of poor learners is passivity. They wait for information to be poured in, but take little responsibility or action in solving problems. *Intelligence grows not by acquiring facts, but by learning how facts are acquired.* Here are some of his major suggestions for enriching intelligence:

• Providing a stimulating environment is not enough; the child must get personally involved.

• Make the child an active partner rather than trying to "pour in" learning.

• Help the child see the reasons behind everyday events. (Instead of just stopping at a stop sign, point out what might happen if cars came from four different directions at once.)

• Help a child get the feel of his body in space. Use the terms "right" and "left," but move with him as he masters them. ("Which way should we turn to walk to Mary's house?" "In which direction is the library from here?")

• Some children may be hard to guide because they easily become impatient. Don't give up.

• Show your child that a deliberate plan of behavior is better than jumping in with random solutions to problems.

• Help your child identify inconsistencies ("Why do you suppose your teacher asked you to bring a raincoat on this sunny day?"), and see cause-and-effect relationships between events.

• Guide the child toward an understanding of relationships whenever possible. Some examples from Instrumental Enrichment are:

1. Parent and child look at pictures of a pot sitting on a stove. First the pot is full of water and then it's empty. The child tries to figure out what caused the change. (The water was poured out, or perhaps it boiled away.)

2. The child looks at pictures of a woman cooking and a man gardening. He is asked, "What is similar about these activities?" (They are both working, etc.) "What is different?"

Multiple Intelligences

Neuropsychologist Howard Gardner also believes we have neglected the spectrum of human intelligence and have unfairly slotted children into a system where their greatest talents may go unrecognized. In studying brains damaged by accidents or illness, Gardner observed separate abilities that function so independently that damage to one often leaves others completely intact. He has identified nine separate intelligences that lead to different types of adult accomplishment:

1. Linguistic (poet, writer).
2. Logical-mathematical (mathematician, scientist).
3. Visual-spatial (architect, sculptor, pilot).
4. Bodily-kinesthetic (dancer, athlete, surgeon, instrumentalist).
5. Musical (composer, performer).
6. Interpersonal (understanding other people, psychologist).
7. Intrapersonal (knowledge of self, personal insight).
8. Naturalistic (botanist, environmentalist, bird-watcher).
9. Metaphysical (clergy, philosopher).

Gardner believes that individuals have a natural affinity toward one or more of these intelligences, probably because of inherited neural patterns. Each intelligence may have a memory of its own; a musician might have a prodigious memory for musical scores but not for spelling. Thus he suggests we ask not "How smart are you?" but "How are you smart?" He urges schools not to force students into the traditional linguistic/logical-mathematical mold and to recognize the importance of artistic and personal skills.

Because it is difficult to excel in two widely diverse talents—art and literature, for example—adults should not expect children to be equally good at everything. Adult models, or mentors, play an important part in encouraging children to fulfill their promise in any area, and early experiences that excite a child about a field may galvanize choices for life.

Intelligence in the Real World

Another innovative thinker, Dr. Robert Sternberg, is also much more concerned with how children solve real-life problems than with how they do on traditional IQ tests. His Triarchic Theory of Intelligence is made up of three basic types: analytic, creative, and practical. *Analytic intelligence* comprises the skills on which most school programs have focused. *Creative intelligence*, which has been neglected in much formal education, may show itself in highly original work in a particular field of interest or talent, or it may pop up when people have to develop answers to new or unusual questions (e.g., "What would you do to detect aliens who had secretly infiltrated your town?"). This ability will be especially important in a rapidly changing world. *Practical intelligence* is simply the ability to function successfully in the world, and Sternberg believes some people have more of it than others. All three forms can be cultivated, however, if we learn to value these styles of thinking and expose children to models and challenges in each. "Successful intelligence," to Sternberg, is the ability to succeed in life by capitalizing on your strengths and compensating for your weaknesses. Thus, respecting the way each child goes about learning, problem-solving, and relating to others is particularly important.

One interesting aspect of Dr. Sternberg's work involves new forms of college admissions testing that improve predictions for success in real life.

"All Kinds of Minds"

Dr. Mel Levine echoes these ideas from his own experience in working with "all kinds of minds." In his book *A Mind at a Time*, he identifies eight neurodevelopmental systems that interact to form an individual profile for each child. To work with any youngster, we must understand her own unique talents and needs—a far cry from simply testing and categorizing. Levine believes that many children who are termed "disabled" actually have very specialized brains that can flourish with proper understanding and teaching. I believe this approach—which refuses to look at a child simply as a label—represents a very promising application of our new understanding of the growing brain.

"Emotional Intelligence"

If you really want your child to be successful in life as well as in school (and who doesn't!), it's worth listening to another view that takes the definition of intelligence in a different direction. After reviewing studies of what characteristics truly predict success, researchers found that qualities Dr. Daniel Goleman termed "emotional intelligence" are actually more important in life than school smarts. For example, no matter what your IQ, interpersonal skills such as the ability to relate to and work with other people and "read" another person's feelings will count even more. Also critical are personal skills such as self-control, the ability to motivate oneself and stick with a difficult task, and dealing with one's own emotions. In this view, parents should coach children in how to interpret the social and personal demands of a situation ("What do you think James really means when he says that?" "What would be a good first step in tackling this project?")

The many different ways of being "smart" may explain why those who are stars in school are not always the most successful in life, and vice versa. Parents who push too hard for traditional academic learning and neglect more practical and broad-based skills may limit their child's success. Schools that value abstract, analytic learning at the expense of the arts, practical experiences, and interpersonal and personal development are at risk of obscuring—and possibly even draining off—a rich pool of talent.

Let's now look at the way environments influence some "basics" of the productive mind: memory, motivation, and metacognition.

MEMORY
Where Is It?

If you were to roam around in the brain searching for a special room labeled "Memory," you wouldn't find it. Human memory depends upon widespread circuits and chemical interactions as well as on specialized areas. Likewise, if you asked me, "How's your memory?" I would have to respond, "For what?" since the thing we call "memory" is really a group of separate abilities. Each has its own neural circuitry, which may change as practice causes memory traces to be moved around and consolidated, making the brain's workings more efficient. For example, studies have shown that chess experts use different parts of their brains than amateur players to remember chess moves. Although some children seem to be born with greater efficiency in acquiring and consolidating certain types of information, many memory skills are actually learned through experience and practice.

Different Tasks: Different Types of Memory

Did you ever feel frustrated during an exam because you could remember the exact place in a book where the answer was given but couldn't recall the information itself? If so, you were experiencing the difference between the two most fundamental types of memory: *implicit*, which happens without conscious attention and is particularly useful for storing background information about space and time, and *explicit*, which requires conscious attention and is associated with more specific learning.

As skills are learned and practiced through explicit, conscious learning, they become more automatic, freeing up conscious attention *(working memory)* for new learning. As we saw in chapter 5, children differ in how easily they are able to transfer skills to "automatic pilot"; a child who readily automatizes routines of handwriting, spelling, and math or history facts may have lasting difficulty using a hammer or reading a map, and vice versa. Whatever the task, automatic memory appears to be facilitated by sensory and motor systems of the brain, which probably explains why teaching through many senses usually works better than using mainly abstract lecture-type approaches.

Memory systems also differ in the type of content they handle. The simplest kinds of content are handled by primitive memory structures that are more like reflexes and that are not unique to human beings. In fact, even a little sea snail with its very simple nervous system (only twenty thousand neurons) can "learn" to alter its customary pattern of gill withdrawal if it is systematically touched. From such experiments, scientists have demonstrated that experience causes chemical and structural changes in even the most primitive brain. They have also illustrated the power of the "stimulus-response" reflex, a connection between events that have occurred together many times—the "lowest" layer of learning.

People also experience such stimulus-response learning of nonintellectual content. "Conditioning" is very effective in training people to behave in certain ways, a process evident during youngsters' play of some fast-paced video games. Most parents also use it instinctively. Your baby approaches the stove, you shout "Hot!" and pull the child away. Eventually a connection is made, even though baby doesn't understand the logic. Babies might "remember" other things, too, such as flash cards, if they are trained to do so. But encouraging too much learning at this level is actually an insult to the human brain and can crowd out more important experiences.

The most irritating parent conference I had one year was with the father of a six-year-old who was doing her best to learn to read but failing to meet his very unrealistic standards. Angry at both his daughter and the school, he shouted, "All you people need to do is give her more *training*! It's your job to *make her remember*."

I nearly shouted back at him, "This isn't a school for animals, sir. We're in the business of *teaching*, not *training* children." I settled for trying to explain the difference between remembering for meaning and merely reciting something that has been pushed in from outside. I know he didn't understand.

In fact, human memory goes far beyond the level of mere association. Parts of the emotionally connected limbic brain filter, allocate, and solidify the formation of memories. Neurochemicals associated with emotional states are part of the "juice" that fuels the circuits, and the *amygdala* causes highly charged emotional memories to take precedence over intellectual ones. The *hippocampus* and cerebral cortex mediate factual memory by receiving incoming information and associating it with previous experience.

Different parts of the brain handle memory for things that have been seen, heard, and physically experienced. Memory for "procedural" knowledge is separate from recall of specific data—understanding what school is for and how one acts there as opposed to remembering a list of dates. Children use many channels to store many little pieces, but meaning is the cement for the system.

How Children Learn to Remember

Theorists disagree about how to chart the stages of memory. One easy-to-understand explanation is of a six-stage process:

1. Sensory memory: registers input for a fraction of a second.
2. Attention: sorts out what goes into the system.

3. Short-term memory: keeps it alive for a brief time; associated with working memory.
4. Working memory: holds several bits of information online until they are dealt with or stored.
5. Long-term memory: stores it from minutes to a lifetime.
6. Retrieval: gets it out of long-term memory.

The only part of the memory system that operates as efficiently in young children as it does in adults is "sensory memory," which registers input for a brief fraction of a second. To keep the brain from being continually overwhelmed, a selection process must be perfected. The brain's attention gatekeeper determines what should be admitted to the next level, and if a child can't pay attention, the material may not reach conscious awareness. Some studies suggest that many stimuli are retained at a subconscious level even though we can't get at them.

The next step is to bring the information into short-term conscious awareness, from where it can be processed by working memory in the prefrontal cortex. Working memory may be thought of as your mental desktop where you keep several things at once temporarily "online." Young children and those with attention problems have difficulty here, apparently related to immaturity or underactivation in prefrontal areas. (The same issue comes up again after midlife, when it becomes increasingly difficult to remember where you put your glasses while you were thinking about what to buy at the grocery store.)

The simplest example of this kind of storage is measured by the span of how many things we can remember in sequence. By three years of age, most children can hold on to one new item of information. This span gradually increases until the adult span is reached: seven items, give or take two. If you look up a seven-digit telephone number, your visual sensory register can hang on to it only briefly unless you do something to keep it alive longer. One way is to say the numbers over and over; this process, called *rehearsal*, is a good technique because it adds an auditory trace to the visual one. Another way to hang on to memory traces is to group or "chunk" them by seeing some sort of relationship among them. The area code may be remembered as one chunk, for example, rather than three.

If the material is of sufficient emotional importance, or if you use conscious strategies to remember, it will move inside the doorway of long-term memory (LTM). Once inside, it may be kept for minutes or for years depending on its salience and the amount of mental effort expended on keeping it there. Children must literally learn to remember, and parents who require them to use memory show them how to increase their ability. Children need special practice at three different levels:

1. Attending to the relevant stimuli.
2. Storing information in LTM.
3. Recalling, or retrieving it when necessary.

Attending to the Relevant Stimuli

Make sure your child is attending to what is important to remember from any situation. If she is admiring her new shoelaces while you are showing her how to regroup in subtraction, you might as well save your breath. One way to focus attention is to ask the child what it is they need to be thinking about, looking at, or listening to in order to gain the information.

Getting It into Long-Term Storage

Individual and age-related differences exist in the size and efficiency of working memory, which can improve with concentration and practice. Although there is a limited amount of space at any one time, a vast reservoir of past experience and learning always lies just under the surface. When college students who claimed they remembered nothing about the houses they had lived in as three-year-olds were shown the blueprints, they immediately identified the rooms. Re-creating the scene as closely as possible usually helps remember anything.

For long-term storage it is important to distinguish between rote-level and meaningful memory. Most of us learned the multiplication tables by rote; if we reuse them on a fairly regular basis, the memory is refreshed and sticks with us. While useful and important for some things, rote learning is very limited in its ability to expand intelligence, which grows through the acquisition of more complex understanding and meaningful connections.

The importance of a child's level of understanding was shown by some experiments in which children were asked to remember patterns of blocks. Young children could not copy some hard patterns, but eight months later they remembered them perfectly. New conceptual growth enabled them to look back and understand—and thus remember accurately. Likewise, adults' memories of childhood events are probably structured by current understanding. The development of language adds an important dimension to memory, and young children are much more likely to remember events that they talk about.

Practice can be valuable for rote-level tasks such as simple memorization of lists, telephone numbers, or math facts. Get the child actively involved and try to attach some meaning to memorization. Interesting or funny poems and songs are appealing and also build language skills. Memorization is facilitated by rhythm, melody, and lots of repetition. Likewise, repeating patterns of movement—finger plays, dance, simple exercises—builds motor memory pathways.

Adults use a number of strategies for hanging on to more complex things they want to remember. You can show a child how to implement them:

MEMORY TIPS FOR ALL AGES

- *Giving new material a meaningful form:* rephrasing it; saying, "What does that mean?" "Why should I remember it?"
- *Using a different sense to practice remembering:* writing down spoken information, making a mental "picture" of a series of dance movements.
- *Organizing, seeing patterns: putting words into categories:* "I need to re-

member five fruits and four vegetables"; "Three of these names begin with *m*, three with *b*, and two with *w*." "These numbers are each 2 larger than the one before"; "This number has a 6 on each end and three 4s in the middle."

- *Rehearsing:* repeating or mentally going over the material several times and then periodically going through it again to refresh the memory.
- *Elaborating:* hooking the material together in some way—making up a story using words that have to be remembered or making a mental picture linking items together; using tricks such as acronyms (the first letters of the Great Lakes spell HOMES).
- *Using visual memory or imagery strategies:* "seeing" yourself following a series of directions; imagining a "mental movie" of the events in a story.
- *Associating material with something already known:* "That new word reminds me of my friend's last name." "That number is my house number turned inside out." "That reminds me of the idea we studied last week in science class." This is probably the most effective method, but it requires a mental scaffolding with lots of "hooks," which are acquired only through active thinking and learning about the world.
- *Understanding connections between events:* Even three-to-five-year-olds remember things that seem logical to them better than things that seem illogical.

Parents Teach about Memory

All of these strategies become more automatic as the child gets older. One reason is that practice improves them. A second is that children only gradually learn what memory is all about. Their memories are potentially just as good as ours, but they lack strategies and the knowledge base to use them as efficiently. If you read a pretend shopping list to five-year-olds and ask them if they think they can remember it, most will blithely assure you that they can. When they get to the "store," they are surprised that they don't know what to ask for. An older child will immediately start to employ strategies ("Let's see, there are meats, canned goods, and bread on the list; eight things altogether . . .") because they are familiar with how to make memory work. Recent studies on the way parents teach children about memory show that using the words "memory" and "remember" and suggesting ways to practice it help a lot.

Children's memory banks are only as good as the deposits of mental schemas that have been made in them. Semantic networks help associate ideas. To help your child develop the best long-term storehouse, review the suggestions for cognitive and language development in earlier chapters.

"I Know the Face, but . . ."

Once something has been stored in memory, the next step is to be able to "retrieve" it, or get it off the proper "hook" when it is needed. You may be asked to do this in two different ways: Given a roomful of people, can you *recognize* the ones you have seen before? Can you *recall* their names? Quite different problems. Recognition is usually much easier; to aid a child's recall, give him a choice to trigger the connections. If he can't remember the name of your street, for example, give him three names from which to choose. Children in school have to take tests that make demands on both recognition (matching, multiple choice) or recall (essay questions, fill in the blanks). If they know about the test in advance, they can study accordingly. Recall is more of a challenge. A child with a large, well-organized base of knowledge has the best chance of digging around and finding what he's looking for.

Growing Memories

Memory changes as children's minds grow. Some abilities are age-related:

By three months: Most infants have recognition memory for mobiles, toys, and common objects. They can remember long enough to distinguish between objects they have seen before and unfamiliar ones. Speed varies among individuals.

Eight to twelve months: Babies can distinguish masks that are more like human faces, showing that they can hold information in their minds and compare it with something new. They begin to show fear of unfamiliar people or objects. They also remember where a toy is hidden—a sign that mental development is guiding memory growth, and probably the earliest development of "working memory."

Preschool years: "Eidetic imagery"—holding a visual picture in short-term memory—is initially stronger than verbal memory but diminishes as the child learns to talk. By age three, children naturally use rehearsal by repeating things they want to remember. Preschoolers also do a lot of "incidental learning," remembering things present when they are learning something else, and they do not restrict their attention efficiently. The preschooler remembers things from her direct experience, but doesn't understand much about how to make memory work. If a four-year-old is shown twelve pictures of familiar objects, she can recall three or four of them, and recognize ten or eleven if asked, "Did you see this one before?"

Elementary school years: By age six, children begin to develop memory strategies. They instinctively rehearse material, and by age seven should be able to see patterns and organize groups of things to be remembered, although even third graders still use inefficient strategies. By this age they should be able to retell a story with the events in reasonable order. Focus on relevant material improves, but children with attention problems take in so much incidental information they have difficulty remembering what is important. By age ten, most children shown twelve pictures can recall eight and recognize all twelve.

Adolescence: This is the age for making new connections as several aspects of frontal lobe function (memory span, planning skills) are still developing. Memory becomes a mechanism for abstract thinking as the adolescent learns to retrieve two or more bits of information and hold them in his mind while evaluating new thoughts. If insufficient groundwork has been laid for understanding material presented in school, now is the time to rebuild. Teenagers should have reached the adult short-term span of seven items they hear and should have numerous strategies for memorizing longer amounts of material. They can differentiate between recognition and recall when studying for tests if someone explains the difference.

Freedom to Remember

Personal interactions, praise, security, and self-confidence are powerful factors in children's memory development. If a child of any age is anxious or overwhelmed by interfering thoughts, the information may not even get by the first checkpoint. Many who have "memory" problems in school are actually distracted by worries or fears. Encouraging a child to express emotions honestly helps all learning.

Helping Children Build Memory Circuits

Here are some helpful activities for different ages.

• Devise games to build visual, auditory, and motor short-term memory. For example, make up a routine of hand movements or patterns of musical tones and see if the child can remember and copy them. Let the child take turns being "teacher" so the situation doesn't become one-sided.

• Having a child rephrase stories or factual information in his own words is a good way to get it into long-term storage.

• Teach children to rehearse by repeating material over and then reviewing it periodically.

• Some studies suggest that music training may help children at any age acquire better memory skills.

• Ask young children questions about events that happened in the near and distant past. Children of mothers who ask this type of question develop better memories.

"Can you recall where I got those cookies you liked so well?"

"Who were the guests at Carlos' party last week? Can you remember the presents?"

"Let's tell about what we did at Disney World last summer. Did you like the rides or the food better? Which ones?"

• Suggest that your child try to remember a series of events in the order in which they happened. ("What happened when we went to Grandma's?")

• Show children how to use recognition cues to trigger recall.

"Leave your skates by the back door so you'll be sure to remember them."

Tips for Elementary School Children

• Memory of visual material is a powerful hook. Show them how to put "mind pictures" to work for remembering.

"Would you please go into the kitchen, put this apple in the yellow bowl, and then close the window? As I say it again, try closing your eyes and making a picture in your mind of each thing I say."

"While you are reading, try to 'see' what the girl is doing in the story."

"Let's pretend you have a chalkboard in your mind. Write the spelling word there in a special color."

• Let children make choices about what and how they will remember. Personal involvement activates "association nodes" in the brain.

• If your child has trouble remembering something, help her associate it with a familiar event, person, object.

• Use several senses at once. Have the child write multiplication facts with a finger on a rough surface (rug, pant leg) in order to feel them while saying and looking at them. Draw pictures of historical events with dates prominently attached. Use color whenever possible.

• Encourage the use of strategies for classifying, grouping, and making information meaningful. Have the child make stacks of flash cards in categories (all I know, all I want to learn; all 5s, all 7s, etc.). Put states in categories (size, location, main occupations, etc.). Label the categories. Count the number in each.

• Dramatize or act things out. Make the scenes funny, surprising, or absurd. The brain remembers oddity, things that don't fit expectation.

• Monitor the noise level in your home. Chronic exposure to airplane noise has led to deficits in children's memory.

Tips for Older Students

• Remember, it is easier to relearn material that is already familiar. When a test is coming up, make a review schedule to go over the material regularly for a period of several days.

• Don't underestimate the value of sleep, which remodels neural circuits in order to fix information in memory. Going to bed directly after learning something cuts down on interfering memories and firms up the new learning. This strategy is good for routine memorization of vocabulary drills, rules, lists, and so on. You may be better off getting a good night's sleep than spending the extra hours cramming for an exam.

• If your textbook contains chapter summaries, use them—they will help you remember the material.

• Similar subjects should not be studied at the same time. Instead of doing Latin homework right after French, separate them with math and English.

• The "slight stress" of a high level of motivation seems to improve the ability to remember.

• The more thoroughly something is learned, the better you will be able to recall and apply it. You may need to "overlearn"—practice more than you think necessary, or keep recalling and rehearsing it.

• Ask someone to drill you on factual material from a study guide you have made of the things you need to remember.

• You will recall better in a situation that is similar to the one in which the material was learned. If you have to write an essay on a test, study for the test by writing practice essays. If it is a short-answer test, make up some questions for practice. Don't study orally for a written test. If possible, study in the same room where the test will be given.

• You will not be able to remember material if you do not understand why it is important or how it is related to the subject you are studying. Get your teacher to help you make study guides that show the main ideas and relationships in the material.

Genius or Fool?

A few individuals termed "savants" show prodigious memories for specialized kinds of material. One phenomenon that has never been explained is "calendar calculation," in which a person, given any date in history, can immediately tell the day of the week on which it fell. Such narrowly channeled abilities, "splinter skills," have been found for mathematics, music, and other special fields. They show up in childhood and are often associated with severely impaired overall intelligence.

There is little danger of mistaking savant memory for that of a normal child, since it usually accompanies peculiar behavior and other signs of abnormality. I mention it mainly because it underscores the bottom line: Intelligent memory is only as good as the whole mind that contains it. Focusing on "splinters" fragments the process.

WHO'S IN CHARGE? A QUESTION OF MOTIVATION

"I give up," roared the high school principal. "This kid simply has no motivation!"

It certainly seemed that way. Danny didn't try—except to get out of work. Long allergic to homework, he had recently stopped even taking his books home. His clothes and his behavior in class advertised his disdain for matters academic, and his curt rebuffs of his teachers' offers of help had alienated most of them. Apparently what Danny wanted most was to be expelled from school, which rendered his father even more apoplectic than the principal. By the time this family got to my office, I could only hope we would all emerge alive!

"Motivation" problems are some of the most frequent—and frustrating—that I encounter in my work with students. Recent research has helped me a great deal in understanding and dealing with them.

Many years ago I shared the common assumption that motivation came with the package: Some kids had it and some didn't. Now I am convinced that all children are motivated until we teach them otherwise. Anyone who has watched young children play has witnessed their innate drive to feel competent by mastering new challenges. They choose their own problems, however, because they find them personally interesting and manageable. Likewise, in order for any of us to be motivated for a particular task, three ingredients must be present: emotional connection, challenge, and payoff. The most effective payoff, however, takes the form of internal (intrinsic) satisfaction rather than external (extrinsic) reward. Teachers and parents need to structure learning situations, but when adults start to take too much control, choose the challenges, and force them on children who aren't ready or able to achieve the personal payoff (success), trouble starts.

Ingredients for Motivation

The *emotional brain*, or limbic system, can either facilitate learning or block the thinking systems. The *hippocampus* mediates factual memory and the *amygdala* attaches emotional significance to experience so that we can quickly classify a stimulus as potentially dangerous. To oversimplify, the limbic system's shout of "DANGER!" may short circuit complex cognitive processing in favor of a quick response to the threat, and less emotionally charged school tasks may never even make it through. For example, when children suddenly develop "motivation problems" at the time their parents are getting divorced, no one is terribly surprised. New research also suggests that *threat* (real or perceived) primes the right hemisphere to withdraw from a situation, which alters the brain's normal learning patterns.

The novelty of these ideas is that emotion may be, after all, superordinate to cognition. The emotional brain does not respond to reason; *telling* it to be motivated is about as effective as instructing a squirrel not to eat the bird food. The moral for parents and teachers is that beating turned-off kids with intellectual sticks simply isn't going to work. Instead, we must create a learning environment minus serious threat, yield some control to the student, and provide some choices and opportunities to rebuild interest and internal satisfaction, just for starters. Until the habits of motivation are internalized, there is little hope that a student will dig into the more tedious aspects of some academic work. Curiously, however, mild stress—such as the excitement of mastering something difficult—actually increases memory and motivation.

The key here is *challenge*. All human beings are motivated by challenge, and, contrary to popular opinion, errors, uncertainty, or failure to reach a goal can all inspire continued effort—but *only* if it is calibrated properly to offer a reasonable chance of success, or *payoff*. Those who have enjoyed many successes are much more willing to take a risk on a longer shot or on dull assignments. The "unmotivated," who may rarely have experienced the joy of mastering a difficult problem, need much smaller and more inviting steps.

Here, of course, is the lure of video games, even (sometimes especially) for those who are otherwise "unmotivated." Challenge, electronically directed to each player's abilities with just the right reward schedule—no wonder kids get hooked! Here's the important question:

Is the player learning anything about getting his own brain in gear around challenges, making wise choices, and developing original solutions? Is he staying attached to a tiresome but necessary step in solving a problem? Real-life challenges demand skills that may not get much practice in an artificially motivating microworld.

What's the Payoff?

Current research suggests that the type of payoff attached to a challenge is key. Many parents and teachers make the mistake of believing that external rewards are a good way to motivate children. While stars, stickers, money for grades, and bribes ("You can have a bike if you get all A's") sometimes work in the short run and with children who have severe behavior disorders, they have the ultimate effect of removing even more internal control from the one who needs it most—the learner. In several studies, researchers have tried giving rewards for good work in tasks that children were enjoying and found that their level of enjoyment as well as their motivation and creativity immediately declined. Instead, we should be trying to move the reward system inside, to the level of personal self-esteem and satisfaction.

Overuse of *extrinsic* rewards imposed by parents or teachers tends to reduce motivation in the long run. *Intrinsic* rewards, on the other hand, come from feelings of satisfaction in a challenge mastered and new competence gained. The best students are those who work, like many of our most successful and creative adults, to gain competence and satisfaction, not, like a rat in a laboratory maze, for a series of extrinsic rewards.

I have explained some of the issues concerning computer use and motivation in my book *Failure to Connect*. Computers for learning can be motivating for the right reasons—valid academic challenges presented in a novel way, such as Internet projects or good simulation games. Conversely, many current software programs actually reduce motivation by relying too much on giving extrinsic rewards—games to play, smiley faces, etc., that are unrelated to the challenge of the learning. When you choose software and observe your child working on the computer, this is an important factor to keep in mind.

When we have an "unmotivated" student such as Danny, it is also important to ask: What challenge is the child responding to, and what is the payoff for his current behavior? In his case, avoiding homework had become quite an amusing challenge, and his payoff was a combination of maternal attention, revenge against a strict and demanding father, and avoidance of humiliation for his poor spelling and handwriting.

Parenting Styles and Motivation

Parenting styles have a great deal to do with a child's motivation for school success. Researchers who observe children interacting with their parents have identified three basic styles:

- **Permissive:** insufficient structure or challenge; inconsistent rules.
- **Authoritarian:** bossy, intrusive, demanding; uses external rewards and punishments; focuses on grades (product) rather than effort (process).
- **Authoritative:** sets clear rules, structure, and expectations but willing to negotiate; listens to child's point of view; offers age-appropriate choices; supports child's autonomy (effort to do it herself); compliments real progress.

In study after study, children of *authoritative* parents come out with higher levels of internal motivation, fewer attention and conduct problems, and better school achievement than children of either of the other parenting types.

RAISING MOTIVATED LEARNERS

Homes and classrooms that raise motivation levels tend to:

- Have a strong commitment to child-rearing, involvement with children, and understanding of the child's point of view.
- Be able to adapt to a child's current abilities.
- Structure clear and consistent guidelines.
- Ensure that the child gets positive feelings of mastery over new challenges met.
- Avoid external rewards and punishments whenever possible.
- Expect children to take responsibility for their own outcomes and gain rewards from internal feelings of accomplishment.
- Provide carefully designed challenges.
- Encourage children to celebrate small successes.
- Avoid insincere praise for poor work (definition of "poor" or "good" depends on the child's ability in this particular situation).
- Focus on effort/learning, not grades/product.

- Offer choices within an overall structure.
- Allow children time to become deeply and independently involved in learning activities.
- Provide a variety of output modes (projects, art, music, dance, etc.).
- Help children see the reason (personal payoff) for completing tasks.
- Maintain a sense of humor.

"It's Not My Fault"

One year I was asked to work with and try to "motivate" a special group of thirteen-year-olds who were labeled "underachievers." They were bright kids but had abysmal academic records and were on the verge of failing for the year. As the year went on, I became more and more frustrated. I was having little success teaching them, and I couldn't figure out what the trouble was. Finally, one day, a girl came into class complaining bitterly about an injustice she felt she had suffered from her math teacher. Deciding to use this incident as an example for problem-solving, I presented the issue to the class. What would they do if they had a problem with a teacher?

"I'd tell the principal."

"I'd tell my mother."

"I'd tell my father and he would tell that teacher off for sure!"

Not one student suggested that they personally assume any responsibility in this situation. Bing! The light came on. These children weren't admitting that they were in charge. I remembered some of the year's other comments:

"That teacher is too hard. No one should be expected to do this."

"I can't concentrate in class. Amy keeps looking at me."

"How can we learn anything when it's so cold in here?"

"My mother says that girls don't have to go to college."

"I don't like grammar and I don't see any reason to learn it. My dad says he hated it, too, and he never needed it after he got out of school."

Unfortunately, my little group was also missing the joys of accomplishment. Even when they did something well, they had trouble taking credit for it.

Meanwhile, I heard a delightful story from the mother of an eight-year-old who had been struggling to complete a science project. In desperation, the mother finally ventured, "Perhaps I should call your teacher and ask if she'll give you some help in school tomorrow." "No, Mom," replied the child, surveying the disaster. "I want to try and tough this one out for myself." I'll put my money on that child!

One term that has been used for youngsters who are unwilling to try and "tough" anything out is "learned helplessness." Students with learning disabilities often display these characteristics because they have failed so often. Homes with either too high or too low a level of expectations also contribute to this problem, as do homes with over-indulgent or chaotic environments. Here are some parental statements that encourage different attitudes toward responsibility, technically termed external or internal "locus of control":

EXTERNAL	INTERNAL
"I'll call Johnny's mother and tell her he didn't play nicely today."	"Let's talk to Johnny and you can tell him how you feel."
"I don't know why these things always happen to me."	"I wonder what I can do about this problem."
"Oh, I must just have been lucky."	"I'm really proud of myself!"
"We can't do anything. We're just ordinary people."	"Let's write a letter to our representative and try to get some action."
"I really shouldn't go through this stop sign, but no one is looking."	"I feel responsible for obeying the safety laws even if no one is looking."
"How dare the school bus driver threaten to throw you off the bus! We could sue them!"	"I'd like to know just what your part in this is. I expect you to follow the driver's rules."

"That teacher isn't fair. He shouldn't have picked Sue for the part. I'll call the school."	"I guess you have two choices. You can accept the decision or go and tell the teacher your honest feelings. I'm sorry you were disappointed, but sometimes life just isn't fair. We have to learn to keep trying."

The Vicious Circle

Many children who are labeled "motivation problems" actually have unidentified learning disabilities. In an earlier chapter we discussed problems with output—particularly written assignments. Even bright youngsters who have such problems learn early on that the challenge is too great, the payoff too uncertain. One of a human being's most basic motivations is to maintain feelings of self-worth. Those who, day after day, do poorly on important school assignments will try desperately to hold on to a positive self-concept, first by making excuses or choosing easy tasks, next by procrastinating, and finally by not trying—because if you try hard and fail it means you're really dumb. In middle school years these self-concepts become deeply internalized, so motivation problems take on a life of their own.

If this section is reminding you of anyone you know, check the following ideas for some beginning steps you might try with a student in middle or high school:

DEALING WITH MOTIVATION PROBLEMS

1. Establish and maintain cooperative contact with the school. Try to uncover the exact nature of the problem: precisely what is the student failing to do (e.g., written work, listening, class participation, social events, reading)?

See if you can isolate any specific areas where challenge and payoff are out of sync.

2. Request a thorough psychoeducational evaluation *even if a learning problem has previously been ruled out.* Psychologists continually refine the diagnostic art, and many bright children have slipped through the cracks. If the youngster has any type of learning difficulty, seek appropriate help at once.

3. Stop shouting, threatening, bribing. They don't work.

4. Sit down and have a conversation, even if you have to rope her in. Tell her you would like to listen to her point of view for a change. Then do so. Practice "active listening": acknowledge and rephrase what she says rather than expressing any opinions of your own. It may take several weeks of effort to get a conversation going, but keep trying.

5. Make yourself available for help at any time, but gradually try to shift the burden of responsibility off your shoulders and onto the child's.

6. Make sure some unpleasant natural consequences for inappropriate behavior are built into the system. What happens to the student at school if he can—but won't—do his homework? What reasonable, firm rules in the household make noncompliance uncomfortable for the child? You would be wise to seek some professional guidance on these matters.

7. Seek a good counselor or other significant adult to whom your child can relate.

8. Encourage the use of technology tools to make learning tasks easier/more interesting (e.g., word processor, spell-checker, calculator).

9. If possible, consider changing to a school that makes a point of engaging students more actively in their learning, and celebrating different types of talent. Be sure your child is a part of the decision. Let him feel that he owns the choices about his own behavior—and his life.

10. Try to relax a little. Many young people go through a period of "acting out" before they finally decide to take control of their futures.

A school principal whom I met recently is directing a program in which students from a wide range of socioeconomic and ethnic backgrounds are encouraged to get actively involved in choosing books to read and topics to research, using technology in the classroom, working together in groups, and expressing and challenging ideas in discussions with skilled teachers.

"I can't believe it," she told me. "I have *no* discipline problems and *no* motivation problems."

Although my friend Danny is still a crusty and difficult youngster, he is profiting from some special help with writing and study skills. We knew his story had started to retell itself when he signed up for the school play. To his teachers' amazement, he applied himself, with just a little prodding, to learning his lines, and showed himself to be a talented character actor with a fine sense of comic irony. The day after the final performance, at which he had received thunderous applause, he volunteered to clean out the family garage.

"He was just floating so high he wanted to do something nice," reported his astonished mom.

Danny's principal was wrong about him. Danny is motivated, but toward goals that are reachable and meaningful to him. Gradually he is taking over more responsibility for his learning—and his life—as he learns to feel the internal rewards of meeting challenges at which he can succeed.

METACOGNITION: THINKING ABOUT THINKING

One way to put brains in charge of themselves is to challenge them to take a look at their own thinking, rather than just soaking up that of teachers or textbook authors. Yet many never reach this stage of development.

Shaneen was an intense, quick learner who studied hard. She always had her hand up in class because she always knew the answer. She possessed one of those brains that just seem to soak up information. At her high school, where this type of thinking was prized, she graduated valedictorian of the class. Accepted at a first-rate university, however, she suddenly began to have difficulty. For the first time in her life she couldn't cope, her grades dropped, and she eventually left the school. What happened?

Shaneen was a victim of a system that trained her to repeat information without thinking deeply about it. It never occurred to her to challenge the facts given—she just dutifully memorized them. In contrast, the university demanded something called "mindfulness"—the ability to stand back and view information from many angles, to examine one's own beliefs and understandings, and to evaluate them critically. When, during the first week of classes, Shaneen was asked to write a critical essay integrating information from several sources, she had no strategies for attacking the problem. When there was no right answer to memorize, she experienced genuine panic.

"Metacognition," a term used to describe thinking about thinking, means being able to stand back and view one's own learning strategies and mental operations. For example, skilled teachers now ask students in math classes to write about and discuss *how* they solved a problem in addition to getting the right answer (and are fascinated by the different processes used by different learners to arrive at the same result). Research also shows that poor readers often don't know what it is that they don't understand; teaching them to ask themselves critical questions as they go through the text increases both understanding and retention.

You can help your child be a "mindful" learner by remembering to ask *how* she learned something as well as *what* she learned. Encouraging children to challenge ideas with well-reasoned arguments is another way (television programs and commercials provide good material to work with). Parents who use terms related to mental operations also help build metacognitive awareness:

"Did you *guess* that, or is it something you *remember*?"

"Wait, give me some time to *reflect* about that *question*."

"Do you have any new *inspirations* about *making plans* for Saturday?"

As we move toward expanding definitions of intelligence in a new century, this capacity for internal reflection may be a major key to keeping all our brains firing vigorously throughout a lifetime.

Engineering Intelligence

Clearly, faddish theories about how to make a child smarter are over-simplifications at best and dangerous at worst. Most of us who study children's minds are not so confident of our ability to force intelligence, and we fear the loss of motivation, reflection, and self-directed attention that results from such efforts. Probably the best argument against too much adult engineering is that it steals control from the most important player: the child.

Attempting to create intelligence also implies a value judgment about the particular set of abilities that compose it. Since we're really not sure what "intelligence" is, it's risky to focus too hard on specialized aspects of it. Experimenting with "genius training" or focusing so hard on testing that we forget to stimulate kids to think, question, and imagine, degrades the brain's natural learning capacity.

Implementing mental ability calls for factors that defy programming into a machine or a brain. Artificial intelligence can't yet comprehend the nuances of human language and thought or the joy of humor, self-awareness, or altruism. Computers cannot imagine or leap unexplored conceptual chasms. These qualities also elude most tests, but they may be, after all, those upon which expanded definitions of intelligence should focus and those that we, as parents and teachers, should prize most in our children.

Part Three

Learning

Applied

Chapter 9

Children Read
with Their Brains

Phillip started to read words on labels and signs when he was two and a half years old. By the age of three he could read out loud from simple children's books, and soon began to spend hours reading anything he could find. One day when he was five his mother was surprised to find him perusing one of her nursing journals—and even more amazed at the skill with which he pronounced the complicated medical terms. Now, at age eight, Phillip is waiting at the breakfast table for his special school van. While he waits, he reads an article from the *New York Times*. He is so engrossed that his mother must remind him when the van arrives. Phillip reluctantly leaves the newspaper, grabs his coat, and runs down the driveway.

"Good morning, Phillip," calls the van driver.

"Good morning," intones Phillip, settling himself in his usual seat. He picks up the ends of his seat belt, regards them with a puzzled expression, and attempts to fasten them—behind his back.

"Here, let me help you," offers the driver, rebuckling the belt across Phillip's lap. "Remember, I tell you every day that the belt holds you and the seat together. You'll get it someday."

The van starts up and Phillip is off to school—his special school for children who are mentally handicapped.

No, I am not making up this story. Phillip is a real child, although his name has been changed. I didn't believe it either until I met him and several others who changed my preconceived notions about early reading. Children who learn to read early are smart. Aren't they? Early reading is a sign of giftedness. Isn't it? Children can't read things they don't understand. Right?

Wrong. Phillip, and others like him, are "hyperlexic," literally, they read too much and for the wrong reasons. Although they develop reading at unusually early ages and perfect their "word calling" to a remarkable degree, that's all it is—calling out words without associating them with meaning. Some specialists call it "barking at print." This type of reading is a "splinter skill," which is compulsive and abnormal, like some of their other behavior. Hyperlexic children have trouble relating to the world around them. They have serious problems with language development and social interactions, and some show symptoms of autism. Hyperlexia is rare, but it raises important questions about what constitutes "good reading" as well as when and why children should learn to read.

Parents have been besieged by conflicting advice about teaching their children to read and helping them after they enter school. You can help your child become an enthusiastic and skilled reader, but not in some of the ways you may have heard. This chapter will challenge many common assumptions by looking at the way the child's brain learns to convert printed words into a meaningful message. Let's start with Phillip's story for some ideas about why children learn to read in the first place.

"A Weird Child"

"Yes, he was a weird child from the beginning." Phillip's mother pauses over her coffee cup as we sit in the living room of their attractive suburban house. "Don't get me wrong—I am crazy about that kid, but he never wanted to be cuddled, and he would never look us in the eye like most children do. His language development was so slow that he wasn't even speaking in sentences at age three."

"But you told me he started to read at two and a half." I was still skeptical, for this was only the first of twelve interviews that painted astonishingly similar pictures of children in a dozen differing environments.

"That's why I was completely amazed when I found out he could read. I had just decided to take him for a full evaluation—you know, to see what was wrong with him—when we were driving home from the library one day. He was sitting in the backseat and picked up a book and started to read some of the words. It took me a minute to realize what was happening, and then I almost crashed into a tree."

"How in the world do you explain it?" I knew that Phillip had, indeed, received several evaluations that placed his overall intelligence well below "normal." His language, despite intensive therapy, was still limited, and he had trouble understanding many things that are taken for granted with most children. Despite high-school-level abilities in word reading, his comprehension was below that of a second grader.

"I don't know. Just to show you how weird he was, he was never interested in toys, never pretended, and never wanted to go out to play. Even in his playpen, he would push all the toys into a corner and lie there looking at books. For a while we thought maybe he was a genius, but obviously we were wrong. I often wonder what would have happened if we had gotten him to play more. We encouraged the reading, but I think it was a mistake. We thought that early reading was always a good sign."

After eleven more interviews and hours of testing these "weird" but engaging youngsters, I was convinced. A few children can teach themselves to read at very early ages even when other development is severely delayed. It is possible to read words perfectly but mechanically. For some reason we don't yet understand, hyperlexic children manage to separate the words from the meaning. Perhaps they fixate on printed words as a sort of "anchor" because they have trouble getting patterns of meaning out of experience. They have excellent rote-level memories, but they live in a world full of things such as toys, seat belts, and people that they are unable to understand. Yet without that ability to comprehend the world and the language used to talk about it, they cannot truly "read" even while flawlessly pronouncing the words on the page. Because they lack the foundations of language and thinking, they are unaware of the real purpose of reading—getting meaning from print.

What Is "Good Reading"?

Good reading involves more than learning to figure out, or "decode," the words. The perceptual channels of the eyes and ears are the entry points into a huge system of meaning, packaged in language, that brings messages from the writer to the reader. Comprehension depends on a background of receiving language messages and connecting them with ideas—which come from personal experience with the world.

Studying hyperlexia has alarmed me about unbalancing normal children's early reading. I believe the lesson to be learned from these unusual cases is that a broad base of perceptual skill plus mental growth is necessary to take reading beyond a hollow exercise. When that base is in place—and only then—do children have the right reasons to read: to find meaning, to learn, and to expand their world. Let's examine the natural course of reading development so you can understand how children learn to read, when and how they should be taught, and your continuing role during a child's school years.

HOW CHILDREN LEARN TO READ
Young Brains Look at Words

"Mommy, Mommy, there's McDonalds! Let's stop!" Is this four-year-old reading the sign? Not exactly, but she is following a natural process that starts children toward reading even before they enter school.

"Cow, cow, pow, pow, pow!" improvises another four-year-old, demonstrating a sense of rhyme, an important reading readiness skill.

"Knock, knock . . ." pesters an eight-year-old, finding wordplay newly hilarious without understanding its link with her reading comprehension skills.

You might not recognize these precursors of reading because they are part of normal language development. The first reading lesson is mastered when the child learns that language carries messages from other people. The second comes when phonemes, the small units of spoken words, are perceived accurately. Next, spoken words become symbols for objects and events ("Let's go to McDonald's!"). Eventually they connect with "pictures" of words ("McDonald's") and finally with letter sounds and word parts in order. Personal meaning meets printed symbol. Ongoing language development and wordplay carry the process forward.

Brand names and logos are easy for tots to remember because they come in interesting shapes and colors. Some children are able to take this visual skill one step further and learn to remember printed words in the same way. The age at which this development occurs varies greatly—and *is not tied to intelligence.* Learning words by "sight," like remembering a picture or shape, is often called "the look-say method" and has been the basis for many early reading programs. Good readers, however, also have a quick, automatic ability to "decode"—to sound out words and syllables.

Preschoolers often spontaneously start recognizing words like STOP, possibly because their right-hemisphere skills are more mature than later-developing left-hemisphere abilities to connect letters and sounds. Before age six or so, children, especially boys, tend more toward visual, pictorial processing. Yet words in books are a lot harder than the colorful shapes on signs. They require sophisticated visual analysis and may all look alike to a young child. If your preschooler does not show an interest in the words when you read to him—if he does not ask you, "What does that say?"—chances are he is not ready to distinguish one from another. He should continue to learn actively from touching, exploring, and figuring out the world, not from being frustrated by abstract symbols. He also needs to be able to recognize, separate, and sequence the sounds in the words he hears before he can transfer this skill to the printed page. Research shows that these skills of phonemic and phonological awareness are a major key to reading success.

With so much necessary preschool maturation and preparation of the brain and language system, it is a real mistake to try and force early reading on children. I have treated six-year-olds who were positively phobic about reading because they already associated it with failure. If only someone had waited until their brains were mature enough to approach reading through the proper channels!

Sounding It Out

How do you read "romchembulate"? Since you never saw this nonsense word before, you probably sounded it out, syllable by syllable, even if the process was almost instantaneous. Doubtless, you also used your familiarity with common word parts ("bulate"). If you tried to read it all in one "picture," by sight, you would miss some of the sounds or get them in the wrong order. Most unfamiliar words have to be attacked through putting letters, sounds, and experience together—combining auditory and visual analysis, or *phonics*. Studies show that quick, automatic letter-sound association is necessary for good reading.

How are phonics learned? In the normal progression of reading, some children figure out sound patterns from the words they have learned by sight. They instinctively generalize the rule that *ph* says *f*, for example, because they can read "phone" or know someone named Ralph. Most children, however, need to be taught the basic letter-sound principles. First, the word has to be visually analyzed: Which letter(s) comes first? What sound does it have? Now the second sound, and the third. Now, look at them and say them in order. Now, keep the order in your head and blend them together (this is *tricky*), say the word, listen to it, and associate it first with something you've heard before and then with its meaning. Not so simple, after all!

Sounding out words meaningfully calls upon numerous brain

areas, particularly in the left hemisphere called the *angular gyrus,* an important junction of sensory areas. It matures early in some children, but not in others. There is good evidence that families differ in the inherited timetable as well as in the size and efficiency of language areas in the brain. Dyslexic people, who have a constitutional difficulty with reading and other language skills, may actually tend to read with other areas of the brain that are not so well suited to the job.

The important news is that good teaching can change this pattern. In one landmark study, a group of second grade poor readers, whose brains were firing mostly in the right hemisphere when they tried to read, received intensive small-group instruction in basic letter-sound correspondence, including emphasis on fluent reading with understanding. Brain scans showed that this intervention actually changed the way they used their brains for reading, and their scores improved accordingly. Likewise, many studies of adults have shown that a brain that has learned to read operates quite differently from one that has not, even though they are equally intelligent. As a result, readers and nonreaders view the world and solve problems in different ways.

Even while children work on automaticity in decoding, or word recognition, they need to focus on comprehension—understanding what they read. Do not encourage your child to be a "word caller" who barks perfectly at the print but neglects the message. Good reading calls upon many areas in the brain working together, and one main way children learn to read is by reading.

Mental Scaffolds for Reading Comprehension

Children cannot understand text that exceeds their language comprehension. For example, a child reading a story about a trip to a grocery store will probably have little trouble with "They paid at the checkout counter," even if she has never seen the words before, because she has heard them many times and knows that this is where we pay. If she has never been to a store, however, or doesn't know the name of the "thing where you give money," she may not be able to decode the words or understand the sentence. Likewise, if she does not know the past tense of the word "pay," she will also be confused.

Learning to decode words is only an access route to whatever lies inside the reader's mind. Reading can add to our wisdom and store of knowledge, but it must connect with ideas that are related to something we understand.

Reading Risks

Children who are too hung up about making a mistake are often inefficient readers. They cling to every word as if they are drowning in an unknown sea. Often they come to me for help with "speed" when what they really need is a solid review of basic skills and confidence that if they make an error the world will not end.

I once had a six-year-old student who looked like a frightened little rabbit every time she opened a book. She was off to a slow start, but her good language abilities made me confident she would soon catch up. As the year went on, however, I was increasingly frustrated by her faltering progress. Whenever I asked her to read, she gazed up at me with large pleading eyes and a quivering mouth. Children do not ordinarily find me scary, so I puzzled endlessly about what the problem might be. Finally, one day, I took her aside and confronted the issue.

"Elizabeth, I have been wondering why you find reading so scary. You are good at so many things, it makes me sad to see you look frightened. Can you tell me what happens inside when I call on you?"

Elizabeth gulped and her chin quivered. "I hate reading!" she blurted out. Gradually the story emerged. "When I was little, Mom had all these word cards pasted all over the house and then she would take them down and see if I could remember them, and I never could and I made mistakes *all* the time. I think I'm really stupid about reading. When you call on me my mind just goes empty."

Further investigation revealed that Elizabeth's mother, a former teacher, had indeed tried to teach her daughter to read at an early age. She genuinely believed she was doing the child a favor, but unfortunately, Elizabeth was one of those who have trouble remembering words by sight. Moreover, it was evident that this was a household where mistakes were barely tolerated. Elizabeth was afraid of playground days when her clothes might get dirty, and she was so worried about having perfect handwriting that she was often behind in her work. While I'm not recommending that you roll your child in dirt on a regular basis, I would suggest that at certain ages a child can learn as much from mud and water as from the alphabet!

Likewise, reading experts are concerned that parents who try to press reading instruction on their children may inadvertently shut down their interest. Many young children have difficulty distinguishing among sounds and need specialized instruction in order to link sounds and symbols. Instead of pushing word reading, teach your child to be a good, careful listener to word games, rhymes, stories, or conversation.

Reading Development in a Nutshell

To help you sort out some of these important ideas about how children become good readers, let's summarize the main issues so far:

- Awareness of the elements of spoken language, *phonemes*, is a major foundation of good reading.
- Decoding words is the entry point. Comprehension must come hand in hand for good reading.
- Learning words in isolation (e.g., on flash cards) removes reading from its normal context of getting meaning from real language. Likewise, don't encourage too many computer alphabet games that separate decoding from meaning.
- Children who don't have a good base of language and thinking skills have difficulty understanding and applying what they read.
- Some intelligent people do not easily remember words by sight. They need to depend on phonics in order to learn to read, and they learn them best through "multisensory" methods that incorporate all the senses (look, say, touch, move/write).

• Many children do not have the neural development required for phonics work sheets until at least age six. For some, especially boys, it may be later. Early childhood programs should focus on specific language and listening skills, not pencil-and-paper drills.

• Reading comprehension is built on mental networks formed throughout childhood from real experiences with the world. Parents who provide interesting activities and talk about them with their child are laying an important foundation for reading skill.

• Poor comprehension may be the result of inadequate experience with the ideas presented.

• A perfectionistic environment where mistakes are barely tolerated may inhibit a child's reading development.

• Early reading is not always a sign of giftedness. If it replaces other activities that are developmentally appropriate (playing, talking), it may be a danger signal. If your child shows symptoms of hyperlexia, delayed language, and extreme difficulty with interpersonal relationships, do not encourage reading. Obtain a complete evaluation of mental and language development, and work on activities more appropriate for early cognitive growth.

• The time you spend reading to your child is the best predictor of later reading success.

WHEN SHOULD CHILDREN LEARN TO READ?
Is Earlier Better?

Will early readers be farther ahead? Will they grab up all the places at the good colleges because they are such academic stars? Let's look at this serious question in light of research in mental development.

Yes, even babies may be trained to recognize word cards. Babies, however, cannot *read*, tapping into a vast personal storehouse of language and knowledge that takes years to build. Most preschoolers, likewise, can be trained through a stimulus-response type of teaching. The human brain can be trained to do almost anything if the task is simplified enough and one is willing to devote the necessary time and energy. Yet the brainpower—and possibly the neural connections—are stolen from the foundation of real intelligence. Reading becomes a low-level skill, and there is a danger it will remain at the level where it was learned and practiced.

I believe that formally teaching reading to preschoolers is a serious intrusion on natural mental growth. Only a few are true early readers who *spontaneously*, motivated by their own curiosity, teach themselves to read *because they want to find out the meaning*. If we get children to "read" words before they have ideas, thoughts, and language to make reading interesting, we hand them a key to the door of an unfinished garden.

The Unfinished Garden

"Look, child, there is an exciting garden of adventure called reading behind this gate. It is important for you to get inside. Here's a key. Let's work on opening the gate so you can enter this wonderful place." The child labors diligently to fit the key into the lock. This is taking lots of time. Is it worth it?

"Of course it's worth it. Entering the garden of reading is the most important thing you'll ever do. You'll be ahead in school and get into a good college. Try a little harder." After hours of effort, the key begins to turn. More hours, and the door opens a crack.

"Whew!" thinks the child. "Now for the goodies! Hey, wait a minute! This is just a big bare place with some little sprouts coming up. This is *boring*!"

"Sorry, kid, I guess your mental garden isn't quite ready yet. If you wait a few years, those sprouts will turn into interesting ideas and then you'll be able to use your reading key to have a lot of fun. I promise you'll love it."

One of the biggest problems in schools today is that children do not like to read. They complain that it is "boring." Is it possible that we have turned them back at the doorway by forcing the key on them too soon?

A True Story

"Stop worrying," Jane told herself as she watched five-year-old Scott intently constructing an intricate block highway system. "He's obviously intelligent and you're just overreacting. So what if Marge is bragging that Erna can read." Still, she found herself reaching for the box of plastic alphabet letters. "Here's a G, Scott," she exclaimed with calculated enthusiasm, laying it on top of his newly designed garage. "G stands for garage. It says 'guh, guh.' "

"Grrrr!" shouted Scott joyously, accelerating a toy car into the garage and knocking the letter onto the floor.

"Look here, Scott." Jane's voice became insistent as she pushed the letter in front of her son's eyes. "Look at the G and say 'guh.' "

"I don't wanna!" wailed Scott, seizing the letter and flinging it across the room. "I hate those dumb letters!"

I know this is a true story because it happened in our home. How well I remember my panicky feeling when our eldest son—at the advanced age of five—wasn't interested in reading. I remember my gentle—and not-so-gentle—prodding, the attempts to teach him letter sounds, and my worry that he wouldn't make the top reading group because he was behind. To be honest, I was also worried about how he compared with my friends' children. I wish someone had given me the facts:

• Many bright, even gifted, children do not read early. Please give them lots of language and listening experiences and let them enjoy stories without an underlying aura of expectation that they cannot fulfill.

• Truly gifted early readers are insatiable in their desire to learn to read. They do not have to be taught, and they make instinctive connections with thought and language. If you have one of these children, share the joy of this natural experience. The way they usually learn is from adults or older brothers and sisters reading to them.

• Early readers do not always win the race. The slower starters, with a wide base of experience and problem-solving, often pull ahead when thinking skills and application become more important around fourth grade.

- Reading problems can be created by forced early instruction. Studies in different countries have shown that when five- and seven-year-olds are taught by the same methods, the seven-year-olds learn far more quickly and happily than do the fives, who are more likely to develop reading difficulties.

- Reading requires an *active pursuit of meaning*. Children who pick up the idea that it is something *done to them* are being programmed as passive readers who will neither enjoy reading nor pursue meaning effectively.

- Forcing or overloading neural circuits may cause the brain to go into "idle" because it cannot handle the load. Don't let your child associate reading with an idling or overwhelmed brain.

Fortunately, my personal story concluded happily. I mustered up enough sense to back off after a few such incidents, and our son had an unusually skilled teacher the next year who repaired most of the damage. Still, it took several years before he discovered that reading was delicious fare for his keen intellect. Now I look back and wonder, "What was the rush?"

I told this story to one mother whose five-year-old is intellectually gifted but not yet ready to read. "I feel so relieved," she sighed. "I just needed some ammunition. I knew I was pushing her too hard, but you hear all these things. . . ."

Hold on to your good instincts about what is right for your child. Don't join the crowd of hucksters who sell keys to the garden of reading before children are ready to use them. There is no justification for turning a treasure into a boring commodity.

Another True Story

Five-year-old Ronee arrived on the first day of school clutching a worn book that she couldn't wait to show her new teacher. "This is my favorite story," she confided. "It's *Cinderella*. I just love *Cinderella*. I'll read it to you if you want."

The teacher, enchanted by Ronee's soft brown eyes and masses of electric pigtails, soon discovered that the child could, in fact, read—not only *Cinderella*, but every book in the room as well as many in the library. Moreover, she could understand them. When Ronee read, she got so excited about the story, she carried on a personal dialogue:

"Oh, no! They're not really going to do *that!*"

"What's going to happen? I'm scared!"

"Oh, that's so funny!"

As she read out loud, her voice got softer and softer until she was reading silently, like a mature reader going after meaning in the quickest way. This reading was definitely not a splinter skill!

Ronee's teacher referred her to the reading specialist, whose tests confirmed that the child could read and comprehend above an eight-year-old level. Most of her reading was based on sight recognition of familiar words or word parts, but she was instinctively using phonics as well. Curious, the specialist asked Ronee's mother what she had done to make her child such a good reader.

"Oh, not much. I always read to her a lot. She just loved her stories, and about a year ago she started bugging me to tell her what the words meant. I showed her how the letters went together to make words. She did the rest herself."

What kind of a reading program should this child have? Some schools put children like this into a "reading readiness" program, where they drill on letter sounds. We should all object strenuously to such pedagogical absurdities. Ronee needs an enriched program where she can use her reading skill to learn about interesting topics and share stories with classmates. She can learn to write stories and plays of her own with "developmental spelling" (see chapter 10), and make books and illustrate them. She can extend her learning by tackling factual topics and reporting on them. If the teacher is overburdened, a volunteer or an older student might spend individual time with her.

Fortunately, Ronee's teacher views her gifted student as a delightful challenge and has arranged a special program for her that includes plenty of interaction with other children. Ronee may be unusual, but she is still five years old. Right now she is working hard, learning about butterflies and also writing a play for her classmates to perform—a dramatization of *Cinderella*.

If you have a child like Ronee, rejoice but keep an eye on what is happening in the classroom. Such children represent a special challenge that many schools are only starting to address. Giving a child like this "reading readiness" work sheets reminds me of pulling the wings off a butterfly.

PARENTS HELPING CHILDREN READ
What Is "Reading Readiness"?

Does caution about early pressure mean that parents should have no part in their child's reading development? Quite the contrary. Parents lay the groundwork that enables the child to activate the system. Above all, children should be shown—by example—that reading is fun. Homes where books, magazines, and newspapers abound, where adults read and talk about ideas, produce the best readers.

To be truly "ready" to read, a child must have accomplished some important groundwork. First, visual development must be adequate for focusing at the proper distance, distinguishing letters and words, tracking in a left to right direction, and keeping place. There is a serious question as to whether many preschoolers have this basic physical ability for reading. Alphabet recognition (saying names or sounds for the letters) is a good predictor of reading ability, but probably because the type of brain that takes readily to these written symbols is the brain that will also take easily to reading. Simply drilling a child on the alphabet is not sufficient! Moreover, if he is not ready to learn it easily, pushing this skill may set up negative associations that interfere with future progress.

Second, thinking skills must be adequately developed to get beyond the physical appearance of words, understand that they have abstract meanings, and connect those meanings to ideas. Many parents are surprised to learn that object manipulation and play are major foundations for good reading.

Language is the third cornerstone. In addition to lots of conversation and vocabulary-building, parents can have fun with one special aspect of language readiness. Before they read well, children must develop what experts call "linguistic awareness," meaning that they know some of the conventions of reading, including what a "word" is.

Developing Linguistic Awareness

• Show your child that a book has a cover, a title that tells what it will be about, and pages that go in order from front to back. Discuss the pictures and their relationship with the story.

• Let your child see that you are reading from the top to the bottom of each page.

• Help your child understand that words have interesting and important meanings, and that you enjoy reading them to get information or to have fun (e.g., use newspapers, magazine articles, recipes, directions, or comic strips).

• Read books without always showing the pictures to encourage careful listening.

• Young children may be unaware that words have spaces between them—both in speech and on the printed page. With a child older than four, call attention to what words look like when you are reading. Without making an issue of it, occasionally trace your finger under the line so the child sees you moving in a left to right direction. Do not quiz or force the child to try and read the words.

• Learning to pay good attention to visual information is important for preschoolers. Encourage your child to look for details in pictures and objects and see how they are related to the whole, as preparation for visual analysis of letters in words.

• With children of four or older, sets of plastic alphabet letters can be made available, but not forced on the child. Remember that "uppercase" (capital) and "lowercase" (small) letters may mean the same thing to you, but they look completely different to the child. Do not expect a child to know that *H* and *h* are the same thing. While some computer software may develop alphabet recognition, "touchable" versions of these abstract symbols are more child-friendly.

• With children of five or older, play games of counting words in short phrases or rhymes. You can clap for each word to keep track. Children will tend to clap for each syllable. The purpose is to show that a word is a unit of meaning, not just a sound. Call attention to individual sounds in words and their order. ("Here's a word: 'deck.' What's the first sound? Last sound?") Emphasize rhyming words and play rhyming games.

• If children spontaneously start to ask about written words, tell them. When youngsters are really ready to read, they become real pests. Take the time to satisfy their curiosity.

Experiencing Written Language

One practical way for parents to capitalize on a child's spontaneous interest in reading is by encouraging him to create his own stories, which you write down for him. Termed "language experience stories," these creations provide an excellent tool for teaching reading; they can be fun at home if the child is interested. Take a large piece of paper and tell the child that you will be the "secretary" for his story. Reserving the top half of the paper for a picture, write down the child's words. Let him watch as you write, saying the sounds (not the names) of the letters in words that can be sounded out. For words like "the", simply say and print the word. Don't dress up the grammar or vocabulary; this story belongs to him. If you can't resist the urge to take over or if the child acts bored, quit. Use uppercase and lowercase printed letters, not all capitals (if you have any doubt, consult your local school for models of the writing system currently in use), or type the story and print it out.

Encourage the child to draw a picture with each story, and soon you will have a collection to staple together into a book: *Charlie's Stories*. Reread each out loud for the author as often as he asks for it. Some children enjoy trying to reread for themselves, and this is one of the best ways to start reading, since children's own words have the most meaning for them. Don't force it, however. While you read, point to each word as you go along. Don't quiz the child, and don't be surprised if he can't remember any of the words in the story. Compliment him on his story, even if it says, "I sat on the grass." It makes his language seem very important—which it is!

Children vary in their fluency with storytelling. You may have to provide some ideas ("Would you like to tell about our walk to the park? What did you see on the way?" "I would love to hear a story about the castle you made in the sandbox. Could a little king be in there?") For most children, language experience stories are appropriate around age four or five.

Incidentally, sometimes we get fooled by a youngster's good memory for familiar stories. Children can look and act as if they are reading when they aren't. For this reason, parents and teachers sometimes disagree about whether a child can read.

Parents Teach Story Scripts

Children pick up a special kind of knowledge in a home where a variety of reading is part of daily life. Sampling rhymes, poems, essays, fables, and folktales builds mental frameworks for the structure of literature. A child who has learned what to expect from the structure of a story—a "story script"—will find reading much easier and more enjoyable. For example, if I told you we were going to read a fable about a fox, the words "sly" or "crafty" would be easier to figure out, and you would expect a moral at the end. Instinctive awareness that a story has a main character, that there is usually some problem, a climax, and an ending, facilitates comprehension. Likewise, a child who has been exposed to picture dictionaries and children's encyclopedias has a good start on using reference sources.

Try telling some stories, too. Don't be embarrassed—you will be surprised that your simplest attempts will enthrall your young audience. All children love to hear stories about when they were babies or tales of their parents' childhood experiences. One father who didn't particularly enjoy reading made up stories about children involved in a wonderful variety of adventures—finding caves in the woods, seeking hidden treasure, or even being chased by wild animals. Eventually he began stopping at the most exciting moment and inviting the avid listener to continue the story. Each one of his children loved the power of solving these problems, but soon learned to create a new climax and hand the storytelling reins back to Dad. Now grown, they still recall the fun of trying to invent the most improbable dilemma for the hero.

The Wiggly Ones

Some children seem to have come from a different programmer. They don't like to sit still and be read to. Capturing one like this is a challenge, and you may need subversive methods. Sometimes postponing bedtime for reading or storytelling works wonders. Look for books that have lots of pictures or pick a subject that is especially interesting. Follow the child's lead—even if she wants to read the toy catalog—and make sure your own vibrations are positive and fun to be around. Our wiggliest one eventually chose to be an English major in college and "discovered" the joys of listening to Shakespeare. It took a little longer for him to get his time into joint—but it was worth the wait!

By the way, reassure your child that you will keep on reading out loud even after she has learned to read for herself. Some children may resist learning to read independently because they fear they will lose the close contact of story time with their parents.

Raising children who read well means raising children who have been encouraged to think well. The following list summarizes the characteristics of homes that produce good readers and good thinkers. You may be surprised how few have to do directly with reading.

HOMES FOR GOOD READERS . . .

- Have a nonpunitive but structured atmosphere where children are encouraged to express ideas and feel part of decision-making.
- Have an absence of unrealistic restrictions, demands, or inappropriate pressure.
- Encourage independent problem-solving. Preschoolers are encouraged to be self-reliant in zipping, tying, setting the table, and other activities. Older children are expected to think through problems.
- Show tolerance of reasonable mistakes.
- Focus on praise rather than criticism.
- Emphasize expanding rather than correcting a child's conversation.
- Do not force early reading.
- Have adult models of reading for a variety of purposes. Pleasure in reading is evident here. Boys and girls see both parents reading, and children tend to copy the attitudes of the same-sex parent.
- Schedule regular time for reading to the child; reading is associated with relaxed and loving contact. Adults in this home stop to engage the child in questions and discussion about the meaning of a story. They may ask the child to explain or summarize a point, but they keep it lighthearted and fun.
- Have books, newspapers, magazines, and interesting children's books readily at hand; "screen time" is regulated.
- Schedule regular trips to the library, where the child is encouraged to select books that are personally meaningful.
- Offer a broad range of experiences, and conversation about them is a reg-

ular part of family life. Adults introduce and explain new vocabulary words.

- Encourage phonemic awareness through rhyming games and careful listening to the sounds in words. (What is the beginning of "look"? What is the end? If I took off the "l" and put in a "b," what would it say? How many sounds does it have? [Three: b-oo-k].)

TEAMING WITH THE SCHOOL
Helping the Beginning Reader

A parent's supporting role does not end when a child starts formal reading instruction, a time of unrecognized stress for most children. Acutely aware of everyone's expectation that they will learn to read, they may secretly worry that they will fail. Parents can do much to allay this natural anxiety, even to the point of articulating for the child how "scary" this new experience must be.

MOTHER: I remember when I started school. It seemed like everyone thought I should learn to read, and I felt scared that I couldn't.
CHILD: Yeah?
MOTHER: It took a while, but I learned. It takes a long time for children to learn to be good readers. Some children start out real fast, but that doesn't mean they're smarter. Everybody has their own special way to learn.

This last message is especially important if your child is in a class with children who are faster out of the gate. We must emphasize the message that slow starters are often just as smart, but on a different learning track for a while. For "lumpers," who favor a holistic approach to incoming information, splitting words up into sound sequences is not natural, and they have trouble remembering in which direction they are going. They would much rather start in the middle than analyze pieces in order. Thus, "was" and "saw," "on" and "no" may be confused. Letters may get turned around—*b* and *d, g* and *q*—because, if you're not into left-to-right sequence, they *are* alike. This confusion is usually not caused by problems in the eyes, but by the brain's difficulty registering and retaining symbols in order. Most children learn to straighten out letters, words, and numerals before age eight, when their left hemispheres take more firm control, and they should be reassured that these normal errors do *not* mean that they are "stupid." Nor do some reversals mean that the child is necessarily going to be "dyslexic." There are other symptoms that accompany dyslexia, to be discussed later in this chapter.

Parents can become too concerned about the normal ups and downs of early reading. Please try to protect children from your own level of anxiety. If early reading becomes associated with stress, fear, or tension, it may retain that negative aura long after any initial problem has been overcome.

Schools that have moved from rigid workbook-type instruction to broader language-oriented methods enable children to move into reading at their own pace in a positive atmosphere. Encouraging the child to write and read about things that interest him, putting "phonics" into a meaningful context, is the best way to begin.

Reading with a School-Age Child

To help the teacher develop your child's reading ability, continue daily story time, express interest and enthusiasm about school progress, and let the child read to you at home. Your job is not to teach, but to reinforce good reading habits. Here are some guidelines:

1. Set aside a regular time to read to your child. As she learns to read, add ten minutes a day when she can read to you. Continue regularly until silent reading ability is established.

2. Make sure that the child is reading from books that are easy and

enjoyable. This is called the "independent" level of reading. If you have any questions, ask the teacher. The purpose is to practice fluency and learn to enjoy reading.

3. Let the child choose the books, as long as they are at the independent level. Children sometimes try to please their parents by selecting "hard" books, but this is self-defeating.

4. As the child reads, listen to determine if she understands the meaning. Clues are found in the way she phrases text, observes punctuation marks, or makes comments about the story.

5. Insert an occasional question that will challenge her thinking. "Why do you think John wanted those shoes?" "What do you think will happen next?" "Let's guess what they could find in the old barn." "What might have happened if he had stayed home from the picnic?" Don't focus on literal-level questions like, "What color were the shoes?" "What did they take on the picnic?"

6. The most common error adults (including teachers) make is helping too much. If the child mispronounces a word, remain silent. Listen to the rest of the phrase or sentence to see if the mispronunciation changed the meaning. For example, if the phrase "a little dog" is read "a little doggy," I recommend that you leave it alone. For beginning readers, confusion of "a" and "the" may also be ignored. If the child makes errors that change the sense of the story, wait for her to realize that meaning has been lost. You want her to monitor the meaning herself. If she continues, stop her at the end of the sentence and ask, "Did that make sense?" Encourage her to listen and reread for meaning. If errors happen frequently, switch to an easier book.

7. When the story is finished, ask her to retell it *briefly*. Help her find only the main ideas and important parts and recall them in order. This process of synthesis is difficult but important. Encourage quality rather than quantity in retelling.

8. If you are both interested, extend your discussion of the story. You could imagine another ending, a different main character, or a different setting. Children enjoy creative projects: making models of

the setting in a shoebox or rewriting the plot from another point of view. Such projects can be taken to school and shared with the class. They are far more interesting than the standard book report.

9. You can help your child with one of comprehension's greatest tools if you encourage mental imagery. Have him practice making "mental movies" of what is happening in the book. Try drawing pictures of what you each "saw" in the story. Use books without pictures or cover them up so that you can make up your own ideas. Research shows that good comprehenders instinctively make mental pictures when they read, and that poorer readers' comprehension can be improved by direct instruction in this important strategy.

10. If your child resists reading to you at home, reflect on the amount of pressure in the situation. Are the sessions too long? Should you get easier books? Are you giving enough praise? Do you take a turn reading now and then? If a real problem seems to exist, go to the child's teacher or the reading specialist with your questions.

11. Encourage habits of independent reading. Extending bedtime is still a good inducement. Turn off the TV and let the whole family read together—silently or out loud.

Neurological Impressions

Some children have trouble picking up the rhythms and patterns of oral reading. One way that parents can help nonfluent readers is called the *neurologic impress technique*, which sounds a lot more complicated than it is. Sit beside your child in a comfortable place. If the child is right-handed, you might sit so that your voice will enter his right ear to stimulate the opposite left (language) hemisphere. The child holds the book (of his independent reading level) and reads out loud. Your job is to read right along with him at a normal pace, providing a feel for the rhythms and phrasing. The child's voice may start to trail off, but keep him going as well as you can. Your voice is the guide; he tags along until the sentences become more familiar.

This technique is appropriate *for children of school age.* Ten minutes a day builds fluency. Repeat each story several times until the child is confident with it. Studies show this type of practice with a teacher improves speed of word recognition. The warm, cozy experience of reading with a parent should be even more effective.

Never criticize a child's reading. Children do not make mistakes on purpose. If he has trouble keeping the place, a file card that follows his progress down the page may help. The latest theories also say that using a finger to keep the place is okay. Most children "subvocalize" (pronounce words out loud as they read) until they are eight or nine. We all have a natural tendency to subvocalize with difficult material. Even older children may need to read out loud when the text is above their independent level.

SQ3R

One nifty technique that is helpful with textbook reading for students nine and older is called *SQ3R*, which stands for:

1. Survey
2. Question
3. Read
4. Recite
5. Review

If your child's teacher has not introduced SQ3R, you can show the youngster how to use it for history, science, literature, or other texts. Here's how:

1. **Survey:** Look over the entire assignment or chapter. Read the title. Read all the subheadings. Look at any maps, charts, pictures. How do they all fit together? Skim the first and the last paragraphs.

Survey study guides at the end of the chapter. How does this chapter relate to the entire book? To the course? Assure your child that the time spent on this step is not wasted, but will cut down on total study time.

2. **Question:** Who wrote this and why? Why am I reading it? (For fun, for a test, to learn about how to make widgets?) What will it be about? Think of some questions inspired by the title. (For example, *Building the Colonies*: What were the colonies? Where were they? What did the colonists need to build? Homes? Stores? Factories? Governments? How did they build them? Who did the work?) Try to guess how to answer the questions. This step gets the child personally involved, setting his own direction and reasons for reading. Turn all the chapter topic headings into questions. Try to guess answers to these and to any questions given in the text.

3. **Read:** Now read the chapter carefully. Writing summaries of each section in the margin is a good habit to acquire. Most students tend to underline too much. Read first, then go back and highlight only the most important points.

4. **Recite:** Without looking back at the text, try to answer the questions you asked at the beginning. How do all these subtopics fit together? What are the main ideas in this chapter? What are the important facts and details? How are the pictures, charts, and maps related to the topic?

5. **Review:** Go back over the material after some time has passed. Refresh your memory of the important facts and ideas. Periodic review is the best way to create memory circuits. Make study guides of facts and ideas that must be remembered.

SQ3R is only one of many practical tools to help students' reading comprehension. Many good teachers now ask students to list ideas, discuss, or write about a topic before starting to read about it, and are finding interesting and motivating ways to combine reading, writing, and reasoning in every subject. Check to see if your school is working on this integration of skills. Encourage teachers to keep up with new research that helps children read with their brains instead of only with their eyes and voices.

WHAT TO DO IF YOU SUSPECT TROUBLE

"Dyslexia," abnormal difficulty with reading, writing, and spelling, is a widely used term guaranteed to inspire terror in a parent's soul. Many good books are available about learning problems, so I will limit this discussion to an overview of preventive measures, symptoms you should be aware of, and ways to go about seeking help if you suspect a problem.

Preventing Reading Problems

Many or even most reading problems can be ameliorated by careful early intervention and reading instruction that is flexible enough to accommodate differing needs. Parents sometimes find themselves at cross-purposes with school personnel who force lockstep instruction on all students; this problem becomes more serious when unrealistic top-down demands for performance are placed on teachers. Such pressures sometimes put everyone into an almost impossible bind. Do not hesitate to complain if inappropriate "standards" are destroying your child's emotional health or enthusiasm for learning.

Early specialized help is important for any child who is having serious difficulty. Do not wait for failure to become a habit. Bear in mind, however, that some bright students do not learn to read until after age seven; if the child is working with a good professional, lay off the demands at home.

Does Your Child's School Encourage Good Reading?

If you want to exert constructive pressure, ask these questions about your school:

At the beginning:

• Are language development and phonemic awareness important parts of the early reading program?
• Is a well-structured, multisensory program in place to teach automatic letter-sound associations?
• Is beginning reading also taught through language experience stories, "big books," spontaneous writing, storytelling, and listening experiences?
• Do children use real books, not just workbooks or computers?
• Is an effort made to identify children's learning styles and provide instruction for varying needs?
• Are teachers able to recognize the bright "unready" child, and can they develop a program to get him ready?
• Is writing an integral part of the reading program? For most children, age five is not too early to start linking reading and writing.
• Are teachers aware of each child's progress and needs, while demands for tests and "standards" are realistic and kept to a minimum before grade three?

In every grade:

• Is silent comprehension stressed?
• Are children allowed to advance at their own pace in reading, while teachers make sure that each step is comfortably mastered before imposing new demands?
• Conversely, are children encouraged to move on to more interesting uses of reading once basic skills are mastered?

- Are instructional groupings ("reading groups") flexible? Is discrimination against the "bottom reading group" absent?
- Does the school understand that boys' and girls' reading styles may vary? Girls may be better at fluency and phonics while boys may favor comprehension. A balanced program will help everyone.
- Are drill and textbook instruction supplemented with a wide variety of "real" reading: quality trade books, newspapers, research materials?
- Is reading instruction thoroughly integrated with writing, poetry, drama, and other creative uses of the language arts?
- Do teachers emphasize expository forms of writing and reading (e.g., essays, information) as well as fiction?
- Is there some system of reporting the child's progress to parents in regularly scheduled personal conferences in addition to report cards?
- Does your child *like* to read?

Skilled instruction that is planned around each child's level of neurological development and learning style can prevent reading problems; patience and skill from both family and school are required.

RECOGNIZING PROBLEMS

How do you know when to be worried? Danger signals differ depending on the age of the child.

Early Signs

- Repeated ear infections; hearing impairment or loss.
- Language delay or problems at any age (see chapter 7). Difficulty with color-naming or rapid naming of familiar objects. Unclear speech. Delayed alphabet recognition (after age five) in a child who has been exposed to letter names.

• Persistent problems with paying attention. Some poor readers show brain wave patterns similar to those of children who have attention deficit disorders. They tend to guess hastily at words instead of using systematic word attack skills. See chapter 4 for suggestions on helping attention controls.

• Uncorrected vision problems. Be sure to have your child checked early for amblyopia (lazy eye).

• Family history of language, reading, spelling, or writing problems.

• Left-handedness or ambidexterity, *if* there are other signals. (Many left-handers are fine readers.)

• Protracted difficulty telling time, learning telephone numbers or addresses, tying shoes, following directions.

• Difficulty processing material quickly through eyes or ears. Current research indicates dyslexia may result from brain-based differences in interpreting rapidly changing signals in both the visual and auditory realms.

During School Years

• Reversals or confusion of letters, words, numerals, directions, or concepts that persist after age seven or eight and are accompanied by other symptoms. All young children reverse letters. It does not mean they will be dyslexic.

• Unhappiness in school; physical symptoms (stomachaches, nightmares, worries) that can't be otherwise explained.

• Eye problems or headaches. Although most reading problems are in the brain, eye problems may also contribute.

• Schoolwork brought home that is consistently too difficult for the child to do.

• Labored oral reading and difficulty with comprehension on material that the school sends home. Slow reading.

• Difficulty getting the meaning while reading silently after age eight.

• Problems with writing, spelling, or foreign languages. Bright children may be dyslexic without showing severe reading difficulty. Their problems with language symbols show up when they have to write them down or master a new system. You will learn more about writing and spelling in the next chapter.

A parent's main job is to stay attuned to the school's ability to meet a child's special needs. If you find yourself forced to teach reading rather than just reinforcing it at home, something is wrong. I can personally vouch for the fact that most parents are too emotionally involved to do a teacher's job with their own children. The parent-child relationship is too precious to clutter up with pressures from inappropriate school demands. If trouble is brewing in your house, go to the school and try to get at the source of the difficulty.

How to Seek Help

As a part-time college professor who teaches teachers to teach reading, I know that most teachers are in the business because they care a lot about their students. When a child is having trouble, they often welcome parental support, but like all of us, they don't take kindly to criticism. Remember that your shared goal is the child's well-being, not an adversarial relationship. Here are a few suggestions if you are forced into the role of troubleshooter:

• Be available for conferences with teachers. Keep a careful eye on your child's progress.

• If you suspect trouble, do not delay too long before you make an appointment with the teacher.

• Present your problem calmly. Describe what you have seen in your child without blaming the teacher. Assure her of your desire to help. Suggest looking for solutions you can work on together. Ask the teacher bluntly if she thinks you are putting too much pressure on the child. Listen to her answer.

• Your most important evidence is (1) your child's negative attitude toward learning, and (2) schoolwork that is clearly beyond the level of his current skill development. Bring in the messy, inaccurate, or incompleted pages. Do not accept—or believe for *one minute*—that your child is "lazy." When the demands are too great, children look "lazy" because it is better to believe that you didn't try than that you are a failure.

• Don't accept "He can do it when he tries." I could run a marathon if I tried hard enough, but I sure couldn't do it every day! Moreover, one of the hallmarks of a child who has a learning problem is inconsistency. Some days things connect and other days they don't. Your mutual goal must be to teach the child at a level where the payoff for trying is sufficient to inspire the effort. Failure does not inspire further effort. Success does.

• Try to work with the teacher to develop a plan of attack that will help your child start to feel successful. This may mean scaling back your mutual demands. Bite the bullet. If your child can't do the work, there is no point in trying to keep up with anyone else. Children learn nothing from work they don't do except how to avoid doing work.

• If your mutual efforts fail to get the child back on course, you should request an evaluation by (1) the school's reading specialist or (2) a school psychologist at the earliest possible time. You can ask the reading specialist for diagnostic reading tests and an assessment of visual and auditory processing skills. If there is still doubt, request learning disability testing from the school psychologist or a private clinic.

• In the meantime, ask if there is any individual help available through the school from a reading specialist, a tutoring program, or a special teacher. Dyslexic children need more expert, direct, multisensory teaching of letter sounds and spelling rules than do others, and it may take them as many as eight times the number of repetitions to become automatic in decoding skills, *even if they are highly intelligent.*

• If the school is unable to provide testing or special teaching, seek help from a clinic or private educational psychologist. If the problem has continued for more than six months in a young child or more than a year in an older one, do not delay. Ask these professionals to work with the school in planning a program to meet the child's needs. The International Dyslexia Association can make recommendations for your area.

• Once you have gotten some help, expect your child to do his part. Having a problem must not be viewed as an excuse for giving up. If the demands are reasonable, you and the teacher may have to provide some structure to undo old habits of avoidance. ("You have a problem, which we understand now. It doesn't seem fair, but I guess that means you'll have to work a little harder than some of the other kids to catch up, but we're all going to help you.")

• A child needs extra emotional support at home if there is trouble at school. Fill up his little spirit with praise whenever you have an opportunity. Many poor readers are whizzes at mechanical things, good artists or designers, fine athletes, or just plain wonderful people. Sympathize with his problems. "I know this is hard, but I love you, and you're okay, and I expect you to keep trying" is the message.

Since children come into the world with different brains, it is not surprising that reading comes more easily to some than to others. If your child is one of those whose talents lie in different areas, do your best, but don't decide that you are a failure as a parent. Some very talented people are simply not facile with the printed word. Reading is not the only important human talent.

REFLECTING WISDOM

Parents are important partners in reading development. They help build frameworks of language and thinking and encourage lifelong attitudes toward reading. They can model and support good reading during school years and be advocates for a child's particular needs. They should protect children from pressures to read too soon or for the wrong reasons. Above all, they can encourage use of this versatile tool to learn, to imagine, and to probe unlimited horizons.

One candid quotation neatly sums it up. "Reading is like a mirror: If a fool looks in, you can't expect a wise man to look out." A child's reading ability is truly a mirror reflecting the background of mental development and interest that he brings to it. Learning to decode the words is the foundation of the process, but understanding and applying them for learning and lifelong enjoyment is what good reading is all about.

Chapter 10

Thinking on Paper:
Writing and Spelling

For many children, writing and spelling turn out to be thorns in the academic rose garden. Parents get stuck trying to help without being very clear either on what the school wants or what they should do about it. Sometimes they feel they are expected to do the teacher's job at the risk of jeopardizing the relationship with their child—who most likely resists their help whenever possible. Other families, not impaled on these problems, are concerned about reports that schools are not teaching children to express themselves well in writing or that none of the younger generation can spell.

Their concerns are justified. An enormous amount of research has been done on how to teach reading, but there is much less on writing and even less on teaching spelling. Yet good spelling and writing (by which I mean getting ideas down on paper clearly, concisely, and persuasively as opposed to handwriting, which we will also address) are important skills even in the era of the word processor and spellchecker. Good spelling instruction can increase reading ability and provide a foundation for foreign language learning. Skilled writing is a tool not only for communicating ideas to others but also for "metacognition": clarifying one's understanding of a topic, experimenting with ideas, or simply enjoying the landscape of one's own mind.

Fortunately, a growing awareness of this importance has sparked some new approaches. For those of us who were brought up to view writing and spelling as boring old educational staples, some may come as a surprise. I love to walk into a classroom and find five-year-olds eagerly penciling stories and poems without any help, a nine-year-old working intently over the fifth revision of a piece of creative writing, a middle school teacher instructing her students on how to write an analytical essay, or students being required on a test to formulate a written answer to a complex question rather than simply filling in bubbles for multiple choice. For schools that have kept up with current research, times are changing fast. Moreover, we now realize that some kinds of parental help are really not helpful. In this chapter I will try to review some important ideas, explain why some people have special trouble with spelling and writing, and suggest some ways to help and avoid the pitfalls.

THE WHAT AND WHERE OF WRITING AND SPELLING
What Are They?

"Writing" means several different things that span the range of mental functioning. First, there's *handwriting*, which is generally regarded as a lower-level skill although it can actually signal quite a bit about some of the brain's important processing functions, such as automaticity. Writing itself runs the gamut from copying all the way up to getting original ideas down on paper or developing a persuasive argument, one of the highest-level processes demanded of children. Original writing requires integrating several mechanical skills (handwriting, spelling, punctuation) with sequentially organized thought and language. No wonder it causes trouble!

Defining "spelling" is confusing. No longer regarded merely as a routine skill, it may reflect a child's ability to use high-level conceptual processes and mastery of rule systems. Research also emphasizes the interrelationship of all these skills with language development. Let's look at the way the brain organizes such varying demands.

Separate Circuits

Some patients suffering brain damage from a stroke can write down an idea but cannot read what they have written. In other cases, people with damage to certain neural areas talk fluently without making sense or read words without understanding them. Damage in another area leaves understanding intact but destroys the ability to express ideas in words. These phenomena occur because the subskills of expressive language are housed in different parts of the brain. Researchers call them "separable processes" or "modules."

The idea of using separate neural circuits for different aspects of reading and writing explains why children may be terribly good at one thing and terribly bad at another. It's not necessarily because they aren't trying, but because those separate skills have different systems of wiring.

In the early years of my teaching I was baffled by some bright students' difficulty with written language. If they were reasonably smart, I figured, they ought to be able to learn these skills with a little bit of effort. Sometimes these same children were also excellent readers, which only made me more impatient. When I began to study the brain organization that underlies all these "simple" abilities, however, I realized how complicated the situation really is.

HANDWRITING
The Mechanical Copybook

Once upon a time, everyone knew what children should learn: the basics of mathematics, reading, spelling, geography, and history. Above all, any educated person needed to practice having a "fine hand."

Schoolwork consisted mostly of memorizing, and hours were spent over the copybook. Soon, however, society became more complex, and so did the demands on education. Now it isn't so easy to make decisions about what children should learn. In the midst of an information explosion, teachers are besieged with new demands and are haunted by the probability that some things they choose to teach may soon be obsolete. Memorized "basics" are only the entry points into knowledge— and what are the "basics" of science, anyway? Of world history? Of philosophy? How can we shovel everything important into those little brains?

Educators agree that children should not spend too many precious hours practicing mechanical skills. Since the fate of the world probably does not depend on handwriting, they now set a more pragmatic goal—legibility. Yet some children fail to achieve even that, and researchers continue to search for the most effective way to teach handwriting. They have found that it has early beginnings.

From Scribble to Manuscript

Preschoolers who are around literate adults soon pick up the idea that writing is important and interesting. By the age of three, most children can distinguish between pictures and written symbols. Often they try "writing" themselves; they scribble exciting—if illegible—messages and act surprised when no one understands them. This "scribble writing" is important evidence of linguistic awareness. Eventually some children begin to identify where the scribbled "words" start and stop by putting spaces in between. Experts believe that scribble writing should be encouraged because it gets the child in the habit of linking ideas and paper without getting caught in complex mechanics. Some parents dignify scribbled stories by encouraging the child to draw a picture on the same page and hanging the masterpiece in a place of honor—on the refrigerator, for example. A young child in an environment that values attempts at written expression has a good chance of excelling later at real writing.

Another important preschool development is copying one's own name, a good example of learning driven by personal involvement. As with any skill, it is wise to wait until interest develops. Children whose perceptual or fine motor (small-muscle) development is not yet adequate to the task find this job too taxing. A sensible parent does not make an unpleasant issue about any aspect of writing! Movable plastic letters can create that all-important name without negative associations.

One problem for young children who are encouraged to write at home is the development of a faulty pencil grip that later is hard to correct. The best way to hold a pencil is to grip it between the thumb and first finger of the writing hand, with the middle finger underneath, supporting the pencil. Have the child make "pinchers" to grab the pencil, then add the "shelf." If your child can't hold the pencil correctly, he is better off not using one. Poor pencil grips cause fatigue and inefficient letter formation. Stick to crayons, chalk, paintbrushes, fingerpaints, or a stick in the sandbox until the hand is ready. Stitchery, cutting with scissors, or other manual activities should help.

Computers are fun, but they do not offer the same opportunities to program into the brain the control of a rhythmic sequence and flow of hand and body movements. A child who does not develop these is at risk for a problem that may extend beyond handwriting, since children with attention deficits tend to score poorly on tests of this sort of motor patterning—although which is cause and which is effect has not been determined.

Almost a century ago the "Palmer method" had children rhythmically penciling forms such as ovals over and over in order to ready the hand for writing. It is curious to read current brain research and learn that this type of skill seems to be related to other kinds of control skills, and to learn that some types of remedial programs for learning disabilities use kindred techniques to develop rhythmic, automatic movements.

Children under the age of six should not be expected to copy sentences. Meaningful copying requires sufficient brain maturation to integrate two or three modalities (looking, feeling, touching, moving, and sometimes even hearing a word). Little ones may be able to copy at a rote level, but they're probably not using the circuits that will connect the words with meaning. Let it wait. Children of this age should not be sitting at desks doing academic tasks. Get their busy hands and brains out doing, learning, and developing neural pathways that lead to smooth body movements.

Perceptual Learning: Auditory and Visual

Children differ in how they master visual information, such as letter formation or spelling patterns, and auditory details of sound sequences in words. Those who are best search actively for clues and details, extracting information from the environment. Some of this ability may be attributed to inborn brain organization, but much of it results from practice with nonliterary materials. You probably didn't realize that helping your child identify details in pictures or examine an ant or a blade of grass builds handwriting and spelling skills, or that repeating nursery rhymes readies the brain for spelling. Any activity that promotes the ability to sort out details and make sense of what is seen or heard helps. Good perceptual learning abilities depend heavily on motivation and the desire to be "in charge" of sorting out information that comes into one's brain.

Practice is the key to perceptual learning, but rote copying or tracing letters is usually not best. Here's an example of a parent helping a child to be actively involved. This youngster wants to learn to write her name, "Maria."

PARENT: Here's what your name looks like when it's written down. [Takes a large piece of lined paper and a colored crayon.] Watch me as I write it. [Names each letter as it is written.] Each one of these squiggles is a letter. Let's point to each one. [Shows child how to identify the five letters.] Now, let's see if any of them are alike. [Helps child see the two *a*'s.] Would you like to try writing it yourself? What color would you like? [Child selects colored crayon.] Oh, that's a lovely color! Which lines will you be writing on? [This gets the child to organize the perceptual field of the paper.] Show me which letter you think comes first. [Helps child identify M. Covers up the rest of the letters so only the M shows.] Before you start to write, can you tell me what that M looks like?

CHILD: Well, it has pointy things on the top. Two sticks. They come together and another point here.

PARENT: You really looked carefully. Why don't you start by drawing the first stick *from the top* to the bottom. [Children are inclined to go "bottom-up"; try to encourage top-down strokes.]

This is the beginning of a lesson that gets the child visually analyzing and organizing the stimulus *before* doing anything with it. She is learning, not only to copy a letter, but to take control and use skills of analysis in perceptual tasks. She is also "verbally mediating." This learning will help her remember better and avoid difficulty sorting out details of similar letters in reading (e.g., *m* and *n*). Most schools still do not teach writing in this way, so it is one place where parents can really help. Please wait, however, until your child is old enough (probably around age five) so that you will both enjoy a successful experience! Getting a copy of the school's letter chart showing how the letters are formed avoids relearning later.

Handwriting and the Older Child

The principles of perceptual learning can also be useful for older children who have missed out on acquiring good handwriting habits. Some children in upper elementary, or even junior high are still agonizing over such details as how many bumps are on the *m* and the *n*. If you stop to think about how these particular letters differ in manuscript (print) and cursive writing, in uppercase and lowercase, some confusion is not too surprising. Most children manage because their perceptual skills carry them through, but "visual memory" for letters and words varies widely among people. It affects writing and spelling just as it does reading.

Accepting this natural variation (without criticism of "dumb" mistakes) can make the difference between a child who is willing to keep trying and one who starts to "lose" assignments and devote her creative energies to inventing alibis for avoiding work. If trouble shows up, go back to the beginning and rebuild her knowledge of what each letter looks like. The first tool is visual analysis, as described above; the next is adding as many senses as possible. "Feeling" letter shapes in sand, in cornmeal trays, in clay, on sandpaper, or on rough-textured clothing helps embed them in the brain. Learning specialist Priscilla Vail suggests, once cursive writing has been partially mastered, that children take three to five minutes each day to simply write the alphabet with all the letters connected, focusing on fluent movement and automatic letter formation. The child can see her improvement as she gets more letters written each day in the same time span.

Handwriting problems may stem from a poorly tuned fine motor apparatus. This selectivity of neural programming confuses everyone by enabling some of these youngsters to be terrific in sports that require large-muscle movement.

The part of the brain responsible for hand movements in writing is very close to the part that organizes the mouth and tongue around speech, and problems with articulation and handwriting often go together. Professionals who do not suffer from the problem are able to pronounce its name—the "articulatory-graphomotor" syndrome. One of the classic indicators is poor pencil grip; the child clutches the pencil at the base of her thumb or wraps it in a contorted fist, a habit that persists even after more mature neural circuits are in place. No wonder writing is laborious and boring. This child needs help from a specialist to help reprogram her handwriting from the beginning. A word processor may be a better solution, although some children who have motor programming difficulty are slower to master rapid keyboarding.

Still another difficulty that some children face is combining perceptual and motor tasks. Copying is particularly difficult for them. If your child has a copying problem, you should distinguish between near-point (close-up) and far-point (e.g., chalkboard) copying, which may operate independently of each other. Since it has been estimated that in some schools seven-year-olds spend as much as 20 percent of their time copying (horrors!), either problem calls for assistance. Using a marker, such as a card, can help a student keep the place for near-point copying. Saying the words to be copied and writing them from auditory rather than visual memory often provides an effective strategy. Helpful adults regard such breakdowns in normal skill development as real problems for the child, accept them without hurling accusations or put-downs, and work for solutions that keep some responsibility in the child's court. Variations in brain organization—not cussedness—are the most likely culprits.

A Crumpled Six-Year-Old

When our middle son, age six, was about halfway through the first-grade year, he began complaining of stomachaches every morning before school. After several weeks I became sufficiently concerned to take him to the pediatrician, who ruled out physical problems and suggested that this reaction might reflect some difficulty at school. When I quizzed Jeff, however, he stoutly claimed that everything was "okay."

The stomachaches vanished at the end of the year, but it took several years for the source of the problem to be unearthed. One evening, as the boys exchanged stories about their early school experiences, Jeff recreated a situation that, even in retrospect, made my own stomach queasy. Unknown to us, his "veteran" teacher was a leftover from a more unenlightened era. When her students trustingly offered up the smudged, uneven products of their attempts at writing, Miss S. would sneer and fling their papers, crumpled, into the wastebasket while the epithets "Messy! Disgusting!" rang through the classroom. When an earnestly clutched pencil slipped below or above the lines, she affixed a large red X to the spot. Only a few technicians made the grade; Jeff's gifts for invention, his creativity—all of his mental abilities—were ignored.

Even today when I think of that woman's assault on those tender intellects, I would like to wring her neck. With a six-year-old's implicit faith in teacher as God, our son took her judgment to heart and decided he was a failure in school. It took years to repair his self-confidence. Now a successful attorney, he still remembers the unrelenting misery of that year—which he was too innocent to complain about.

I wish now that I had possessed the confidence to unearth the truth and march on the principal's office. Parents can intervene if they suspect that a young child is being brutalized by inappropriate demands from a teacher. Insistence on neat, perfect penmanship from six-year-olds certainly falls into that category! I wish all adults could look first at the product of the child's mind, and only secondarily at the output from his fingers.

SPELLING
When a Fish Is a GHOTI

Spelling our language presents inherent difficulties. Although our alphabet contains only twenty-six letters, we use some forty different sounds in speaking; thus some letters must do double or even triple duty. Children who are poor spellers might be delighted to learn that a computer, programmed with all known spelling rules, could score only 50 percent on a standard spelling test! The inconsistencies are illustrated by George Bernard Shaw's example of spelling the word "fish" as "ghoti." How? Take *gh* as in "rough," *o* as in "women," and *ti* as in "nation." Don't ask why some kids have trouble spelling.

As in reading, there are two basic ways to approach spelling. One is through visual analysis and memory, which is needed for irregular words such as "says" or "could"; the other is through auditory analysis, phonics, and a knowledge of the basic rules of English orthography (spelling). Knowing phonic and basic spelling rules (change the *y* to *i* before adding a suffix beginning with a vowel, *i* before *e* except after *c,* etc.) can take care of about 80 percent of the words that children need to spell if, unlike the computer, they have mental structures for writing real language. Yet most top-notch spellers also have a good visual memory for verbal symbols. When in doubt about how to spell a word, do you write several versions in the margin and then use your visual memory to choose one? Some children lack that equipment, and as a result spelling is difficult for them. This ability is located separately in the brain from visual memory for places and things—at which poor spellers are often very adept.

How They Learn to Spell

The natural progression in spelling is opposite from that in reading, but good spelling instruction that focuses on the basic rules of our language helps children decode words more easily. Although young children may try to reproduce a visual icon such as STOP when they want to write a story, they first tend to spell mainly with sounds. As maturation speeds the interchange of messages between the visual and verbal areas of the brain, sight and sound are integrated. Simply, children learn to spell first by careful listening to the sound patterns in words. Then they master word parts from systematic instruction, by writing, and by looking at words many times in books. Since children with immature phonemic analysis skills (see chapter 9) are often unmotivated readers and writers, disuse of visual-verbal memory circuits compounds their problem.

Some good readers, too, have trouble with spelling. This apparent inconsistency can be explained by the fact that reading is a recognition skill; the printed words are the clues. Spelling, on the other hand, demands pulling something out of memory with no visual cues. When you write those words in the margin, you make the job easier by changing it from recall to recognition memory. See how specific these abilities are? The first step in trying to help is getting the child involved in solving the rule mystery.

Rule Detectives

Traditional approaches to spelling have settled for rote-level drills such as writing a word ten or twenty times, hoping to fix it permanently in the mind. Research has shown that writing the word correctly two or three times works, whereas more repetitions tend to be less effective and certainly more boring. Writing a spelling word works better if the child spells or says the sounds out loud while writing each letter and does not practice an incorrect version as a result of copying it inaccurately in the first place.

In another drill format, students are given a list of unrelated words at the beginning of the week for a spelling test on Friday. Unfortunately, these words are often learned without meaningful context, and the students—after getting them right on the test—turn around and misspell the same words in their writing. Current research suggests that there are better ways of learning to spell. Even if your child's school is still stuck with these outdated methods, you can help at home with more current techniques.

The first thing to check is whether your child can easily read all the words on the spelling list. If not, it is bad teaching practice to give him these words to spell in the first place. Next, focus on groups of words that have similar spelling patterns. Good spelling instruction teaches directly and has children practice spelling principles such as syllable patterns ("tion" as in "vacation"; "ough" as in "rough") and orthographic rules (bat + ing = batting because the consonant is doubled before adding an ending that begins with a vowel). Schoolchildren must absorb and generalize rules that govern spelling patterns just as two-year-olds learn the rules of language. Both must observe and use many individual examples before internalizing them into rules.

When children learn the rules, they remember them even better if they do some of the detective work. For example, I have endlessly taught first graders about the "silent *e*" at the end of a word, making the vowel "say its name." Sometimes I feel like bashing my head against the chalkboard when each class keeps forgetting it. Are these children stupid? Not at all. I have inadvertently encouraged them to remain passive while I tried to do all the work! Now we know that the teacher's job is to get the children to analyze and apply the rules:

ADULT: These words all have something about them that is the same. Can you see what it is?

CHILD [who may take some time and need guidance to come up with this generalization]: They all have an *e* at the end.

ADULT: I wonder if we can find out some rule about what that *e* is doing to the other vowel in the word. . . . [and so on].

Most children are not ready for this abstract type of rule generalization until they are at least seven, and many still need a lot of help even then. As with all learning, however, getting the child to be the active thinker should be our goal. If you start by pushing words in, don't be surprised if you end up with a passive child who regards correct spelling as something for which others are responsible.

Careful Listeners: Good Spellers

The most fundamental skill for spelling is the same phonemic awareness encountered in the last chapter—the ability to discriminate and order the sounds of oral language. Children who have inadequate early experiences in careful listening, including those who suffered hearing loss from ear infections, may have difficulty with spelling. Check back for suggestions on building these important skills.

"Wnsupnatim Thr Wz a Monstr"

I often get a shock these days when I walk into the early classes at our school. Among whirlwinds of active learning there is always a group of children bent earnestly over paper and pencil, writing original stories.

THE HURT
Oh, oh, oh, it hurts.
My dad fixed it.
Now it does not hurt.

(Age 6)

They rarely ask how to spell the words, and they are so excited over their creations that they clamor to read them out loud to the class. But many of these five- and six-year-olds can't read yet! What is going on?

"Developmental" spelling, in which young children are encouraged to write stories using the letter sounds they know—without hassling them over perfecting the spelling first—is based on research showing that this is the natural progression of children's spelling acquisition. No one is pushed, but most children are eager to try, even if it is with "scribble writing." First "words" are usually single letters or jumbled combinations, but it is astonishing how quickly sounds and the rules are mastered by most youngsters. Emphasis is on written language as communication. Gradually the child moves toward the correct form. A typical progression for developing the spelling of the word

My puppet is a princess.
She is pretty because
she has long hair.
She has new slippers.
They don't fit.

(Age 5)

"liked" went like this in a single year: "L-LT-LKT-LAKT-LOKT-LIKT-LIKD-LIKED."

A program like this is highly motivating and gets children to focus on accuracy and order of sounds in words. It is also an excellent diagnostic indicator of just how much phonemic awareness a child has mastered and gives a clear indication of who needs some extra help in this area. Most children gradually make the transition into standard spelling, but some need extra instruction in hearing the sounds accurately in order and re-producing them on a page. Direct teaching of letter sounds and exposure to lots of common word parts, language experience charts, or "big books" should also be part of this introduction to the spelling process.

By age seven most children should be making the transition into standard spelling with an increased emphasis on accuracy, although they will still make mistakes on more difficult words. Those who lag behind should continue to receive special attention, as they are also very likely to be experiencing problems with reading.

This system can also be used at home *if* a child around age five wants to write. The most important hurdle to get by is worrying about whether a word is "right." If the child knows what it says, it is right! Do not crush enthusiasm by insisting that every word be spelled cor-rectly at first. Say to the child, "Let's listen to the sounds in your word. What sound do you think comes first? Do you know which letter makes that sound?" Of course, no wise parent would force this activity and create negative connections for future learning.

Poor Spellers

Most people are not aware that dyslexia in bright youngsters does not always show up as a reading problem but as difficulty with spelling and writing. Poor spellers may also have been taught incorrectly before their brains were ready—or interested—in making sense out of letter patterns. Spelling remains an irritation to them. When they write they make dozens of "dumb" mistakes and don't seem to care about cor-recting them. Sometimes it seems as if they have given up completely.

Caution!

Some children need much more direct teaching from the beginning if they are to learn to spell and write. Youngsters with any signs of dyslexia should have skilled instruction with multisensory teaching of letter shapes, sounds, and spelling patterns. If your child's school does not provide it and your six-year-old is floundering, seek special help.

Severe spelling problems are hard to cure. Schools can work to prevent them by intervening early and using systematic teaching of spelling patterns and rules while still encouraging the child's enthusiasm for free writing. Here are some ideas for helping your child at home.

Helping the Poor Speller

Things that don't work:
 • Expecting that your child doesn't need to spell because he will have a word processor. Not only do you need a certain level of skill before you can even use one, but also the process of learning the fundamental rules of orthography improves reading skill and the ability to work with abstract rule systems, which will be important in math, science, and foreign language learning later on.
 • Assuming that spelling ability is a sign of overall intelligence. It isn't.
 • Shouting at or berating the child for making errors.
 • Telling a young child to "look it up in the dictionary." Poor spellers often have a terrible problem with alphabetical order.
 • Drilling in only one sensory modality (i.e., parent says word out loud and child spells word out loud, *or* child copies list of words without saying them out loud).
 • Insisting on perfection in spontaneous writing. This has the unfortunate side effect of corking up written expression.
 • Putting emphasis on mechanics instead of the quality of the child's thought.

Things that might work:

- Praising the child's good ideas before starting to correct errors.
- Looking for patterns and rules in spelling. A source of useful materials is given in the bibliography.
- Using visual analysis: "Is it 'bad' or 'bed'? How are 'chip' and 'check' alike? Different?"
- Encouraging auditory analysis by saying the sounds in order *before, during, and after writing the word.*
- Encouraging visual memory with this six-step procedure:

  1. Examine the word for any recognizable parts (roots, suffixes, prefixes). Relate letter patterns to words already known.
  2. Cover the word.
  3. Visualize the word. Imagine writing on a chalkboard in colored chalk or on a big piece of white paper with crayons.
  4. Ask the child to say the sounds, not the letters, out loud while writing the word. If an error occurs, stop immediately. Don't practice wrong spellings.
  5. Have the child check the spelling.
  6. Repeat steps 2 through 5 several times.

- Get the senses of touch and movement involved in spelling by writing the word on a rough surface with a finger.
- Play spelling games. Commercial games and computer software are available, and old standards such as Anagrams, Hangman, and Ghost get everyone involved.
- To help children with auditory analysis, play with rhyming, tongue twisters, pig Latin, or Hinky Pinky.
- Older students can and should use a dictionary and/or a word processor that has a spell-checker. Get them a "poor speller's dictionary" that helps them find words.
- Be wary of French with its irregular spelling patterns, which often cause horrendous problems for poor spellers. Spanish or Italian are more orthographically regular modern languages.

Entymology Etymology

This week I wandered into a classroom and found a teacher and a six-year-old bent over a pile of large, colorful pictures of different types of insects. The little girl was sorting the pictures into piles according to categories she had selected. She first made two piles: "insects that suck blood and ones that don't," then she resorted them into "with and without wings," and then "skinny and fat." As I watched her analyzing and categorizing visual details, I suddenly realized this child was building skills for spelling. As with letter patterns in words, she was learning to pick out, classify, and derive rules from visual details. Parents who encourage this kind of active perceptual learning are laying a far better foundation for intelligent spelling than those who encourage passive copying.

WRITING

The Topmost Skill Starts at Home

Having to express ideas in writing is the final test of a child's background of thought and language. A writer must: (1) understand and pull together ideas or information; (2) formulate an original statement; (3) find the right words; (4) get them in order; (5) call up the mechanical skills while holding the ideas in working memory long enough to (6) get them down on paper. A child's ability to perform this sophisticated exercise depends on three abilities: comprehension of ideas, expressive language, and facility with mechanics. If you have read the preceding chapters of this book, you know that parents have a major role in the development of all three.

Children first begin to write stories about their own experiences. Later they tackle imaginative stories, poetry, and "expository writing"—reports, essays, and research papers. Only a few master formulating an original thesis statement and supporting it with research, or writing satire, drama, or short stories. Children who have been surrounded by reading, storytelling, and involvement in conversation with adults have a head start, but many teachers are concerned that students' level of language use overall is declining. A child who cannot easily express ideas when speaking is almost sure to have trouble when trying to write them down. No amount of teaching can make up for an impoverished language environment!

Too Much Lost Time?

Toni was a skinny little eight-year-old who came closer to making me cry than any child I've worked with. Her first six years of life had been shaken by her mother's serious illness and frequent hospitalizations, and eventual death. Her father, sincerely concerned about the child, was so personally overwhelmed that most of Toni's upbringing had been taken over by housekeepers. Although competent, they had done little talking or reading with her. I worked with Toni one summer because her teachers were worried about her reading comprehension and appalled by her writing; although her handwriting was fine and she had learned to sound out and spell words, she simply couldn't write anything original. A psychologist had suggested that she might be blocking overwhelmingly painful emotions, which would not have been too surprising!

As I had anticipated, Toni was intrigued by my suggestion that she tell a story while I typed it. We settled ourselves in front of the computer keyboard and I asked the standard question, "What would you like to 'write' about?" Instead of the usual barrage of words and ideas, silence reigned. Toni stared helplessly up at me. "Would you like to make up a story?" I prodded.

Large eyes searched my face. "How?" she asked.

As the summer wore on, I became more painfully aware of the gaps in Toni's learning. She had been taught the mechanics at school, but the purpose, the structure, and the intimacy of written language had been left out of the package. We worked many hours that summer, but I knew that one thing was missing; I could never provide those lost years of snuggly story times. Is it too late? Toni's dad and new stepmother are trying hard; perhaps she may yet be able to write a happy ending.

Encouraging Children to Write

Don't lose time for your child's learning if you can help it. Here are some suggestions for starters:

• Read aloud on a regular basis, even with older children. Delve into poetry, literature, essays, and good journalism. Don't be afraid to broaden your own tastes. Your librarian can advise you. Do not waste time on watered-down versions of classics that use "pop" language. You'll be surprised by how much children can understand and enjoy (even Shakespeare) if it is read to them dramatically in a pleasurable atmosphere. Look for books that have good language use, lots of interesting and challenging vocabulary words, and varied sentence structures as well as a good story that has some "meat" to it to promote discussion.

• Encourage clear expression of ideas at all ages. After you read a story, ask, "Can you tell me what was important in the story? How would you put Peter's feelings into your own words?" Practice describing pictures and daily events. Check for more suggestions in chapter 7.

• Write notes and letters to your child. When he is old enough, encourage him to write back—first with pictures and scribbles, then with words. Don't criticize. Enjoy the message.

• Create a writing environment. Equip a "writing table" with lots of paper (lined and unlined), pencils, felt-tip pens, crayons, a stapler, wallpaper samples and cardboard for book covers, a hole-puncher, scissors, paste, a wastebasket, and a bulletin board. Encourage ideas by clipping pictures from magazines, cartoons, or items from newspapers. Get excited over any writing that is produced. Praise your child for wanting to exercise his creativity.

• Get a couple of clipboards and take your child outside to write down names of things that you see on your walk. When you come in, your child may want to use these words to tell a story that you can write down and reread.

• If your child is struggling for a topic to write about, suggest starting with an experience that is personal and meaningful. Drawing a picture or brainstorming works for some. Try Rico's technique of "writing the natural way" (to be described shortly).

• To develop a story starter, brainstorm answers to the key "W" questions: Who, what, when, where, why (e.g., a brown dog—flies— in the future—to Mars—to see if there are any dogs there and what they're like). Once begun, the story may take off by itself.

• Suggest that the child use a tape recorder to talk about the topic, and then write down the ideas after the tape is played back.

• Always have a dictionary and thesaurus (synonym dictionary) on hand. Both are available in editions for younger or older children. A thesaurus is particularly useful for building vocabulary. A child can use it to learn new words and "dress up" the language in his writing.

• A child's vocabulary knowledge is a huge factor in school success and is directly related to the quality and variety of words used in the home. Children learn words best by having them explained. Encourage your child to ask you about any word she doesn't understand.

• Sometimes children try to use fancy words they don't under-stand—and end up sounding ridiculous. Help them with new words by explaining their meaning and showing how they sound in sentences.

• Develop the habit of mutual storytelling. Tell a round-robin story with all the family members. Use interesting words. Accept the child's ideas and have fun. You don't have to be a teacher. Enjoy!

Writers Need Readers

Personal journals can "turn on" a child of almost any age to writing, once the language and thinking foundations are in place. Some preschools have initiated a delightful exchange in which a child carries the journal between school and home. There is no pressure, because parents and teacher do the actual writing. If you and your child's school are interested, here's how it works:

Staple several pieces of unlined paper together into a book. Once a week or so, help your child choose a topic, draw a picture, and dictate a language experience story following the guidelines in chapter 9. Ask the teacher if she would be willing to let the child share it with her, and then dictate one at school, too. Some topics for starters can be: "Friends at Home, Friends at School"; or "My Birthday at Home, My Birthday at School." Preschool teachers and parents who have used this idea are enthusiastic, and children love to feel that their own words and ideas are important.

Play at School

I like to play in the sandbox. I like to play with the thing you put the sand in and then it all comes out.

Play at Home

I LIKE TO PLAY ON OUR SWING SET WHEN I AM AT HOME. I LIKE TO SIT ON THE TOP.

Journals are effective tools for developing writing at any age. One unusually persuasive mother, concerned that her daughters' school was neglecting writing in the primary grades, instituted a lasting tradition of journal writing on their frequent family trips. Every morning after breakfast, wherever they are traveling, the whole family sits down to write in their journals (spiral notebooks). A child too young to write draws a picture. Even Dad, who had to be cajoled mightily at first, admits that he began to enjoy this time for reflection, and he loved hearing the different perspectives each family member brought to a situation. Now that the girls are adults, they still reread these often hilarious records of their times together and are convinced that the effort was worthwhile.

Cluttered Thinking = Cluttered Writing

Output problems, covered in chapter 5, afflict many reluctant writers. These children need organizational aids, such as sentence and paragraph frames used by writing teachers, to make their ideas clear—even to themselves. A simple frame for an expository paragraph contains: (1) a topic sentence; (2) three main points; (3) a conclusion. Then the student can go back and add supporting details. Starting with a small, manageable task is important.

Children who have avoided practice or who have a disability in writing often lack automatic use of the mechanics, a deficit that impinges on expressing even the best ideas. I have often seen a child get a fantastic thought, start to write it down, then get trapped by some mechanical problem. By the time she returns to her idea, it has fallen out of her head. Reread the section on automaticity in chapter 5 if you want to understand this issue better.

Likewise, parents and teachers wail, "He spelled it perfectly on the weekly test and then turned right around and misspelled it in his report. Careless!!" Not necessarily. Stop and think for a minute about the demands on working memory in a spelling test—where all attention and higher-level reasoning is focused on the words alone. Then compare these demands with paragraph writing, when higher brain centers must focus on ideas. This child may not be purposely careless; he simply can't think about spelling, content, and organization all at the same time. In addition to continuing to work for automaticity in basic skills, here are four constructive approaches for such problems.

1. Encourage children to get their ideas down in a *first draft* without emphasizing mechanics. "First draft" writing is an often-neglected process that forces the writer to discover what he really knows (and doesn't know) about the topic and to organize and clarify ideas. Allow the child enough time to tidy up the work with successive drafts and produce a piece of writing of which he can be proud.

2. For older children who have adequate keyboarding skills, a word processor may increase fluency, organization, and accuracy. Software for developing essays or paragraphs may provide an organizational structure. Young children, however, should start with the physical, multisensory experience of feeling, moving, seeing, and hearing the sounds in the words as they write.

3. For any writer whose thinking style does not naturally organize ideas into a logical, related sequence, various kinds of "mind maps" as sampled in chapter 6 (there are an endless variety) can become routes to clarity. Most schools are now teaching these techniques; encourage your child to use them.

4. Parents can serve as proofreaders for students who have problems with mechanics. Some suggestions follow for ways to assist without taking over the job.

Helping Your Child Proofread

• Always start by finding something to praise at the beginning and the end of the session. Be sure to show more interest in the ideas being expressed than in the handwriting, spelling, and punctuation. Then offer to help polish the work so it will be "even better."

• Encourage the author to make the corrections. You might develop a system of making marks in the margin that indicate a certain type of error in a line (e.g., "sp" for spelling, "p" for punctuation). Work with the child to help him find the error and correct it.

• If the child has trouble with wording, have him read it out loud to see how it sounds. If he thinks it sounds fine, suggest another form. Have him listen to the difference. Suggest reading it into a tape recorder. Play it back. How does that sound?

• If you are unsure of writing rules, ask the school or a bookstore for a style manual. Your interest in informing yourself will be a powerful example for your child. Never be embarrassed about seeming "ignorant." Figuring out the rules together will make them "stick" for both of you.

• Remember that good writers make many drafts before they are satisfied. An original draft must "become messy before it becomes clear."

Electronic Secretaries

Typing words into a computer's memory eliminates many of the demands on the human brain that make writing difficult for some people, and leaves the working memory free to organize ideas and construct sentences. Spell-checkers that force the child to check and respell the words are powerful inducements to first-round accuracy and also teach the correct patterns. Computer printouts look wonderful, a real blessing for a child whose own handwriting creates instant nausea in readers. The pride children feel spurs them on to correcting and rewriting, and the computer frees them from laboriously having to recopy each corrected draft.

A question still exists about when children should learn touch typing (keyboarding). If they begin with "hunt and peck," they program an inefficient method into their neural circuits (some skilled hunt-and-peckers disagree). Vision is a dominant sense, and searching for keys visually not only is slower but leaves less cortical energy available than do automatic motor patterns such as touch. Some educators have suggested that even six-year-olds can learn keyboarding skills, but most educators feel that fourth grade is the earliest time children have the motor control and motivation to learn keyboarding without too much fuss. In many schools, it is even later—around sixth or seventh grade. I wish we had definitive research on this issue as computers become fixtures in most classrooms.

Bringing More of the Brain into Writing

Some people write better when they combine language with the visual, holistic approaches associated with right-hemisphere processing. One interesting technique encourages children of all ages to start writing by drawing pictures and describing them. This sparks ideas and forces some preliminary organization. It is especially effective with a young child who is having trouble finding something to write about or with an older one whose learning style tends to be more visual than auditory-verbal.

Gabrielle Rico is a brilliant writing teacher who believes her technique, "Writing the Natural Way," brings visual creativity into the

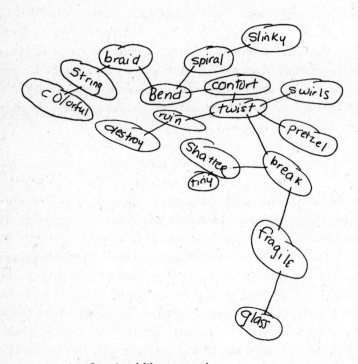

It twisted like a pretzel,
Broke like china.
It swirled into many colors,
Shattered, as of fragile glass,
Was contorted, then destroyed.
With the wind, the shattered pieces
Blew into the sunset.

(Age 13)

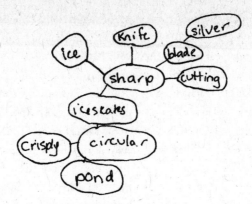

Circling around the pond, cutting crisply into the ice with its silver blades. The sharp blades of the ice skates are like knives cutting steel. Its circular pattern steadily follows the same pace until the blades hit the ice once again. *(Age 13)*

process. She has achieved impressive results by using imagery and free association with adult writers who were "blocked." Here's the way Rico's system works: A web of personally associated words is developed for one special word or phrase; the writer relaxes, lets his mind come up with connections, and then "mind-maps" the ideas around the kernel idea. Once the visual outline is created, writing begins immediately; the goal is to let ideas flow rather than to worry about form or even content. I have seen extraordinary results from adults trying this system for the first time and was anxious to try it with some students. I have included some examples from thirteen-year-olds who thought they "couldn't write." The core words here are "bend" and "sharp."

A parent and a child can try this system together. If you can free your mind from remnants of copybook experience, you may be astonished at your own networks of creativity!

If you recall the importance of appealing to emotional centers in the brain, you will see one possible explanation for the success of a method called "process writing," which gets children willingly to write, rewrite, and polish as many as six or seven drafts. An integral part of the process is having the young authors read their writing to the teacher or other students in the class for suggestions. One parent whose child was taught by this approach told me that her son was transformed in one year from a child who hated writing to a budding author who now keeps a daily journal *because he enjoys it!* Of course, it is also important to teach children of this age how to write different types of expository text as well as how to write creatively. Specific rules can help students put together a coherent, logical essay or factual report. We now know that all these different forms must be read, modeled, and taught. You can encourage your child's school to make writing a central part of the curriculum rather than a stepchild. In an era when people read less and view more, inadequate writing instruction cheats every student and may ultimately rob us all of our cultural voice.

A Writer's Voice

To write well, children must learn to carry on a personal conversation inside their own heads. Good writing has a unique voice that is different from "talk written down." The only way to pick it up is from reading and listening to quality writing. To illustrate how parents give children a chance to develop a "writer's voice," author Eudora Welty recalled the wealth of language and the love of books with which she was surrounded during her childhood. Immersed in their sound, she found her special "writer's voice," which was a constant guide. I often worry that writers' voices are becoming scarce commodities as I work with youngsters who lack even a basic sense of what sounds good on paper.

Proficiency and pleasure in reading and writing evolve from the foundations of listening and speaking. Whatever your child's age, don't miss the opportunity to enjoy poetry, essays, opinion pieces, humor, drama, and good literature together. Expand everyone's vocabulary by noticing and using interesting words. Make writing a part of everyday life—a lively, personal mental adventure. It is never too late to settle down together and venture into the treasure-house of the literate mind.

Chapter 11

Parts into Wholes: Building Math and Science Skills

Recently I met my neighbor Steve in the checkout line of our local supermarket. Enthroned in his cart, four-year-old Deborah joyously clutched a new workbook filled with number facts and simple equations. Knowing my interest in math learning, Steve was delighted to point out that he was getting his daughter off to a good start. I wanted to share his enthusiasm, but I hope after he reads this chapter he will realize that the supermarket contains raw material infinitely more important to Deborah's future math ability than her new workbook.

Likewise, a disturbing experience when I was observing a seventh grade pre-algebra class showed that even some teachers need to bone up on current research about mathematics learning. Mr. S., a veteran teacher, wrote a problem on the board and asked for volunteers to solve it. Since I had already noticed that he tended, doubtless without realizing it, to call on boys more often than girls, I was pleased to see him recognize Marla. An insecure but highly motivated math student, Marla started toward the board, venturing, "I'm not sure, but I'll try."

"I don't want TRY!" roared Mr. S. "Who knows how to do this problem?"

Ouch!

Mathematics causes parents more anxiety than any other school subject. It is the only area of the curriculum with an identifiable "phobia" attached to it. Math homework takes the prize as a cause of family shouting matches and parental feelings of inadequacy. Likewise, science, for many of us, meant boring memorization of confusing terms and symbols, and it is still poorly taught in many schools. What can be done to demystify these topics of ever-increasing importance in our technological world? How can parents help when they feel less than competent? What do they need to know to intervene in a school like Marla's, which is seriously behind the times? Good news! Even if you can't compute the Pythagorean theorem, calculate when two airplanes will meet over Chicago, or remember the table of chemical elements, you can help your child build a foundation for excellence. Understanding the two ways in which the brain processes technical information is the key.

RULES VS. REASONS

Most people think of math as arithmetic, the study of numbers, and the rules or operations such as addition and multiplication that we use to manipulate them. Guess again! Mathematics is a much greater science of relationships, which uses numerical symbols to describe fundamental truths about our universe. Science likewise is much more concerned with understanding relationships than in manipulating data. The numbers or symbols on a page represent powerful abstract concepts—but they are rooted in concrete experience. Mathematicians and scientists of all ages begin by asking questions about the world: soap bubbles, pendulums, swings, pretzels, patterns of spider webs, springs, seashells, ants, stars, and the leaves on tree branches are all raw material for brilliant minds.

For success in math, the child must develop two separate abilities that are linked throughout the study of arithmetic, algebra, geometry, statistics, trigonometry, and calculus. First and probably most important is the ability to comprehend relationships, to reason abstractly, and to solve problems. "Spatial-temporal" thinking, or the ability to mentally manipulate relationships, such as mass and velocity, in time and space is a critical component. Some aspects of computer science, such as the envisioning of a new way to organize an Internet system or design a new application, also fall into this category, as do many aspects of physics, biology, and the other sciences. The other side is the ability to follow the rules, to analyze, and to compute accurately; to observe carefully, form hypotheses (educated guesses), and sustain an orderly line in problem-solving.

Recent research suggests that these abilities are mediated by different cortical networks. Areas in the right hemisphere, good at seeing the whole puzzle, contribute much of the understanding of the *reasons*—the big, global concepts and observations that are rooted in visual-spatial processing. Left-hemisphere areas, on the other hand, enjoy following rules—analyzing the pieces, solving problems in an orderly manner, and understanding the language, or sequence, of math, of an experiment, and of computers. Studies show that even such similar skills as multiplying and subtracting are located in slightly different parts of the brain. This sounds like a pretty complicated business, especially since all these networks must learn to work together efficiently. In this chapter we will look at some examples of how these thinking processes develop, and discuss specific steps that parents and teachers can take to ensure that all parts of the child's brain are ready to join up for the demands of a technological world.

FINDING THE ROOTS OF MATH AND SCIENCE
Active Explorers

What can we learn from thirty-two boys and girls, ages two to three and a half, who are allowed to explore a room in a museum or follow a route through a specially designed playhouse, about the way children develop these skills? Some provocative findings came from a study that measured these youngsters' exploratory behavior and their visual-spatial abilities, or how well they could relate their own bodies to objects outside themselves. The children who explored more actively proved significantly better when they had to reverse their path back through the playhouse; their "cognitive mapping abilities" were superior to those of children who were passive explorers or who depended on a parent to guide them. Researchers were surprised that children this young could hold a mental image of the route they had taken, apparently by associating it with their own body movements. The key was not how much movement they made, but *whether the children themselves were the initiators*. This study is one of many showing a link between early behavior patterns and later ability with spatial relationships, one of the best predictors of math, physics, and engineering aptitude.

Reasoning Spatially

There are practical reasons why a child's active physical exploration builds spatial skills. Concepts of the physical universe that we as adults carry around in our brains depend on getting the "feel" of objects and their relationships in space, distance, quantity, and direction. Awareness of time (temporal) relationships may also be gained in the same way. For example, if you were asked to describe the route from your house to your office, you would probably use both your visual "mind's eye" and some slight body or head movements to get the directions right and recall whether you pass the drugstore before or after the park. Similarly, if you are asked to subtract 57 from 321 in your head, you may employ similar strategies to form a visual image, borrow, subtract down, go back up to the 10s column, go down, and then back up again, although some mathematicians have such a good feel for numbers that they get the answer in quicker ways (e.g., subtract 57 from 100 and add 221 or, minus 21 to 300, then minus 36). An individual who has trouble with spatial relationships may find mental computation very trying.

Children in school who have a poor sense of spatial relationships for symbols have difficulty with place value, directionality (subtract down, but multiply up), fractions (which numeral is on top and which is on the bottom?), estimating (is it higher or lower?), and geometrical problems, and may be baffled by charts, graphs, and maps. Later they may falter on abstract relationships in algebra, trigonometry, physics, biology, or other sciences.

Some people's brains simply seem better attuned to this kind of reasoning from the beginning. Moreover, there are many different types of "spatial skills." Dyslexic individuals may excel at some spatial reasoning—possibly because their brains are predisposed to trade off competence in left-hemisphere analytic and language areas for power in the right side—but have difficulty with place value or writing out the symbols in a sequential, linear equation.

It's worth paying attention to spatial skills, and environments make a difference. For young children, toys and other experiences that don't always seem to be directly related to math and science are far more important than early "learning" software, workbooks, and other commercial programs that try to push elementary school math down onto younger children. Large blocks, mechanical building toys, and age-appropriate carpentry tools are effective as are sand, clay, and water play. A child building with wooden unit blocks, boxes, spools, or other objects that have shapes of varying sizes is also building the concept of *seriation*, the ability to make a "stairway" out of graduated-size objects, showing understanding that a block, or number, can be bigger than one neighbor and smaller than the other—all at the same time. This seemingly simple—but actually very abstract—idea is usually not fully mastered until after age five or so, yet is prerequisite to a true understanding of counting.

Feeling and figuring out how parts go together help budding reasoning abilities. A child measuring a rug by using units of interlocking cubes, assembling a picture from pattern blocks, or taking apart a castoff clock or radio with a screwdriver is learning more "basics" than one who is doing pagefuls of sums. Never underestimate the value of "junk" as raw material for learning.

Children need to climb, crawl through things, and explore new paths, firming up notions of direction and relationships in space and distance by physical means. Making mud pies, believe it or not, is a readiness activity for algebra—the science of describing relationships of quantity. Measuring or comparing distances and sizes of objects is also important. During school years, team sports encourage an understanding of position on a field and the relative movement of players. Remember once more that the child's active physical involvement, linking subcortical and motor areas with higher reasoning powers, is paramount. For most of us, learning comes first from doing it, not from watching it happen.

A SAMPLING OF PLAY ACTIVITIES FOR BUDDING MATHEMATICAL BRAINS

- "Feely"box: Cut holes in opposite sides of a cardboard box and place objects of different shapes inside; cover the box so the child can't see the objects and ask if he can tell what they are by feeling with both hands. See if he can count the number of objects inside.
- Counters: Small objects such as poker chips, beans, or anything else to count, arranged in symmetrical patterns. Take away or add items and count the result. Even plastic utensils can provide a math lesson while you await your food in a restaurant.
- Unit blocks: Count, measure, make patterns, make symmetrical structures, follow a sequential pattern (e.g., two short, one long, two short, etc.)
- Cards with numbers or spots: Play games such as "War" or "Go Fish." Arrange cards in numerical order.
- Dough pounded or rolled into different shapes, cut in halves, quarters, etc.
- Board games and dice: Counting spaces, learning which is "more," following a sequence and rules.
- Toys that snap together to make different sizes or patterns: cubes, train tracks, beads.
- Sorting, classifying: Almost anything can be sorted and classified, from butterflies to rocks to socks to pattern blocks. Color, shape, size, or any

other attribute can become the basis for a category: "small," "pink," "funny-looking," "soft," "not round," and so on.
- Toy or real clocks—the ones with faces and hands that the child can manipulate.

Are Girls Different?

Some theorists have suggested that the different toys and play activities of boys and girls may explain why boys invariably score better on certain spatial relationship tests than do girls. One study showed that girls who later excelled in math and science had been allowed to explore actively and solve problems themselves, and to play with "boys'" toys as well as with more traditional female ones. Both boys and girls who had low scores were more passive in play activities and tended to be dependent on their parents.

Parental expectations that girls will have trouble with math and science tend to be a self-fulfilling prophecy. The behavior of teachers, such as Mr. S. at the beginning of this chapter, can also have a profound effect in crushing or encouraging girls' learning. Current studies show that teachers who encouage students to try even though they don't know the answer, and who regard mistakes as good opportunities for learning, get the best results from everyone. Some studies have shown that girls approach math more positively when they can work together in collaborative groups and are encouraged to verbalize concepts and processes.

When Steve takes Deborah home, will she be encouraged to sit quietly with her new workbook or to explore and play actively? Does she always ride in the shopping cart or sometimes navigate the grocery aisles herself? Does Steve ever ask her to get a box of cereal or a certain number of apples and then find her way back? These challenges are more important at age four than learning to write numerals or recite the answer to $2 + 3$.

SKILLS THAT AREN'T IN THE BOOK

Authors of textbooks try hard to convey all the basic skills that will produce good math and science students, but they get frustrated because they know that some of the most important abilities resist encapsulation on the printed page. These are the attitudes and problem-solving skills that children have developed before they march, creep, or get dragged through the classroom door on the first day of school.

Taking a Risk

Several years ago a worried father came to me after a parents' workshop at a school in an affluent neighborhood. The discussion that evening had focused on problem-solving skills and the fact that children who learn to meet challenges and develop strategies are better students. As I often do, I had used the example of climbing trees as one natural way to develop these skills as well as those of relative distances, spatial-temporal relationships, cause and effect, and other important concepts. This dad was worried about his daughters' problems in math. "They've never climbed trees," he lamented. Then his face brightened. "I'm going to buy some trees tomorrow!"

What do you do when you don't know what to do? These are problem-solving skills, the crux of scientific and mathematical thinking and the key to success in an information age. Yet these capacities are at risk in a childhood of electronically programmed challenge that can be turned off if they start to feel the slightest bit "hard." Students at all grade levels now seem to have increasing difficulty figuring out what to do when confronted with a math problem, even when they are adept at subtraction, division, and other types of computation. They have trouble developing strategies to solve story problems. Science teachers—who now understand that hands-on problem-solving should be their goal—also find too many students who become frustrated if they can't memorize a simple answer. Dutifully finding the "right" answers no longer works in our increasingly complex world. The human brain must think up the problems, try new solutions, and approach questions from different angles. It is important to learn the rules, but we must teach our children to move beyond the "one right answer" mentality. For example, good mathematicians frequently estimate (primarily a right-hemisphere skill) to anticipate or check the accuracy of an answer. Good scientists are noted for their ability to risk a "guess" (hypothesis) that links previously untested relationships and that may turn out to be wrong. Some children are such reluctant problem-solvers or so fearful of making a mistake, however, that they are unable to estimate or form a hypothesis.

HELPING CHILDREN SOLVE PROBLEMS

1. Encourage questions, preferably ones to which *you* don't know the answer. ("I'm not sure why leaves have different shapes—let's collect some and try to figure out some reasons.")

2. Ask open-ended questions and welcome innovative responses. ("What do you think these woods will look like a hundred years from now?" "What would children be like if there weren't any schools and everyone stayed home and learned from a computer?")

3. Encourage divergent approaches to everyday situations, within reason. (If the child can think of a reason for setting the table in a new and different way, why not?)

4. Help your child to tolerate some uncertainty—effective thinkers can delay the best solution to a problem until they have tried out several hypotheses.

5. Provide toys and games that encourage play that the youngster creates himself; praise and admire innovative uses of play, construction, or game materials.

6. Show your child how to estimate. ("You have nine pennies in your bank—that's close to a dime." "We have to drive 295 miles to grandmother's house—that's almost 300 miles.")

7. Practice thoughtful "guess and test." ("I'm not sure what will happen if we put lemonade in the Jell-O instead of water—let's guess some possibilities and then see what happens.")

8. Avoid using the words "right" and "wrong" unless a moral or safety issue is at stake; take time to listen to the child's ideas before passing judgment. Try out the phrase "That's an interesting idea/answer—tell me more/tell me how you got it."

9. Model adult problem-solving. ("This looks really hard, but I'll try some things and see if they work.")

10. Help your child feel secure enough to take sensible risks.

One study of school subjects found that children who tended to depend on an adult for guidance were particularly put off by math because it usually seems more confusing than other subjects at the beginning of a new topic. Children who were described as "mastery oriented," who felt capable of meeting a challenge, did much better.

Although some children come into the world with right hemispheres that are better equipped to master visual-spatial challenges, each has a level at which parents can help build a base of security for this important assignment.

The Magic Chalkboard of the Inner Eye

"Mary has 36 apples in a basket. She wants to put them into 4 equal bags. How many will be in each bag?"

The largest chalkboard in my classroom is an imaginary one that soon becomes familiar to children who come to me for help in math. Repeatedly I find that these youngsters lack another skill that can't be taught in books—visual imagery, the ability mentally to "see" something that is not actually in front of them. Not only do they have trouble with mental math calculations, they are also unable to create a visual representation of a word problem, to remember or relate the important elements. Instead of "seeing" Mary divide up her apples, they may take a chance and add 36 + 4. Often they do not remember the numbers in the problem.

When I teach these children, I put aside the textbooks and go back to the beginning—what does this *mean*? Our first job is to imagine Mary and talk about what she is doing. If the child is unable to visualize the situation, we may draw a picture of Mary, the apples, and the bags. Often we act out the problem first, using paper clips or chips as apples, getting the body involved in this important step.

Next we try to figure out a mathematical sentence (equation) to connect with our story. What is Mary's problem? How does she get the apples into the bags? Oh, she needs to *divide* the apples! Show me on your paper how we say that in math ($\div$ or $\sqrt{}$). And so on, slowly, until the equation is developed.

Once the facts and the process are understood, we go back to imagination. "What color is your chalkboard today?" I ask, as the child closes her eyes and selects from a delicious mental rainbow. "And what color is the chalk?" Then we "write" the equation in these wonderful colors, saying and imagining the numerals and the process. Repeated practice may form a habit that makes computation more manageable. The imaginary chalkboard with its vivid colors also helps children who have difficulty remembering the "facts": $8 \times 7 = 56$ written in the mind in blue, purple, green, and yellow sometimes sticks. Meanwhile, the emotional brain is really turned on by all that color!

When parents encourage their children to picture ideas mentally, they help visual imagery develop. After Deborah has explored the cereal aisle in the grocery store, Steve might devise a game in which they close their eyes and try to remember what it looked like. Where were the cornflakes on the shelf? What color was the box? Can they remember the picture or any of the numbers? Was the oatmeal above or below the Pop-Tarts? Now let's imagine a giraffe walking down the aisle. Let's put three children on his back. What do they look like? As long as the child is having fun, parents have many opportunities to help develop the "inner eye," a big part of the "big picture" of learning ability.

Concrete–Symbolic–Abstract

The ability to create and hold mental pictures is related to development of symbolic thinking. Remember the toddler who was talking to a pretend granddad on a toy telephone? Or knowing where the cookies are in the cupboard even though they are out of sight? He has mastered the first step in a natural progression from concrete to abstract thought.

In the growth of symbolic/abstract reasoning, the concrete building block is the foundation. Seeing and touching come first (three real cookies), then understanding that things (or pictures or numerals or words) can stand for other things (a "3" for the idea of three cookies). Only after these stages are mastered through many individual experiences and the accompanying brain maturation occurs can children start to move to abstract thought (x = 3).

Abstract thinking requires reasoning with symbols, or understanding that one symbol system (algebra, formulas for chemical reactions, or sentences) can stand for another (numerals, substances interacting, a simile). Since this type of reasoning isn't well developed in most people until at least their teen years, moving down a level on the hierarchy makes a problem easier. For example, dividing up real objects—counters, pennies, matchsticks—is a concrete task easily understood. If we make these objects "stand" for apples, we have entered the abstract-symbolic level. Likewise, to draw (symbol) Mary and the apples is difficult for little children, but it helps those who are teetering on the brink of abstract-symbolic thought. Creating graphs and charts to illustrate more complex problems accomplishes the same purpose, and I love to walk into a second grade and see a bar graph tallying class preferences in ice cream flavors or pets. The teacher may also be using computer software for such activities, but it is critical that real, hands-on tallying—counting and marking off a certain number of squares for each category—helps ground the symbols. The more channels through which experience comes in, and the more firsthand meaning it repre-

THE BUILDING BLOCKS OF THOUGHT

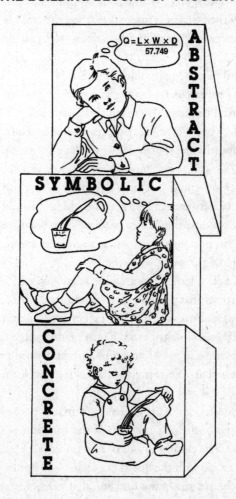

sents, the more likely it is to stick and provide a base for more advanced reasoning.

For fractions, endless pies can be divided—first, real ones with a knife, then paper pies or other shapes with scissors, then figures drawn on the real and imaginary chalkboards and images on the computer screen. Finally the concept is internalized, and the child is ready to use it for solving increasingly complex equations—with no pictures and no scissors!

If your child is having trouble with fractions, you may need to revert at least to paper cutouts and start working up—being careful to use mathematical language ("Let's cut this square in half. Now let's divide each half in two—how many pieces do you have now? [Four.] So each one is a fourth, one-fourth. How would you write that [one piece out of four]? We call these "fourths." Now show me three of them; three-fourths. How could you write a fraction to say "three-fourths?") Good computer software can help here, but things that can be seen and touched are the foundation. Later on these same techniques may help the student learn percentages, which are really just another way of expressing fractional parts of a whole.

Likewise, take a look at your child's science classes. Do they start with real questions that intrigue the children, and materials that they can understand and manipulate? It is tantamount to child abuse (and science abuse!) to teach science in the early grades with textbooks, having children memorize rules and terms without providing interesting firsthand experiments. Even high schoolers seem to learn best with a combination of real and virtual experience.

Young children can, with guidance, form a hypothesis and test it with rudimentary scientific methods if the question is one that intrigues them. Once during my days as a principal, a group of third graders came to me with the question of what soft drinks would do to their teeth. I figured this was a question that might interest everyone, so I posed it to a school assembly. Together we formed a hypothesis: "Lots of soft drinks will have a bad effect on children's teeth," and we developed a method to test it. Several first graders brought in second-hand teeth and we set up two experimental conditions: one group of teeth was submerged in a glass of water and the other in a glass containing a popular soft drink. The glasses were placed in an area where the children could view them every day, and it didn't take very long before changes in the soft-drink teeth began to show up. By the end of the experiment, the teeth in the water were the same as before, but the soft-drink-exposed ones had become soft and mushy. ("Oh, YUCK!") Years later, as high school students, they made a point of informing me that they still remembered that experiment!

At any age, science learning (and math, too) starts with curiosity; good curricula are based on the fact that real science is about testing informed guesses—trying to add to knowledge that is constantly being expanded and revised. Science fairs can encourage this attitude—but *only* if the process is more important than the product, *and* if parents don't take over!

If all students were taught from the bottom up rather than by bafflingly abstract rule systems, and also taught (in higher grades) to read real scientific studies and grasp the fundamentals of probability statistics, we would live in a culture much less gullible to media "hype," and people would be far more skeptical of irrational claims surrounding diets, medical fads, and even politics.

THE LANGUAGE OF MATH
Understanding the Puzzle

Even teachers get stuck with the idea that math consists only of numbers, forgetting about the important roles that words and language concepts play. Although experts debate whether it is possible to engage in visual-spatial reasoning without using any words, mathematical learning definitely uses a combination. Much of language, as we have seen, is mediated by the left hemisphere, but some of the most important linguistic concepts in mathematics are probably still based in the right.

Language in math takes two forms: (1) words that describe abstract concepts, such as "equal," and (2) grammatical statements, such as "Four take away two equals two." As in other language processing, the right hemisphere helps with the conceptual understanding, whereas the left is adept with the sequence and the grammar.

Many of the words used in math stand for abstract concepts, but the way the child learns them is—guess what!—through physical experience with objects and events in daily life. Some of these concepts are: **equal, greater, less, more, bigger, smaller, plus, take away, multiply, divide, when, until.** Steve might ask, "Which box is **bigger/smaller**? Which holds **more/less** cereal? Let's see if these oranges are **equal** in size/weight. I have **too many** cans of tuna—let's **take away** some. Do you think we can **divide** these cookies into two **equal** bags?" Prepositions are important words when learning about relationships. How many ways can you expose your child to the ideas of **up/down, before/after, above/below**? Anytime such ideas can be tied with language to everyday experiences, they become understandable.

Especially in a child's early years, computer software simply can't do this job. By the time a child is seven or so, good software, spreadsheets, and databases can effectively supplement learning. Middle school students profit from good software programs—especially simulations that enable them to manipulate abstract ideas on the computer screen: proportion, velocity, or geometric/spatial relationships are a few of these—but only if there is also a good teacher to explain concepts, make the learning meaningful and relevant, and help students talk about what they are learning.

Because Why?

Even larger mathematical and scientific concepts are also represented in language. One of these is "because." Most children do not fully grasp causation until well after the age of entering school. In order to understand our systems of math and science, one must grasp three related ideas at the foundation of much of Western thought: (1) events have causes, (2) causes precede effects, and (3) there is a link between cause and effect. While we adults take this knowledge for granted, a child experiences many causal situations before getting an intuitive notion of its meaning. You may have noticed that, in the meantime, their understanding of "because" and "why" are a little shaky. One smart and vigorous four-year-old who had experienced a fair share of time-outs in his room consistently prolonged the disciplinary time by continuing to fuss in spite of his Mom's patient explanations of what was expected. Only when he was almost five did he finally turn to her one day and say, "Oh, I get it! If I want to come out, I need to settle myself down," and he immediately proceeded to do so.

Clearly, even personal experience won't ingrain complex understandings until a certain degree of maturation is present. As we saw in chapter 3, adults can help by asking the right questions. Here are some involving cause and effect: "If I pull out the bottom block from the pile, what will happen?" "What made the light go on?" "Why do you suppose Maria started to cry?" "Why do you think Mom got angry?" (Be prepared for "Because she's a mean mom.")

Piles of Ideas

Abilities to categorize and classify are intrinsic to science and math. Caregivers have ideal opportunities to develop these skills between the child's ages of three and seven. After Steve gets the groceries home, he and Deborah can sort them into all kinds of categories—boxes, bags, cans; square, round, rectangular; large, small; heavy, light; vegetables, meats, fruits, grains, things Deborah likes and doesn't like; things for breakfast, lunch, dinner. Here the child is developing a basic understanding of "sets"—groups of similar objects. They might put cans and boxes, for example, in separate piles, and then draw a picture diagram using small circles and squares to represent them, finishing off with a big circle around each set. For older children the idea of overlapping categories (interesecting sets) can also be illustrated—fruits and vegetables, for example, with the two circles intersecting around "ones I like." This is also called a "Venn diagram" and is used to teach logic, even to adults.

You can classify leaves, flowers, insects, or other items found on walks. Adding a chart or graph in some simple form will build visual organization skills as well as the notion that symbols can stand for concrete objects. You might make a bar graph by coloring in a square on large graph paper for every leaf you find, using a different color bar for each type. You might trace different leaves and record the number found. If you also let the child think up new and interesting ways to create charts, you may get a creative surprise. If it isn't perfect, wonderful! It's better for a good scientist to figure out what doesn't work, and why, than to be shown only what does. Classifying objects also offers a good opportunity to discuss likenesses and differences, shapes, and symmetry. Practicing these visual discrimination skills will also contribute to the child's ability to recognize the form of numerals and geometric figures.

ANALYZING THE PIECES

Where are the numbers? So far we have been concerned with holistic skills. Another quite different set of abilities is also important in the first stages of learning. Counting, learning basic math facts, following steps in an experiment, and calculating are probably handled mainly by the sequential, orderly, and analytical left hemisphere. Left-hemisphere skills produce accuracy in computation and help with understanding the "grammar of math": the order in which propositions are expressed, such as "Two plus three equals five." Nonetheless, both hemispheres must work together if the child is to understand what this means.

Can He Really Count?

Counting is one of the first elements of arithmetic that parents consciously teach. "Billy can count to twenty!" exclaims an excited mother of a three-year-old. What she means is that Billy has learned to recite the numbers from one to twenty. She would be surprised to learn that he cannot actually count, since there are several aspects of this skill that he will not master for another year or two.

1. Reciting numbers in order.

2. Pointing to a few objects in a row and saying a number while touching each object; starts around age three.

3. Accurately counting, or enumerating, an array of objects; this ability is called rational counting with one-to-one correspondence; it does not usually develop until at least age four and often later.

4. Mentally counting a number of objects without touching them; the child has internalized the idea of "number." By age five children may be able to "see" how many are in groups of up to six.

5. Understanding the difference between being fifth in a line and representing the quantity "5."

6. Being able to add or subtract from a given number. While even infants seem to have an innate sense of numerosity (how many), it takes about five years for children to solve oral problems of add and take away by using counting strategies. ("I've got six oranges in the bowl; if we eat four, how many will I have left?" "Yes, you'll always be two years older than Matt. When he is seven, how old will you be?")

Most children between ages three and five have some definite ideas about what counting is; they believe it is necessary to go from left to right, start at the end of a line, and go in order. Only later do they begin to grasp the concept of numerosity so that they can size up an array of objects that are not in a row or tell you how many marbles you are holding in one hand. In fact, although some twelve-month-olds can tell the difference between three and five objects, the abstract notion of "number" is slow to develop. Many of us were taught in school that the word "number" means the printed symbol on the page, but now we call written figures "numerals."

The "One" Idea

What does "one" mean? Think of one pencil, and then of one world, and you will begin to understand why grasping number concepts takes a certain level of mental maturity. As in all other learning, children gain these ideas from lots of practical experiences with sets of objects. You can help your child by not only teaching numbers in order, but also by asking, "Please bring me 3 pencils." You might have a scavenger hunt outdoors: 6 acorns, 8 leaves, 3 stones, etc. Again, a trip to the grocery store offers innumerable chances to count objects and money. Once the child masters one-to-one correspondence up to 10, you can start asking questions such as "If you take away 4 of those acorns, how many will be left?" and encourage the child to use the objects as "counters." Such activities are infinitely more valuable than trying to teach answers to written equations, because the child develops a working understanding of what the number facts mean.

Teachers use various objects that they call "manipulatives," such as rods, cubes, or beads, to build numerical understanding. If your child's school has young children glued to workbooks without hands-on experiences in math, you should complain. You may avoid an incident such as the one in which a six-year-old, when asked what he had learned in school one day, replied, "I learned that three plus four is seven. Mommy, what's seven?"

Once most children have enough concrete experiences, ideas of numerosity will be internalized, but the ease with which this happens varies widely. I have worked with bright elementary school children who still do not have a "feel" for such ideas as the relative size of numbers ("Which is bigger, 28 or 32?"), or the fact that 13 means 10 + 3 rather than a 1 and a 3. We get out the manipulatives to build the missing concepts. Anything that can be counted works; things that can be put into bundles of 10, such as straws, will help with *place value*. For example, 2 bundles of 10 plus 3 single straws equals 23. Such grouping helps the child see why different numerals go in different columns—a difficult abstract idea.

Don't be surprised if your child has trouble with the notion of "zero" or the "empty set" until at least age seven, and perhaps later. It is especially hard to understand when 0 is used as a place holder, as in 107.

Parents always wonder if their children should be allowed, or even encouraged, to count on their fingers. As a teacher, I am convinced that (1) they will do it whether we like it or not, and (2) fingers represent the original manipulatives.

Beyond the "Facts"

Children eventually need to master the use of a personal calculator and computer to help with computation, but they also need to remain smarter than the machines. To do so they must have a thorough familiarity with basic number facts ("tables") and hands-on written practice with the processes involved. When calculators were first introduced into elementary classrooms, some educators cheered because they felt they would no longer have to drill their way through the "basics." Unfortunately, it didn't take long before kids started arriving in pre-algebra without the slightest idea of what division really means, that 7×6 isn't 48, that gasoline is unlikely to cost $18.40 a gallon (yet, anyhow) or that there could not be 5,743 days until the end of the school year ("Hey, I put the numbers into the calculator and this is what it says. . . ."). Now we recognize that the grit-work of learning the "facts" and the processes firsthand is a necessary step toward making sense of mathematical questions and knowing how use our electronic servants intelligently.

In several of the above cases, estimating an approximate answer before starting to work out the problem would have alerted the student to a foolish answer. Estimation is in part a metacognitive skill, which moves processing up into the prefrontal cortex and provides important exercise for higher control centers; one objection to too much calculator use is that it may remove the necessity for such metacognitive processes, which are integral to attention and genuine problem-solving. Estimating is now an important part of good math instruction.

One reason some children have trouble learning math combinations ("tables") is a basic lack of comprehension of the relationships involved; if you don't understand adding and multiplying, it is hard to sort out + and ×, or to figure out that 4×3 really means four 3s added together. Without meaning, isolated drills will be of limited value, and "memory" will be undependable. The human brain tends to remember material that (1) it is ready for, (2) has meaning, (3) can be arranged in patterns, and (4) can be linked to some previously learned information. Thus, Deborah's new workbook of equations may actually be counterproductive until she has gained more understanding. Drilling on $3 + 4 = 7$ seems silly if the child doesn't understand what 7 is, and a middle schooler should realize that the decimal point needs to be checked if gas costs $18.40 a gallon.

Number Facts: Becoming Automatic

Number facts are a good illustration of a skill that requires automaticity. To foster any automatic skill, four things are important: (1) motivation and involvement by the learner, (2) repetition, (3) novelty, and (4) presentation through different modalities. How can a parent help? To increase the child's involvement, it is important to allow for some choices and to keep the task manageable. With flash cards, for example, the child might choose which set of combinations to learn first, grouping the cards in bundles of "known," "not known," and "next to learn." Personally making the flash cards gets the student involved.

Time spent riding in the car can be used to repeat multiplication tables forward and backward. For additional novelty the child might make flash cards in different colors or with pictures on them representing each fact (8 pizzas + 7 Cokes = 15 [stomachaches?]). Pictures link drills both with meaning and with a visual image. Computer programs for drill and practice are useful because they blend novelty, which appeals to attention-regulating brain areas, with repetition through several senses. Just make sure the "reward" is personal improvement, not some trivial game that distracts from the challenge of solving harder problems.

Presentation through different modalities involves looking, saying and hearing; touching; or body movement. For example, the child might say $7 \times 8 = 56$ while writing it on a rough surface (living room rug, corduroy pant legs, fine sandpaper). Singing frequently works for rote memory skills, and tapes are available for almost everything that needs to be memorized. Or encourage the child to make up his own rap with the facts involved. Writing it in the air with the foot, head, or shoulder gets the motor cortex involved. The more senses that can be activated simultaneously, the better the fact will stick. Some experts have even recommended gustatory experiences, if you feel like baking cookies in the shape of multiplication facts.

Different Strokes

Many potentially gifted students are global thinkers who have genuine difficulty with sequential details. One algebra teacher told me that the most gifted student he ever had could/would not write out an equation in order, even though he almost always had the correct answer. When he described the process by which he arrived at the answer, even the teacher had difficulty understanding it. This youngster is now a PhD student in astrophysics. I assume that at some point he mastered the multiplication tables (probably when he felt he needed them.)

Knowing the answer but being unable to write out the equation does not necessarily signal carelessness, just difference. You may be interested to know that Einstein's wife had to check all his computations before he published a paper. "Careless" students can be difficult to teach, but we shouldn't give up on trying to help them master the mechanics as well as the concepts. They will need notation to communicate their good ideas to others. Technology may give them a chance to shine by helping them order the symbols. Younger ones may respond well to movement or visual cues; acting out, drawing pictures, or making diagrams to help identify the sequence of a problem. Some tutors have special techniques that can help.

On the other hand, there are many children who compute accurately and neatly, but don't "get it" when story problems or concepts are involved. This situation is actually harder to deal with. Such problems, sometimes falling into the category of a "nonverbal learning disorder", demand special remedial techniques. You might refer back to the "splitter" in chapter 6. Some computer simulations may help broaden the conceptual base for youngsters of middle-school age.

Real-World Math: The Bottom Line

Far more important than simply memorizing "facts" is solving problems using addition, subtraction, multiplication, and division in real-life situations. Simply by following one rule, such as subtracting with regrouping (borrowing), one can do pages of problems without understanding the process or the reasons. Many children perform math in this manner, but the minute they have to switch approaches or apply the knowledge, as in a story problem, they become confused. They also find math "boring." We are now attempting to replace this kind of "mindless computation" with mathematical reasoning. For example, a new math test might challenge seven-year-olds with problems like this one: "Three boys have two apples. How can they divide them up so that each boy gets the same amount?"

Many of the newer tests in the United States place more emphasis on mathematical reasoning in such practical situations. Interestingly enough, cross-cultural studies have shown that in countries like Japan, children are carefully grounded in understanding not only how to compute, but also why different problems are approached in different ways. Japanese elementary teachers commonly spend more time on one complex problem, encouraging the children to reason mathematically and discuss alternate approaches rather than just searching for the right answer and covering lots of problems.

Good science classes also strive for this type of deeper analysis combined with relevance to real-world questions. Students at all grade levels plan and execute experiments and projects that reflect important scientific questions.

If your child's school lags behind current research in how to teach math and science, you have a right to start asking questions! I hope the information in this chapter will help you present your case.

"Seeing" the Problem

You may notice that some children verbalize steps as they go ("You can't take 7 from 3, so go to the 10s column. . . ."), which engages the left hemisphere. Such verbal mediation strategies are good for children who have difficulty paying attention or remembering the steps and can also help with directionality. ("The sign says subtract, so I will start at the top and go down.") Some children need to write problems on graph paper that has large squares in order to keep columns organized. Some children's attention problems seem to reflect visual-spatial confusion—the page makes no sense to them, so they don't know where or how to begin systematically.

Some kids have difficulty distinguishing similar signs (+ and ×, for example). Many children reverse or invert numerals such as 6 and 9 until they are about seven years old and may become frustrated if too much pressure is applied before they are neurologically ready to see the difference. To build skills, help children get meaning out of unfamiliar symbols (e.g., codes) or a mass of visual information ("hidden pictures," puzzles that have small details, mazes, or any activity that involves making sense of an array of dots, for example). Looking for constellations in the night sky is one natural example. Math and science have been defined as "a search for patterns"; in this area, parents are important teachers.

Math and science textbooks and work sheets also require certain visual organization skills that may cause trouble. When looking at books with your child, you might occasionally discuss the way the pages are organized ("Why is this line here across the middle of the page?" "Let's look to see how many activities are on this page." "How many pictures are here, and how many captions—what can you tell about the way they go together?"). Older students can be encouraged to describe graphs, geometric shapes, or numerical arrays in words. It helps them get some feeling of control over a confusion of visual elements.

BUILDING BRAINS FOR THE FUTURE

Good preparation for success in a technological society does not rest primarily on high-tech experiences in childhood. Parents' major role is to use interesting and meaningful everyday activities to build their children's self-confidence, concepts, and foundation skills. Remember, creating an atmosphere in which *wrong answers* are viewed as a learning opportunity and where children are encouraged to take *intellectual risks* may be the most important factor of all. Here are some activities that help:

Family games involving cards, numbers, or money promote an understanding of relative quantity and build computation skills. Games requiring visual organization or strategy are also valuable.

Cooking (under adult supervision, of course) offers a wealth of possibilities for understanding the important ideas of quantity, measuring, sequencing steps in a problem, following directions accurately, fractions, and testing hypotheses. Here is an enjoyable, meaningful, and delicious learning experience!

Shopping offers chances to compare prices, shapes, learn about decimal places, and practice computation in a meaningful situation. Catalog shopping at home can become a math game—figuring out how many items can be purchased for a certain amount, for example. Every school-age child should have some sort of **allowance** to manage, however small, so he can get real experience in buying small items and getting change. Older children can learn about interest in a natural context from a bank or if they need to borrow from the parental exchequer.

Travel games, such as license plate bingo, keeping mileage records, or even computing gas mileage can be fun. Working with maps builds graphing and directional skills and can make a child feel very important. Letting the child figure out how much tip should be left in a restaurant or how much sales tax will be added teaches percentage, and they can check bills for accuracy. Electronic amusements during car trips keep children quiet, but you are losing a valuable opportunity to expand their minds and also help them learn how to improvise, negotiate, and manage feelings and interpersonal relationships.

Computer use is especially helpful in the service of real-life needs. For example, elementary school children can help research and plan family trips by figuring mileage for daily driving or flying between desired stops, comparing hotel prices, making gasoline and food budget estimates, etc. Would it be cheaper for us to drive, fly, or take the train? Youngsters can use a spreadsheet to keep their own allowance budgeted or even help with some aspects of tax preparation (also a good opportunity to discuss citizen participation in government). If you stay on the lookout, innumerable opportunities present themselves, and doing an important job for one's family is a magical experience to build kids' self-confidence.

Music lessons have been shown in some studies to improve spatial and mathematical skills. While these results are still tentative, the rationale is that the spatial intervals and interhemispheric coordination of playing the piano with both hands, for example, or mentally converting pitch into a spatial map (where is it—higher or lower?) stimulate spatial-temporal processing in the brain and thus transfer to math ability. Listening to music, as important as it is, does not have the same effects, nor do computer simulations of similar activities. No study has determined either the optimum age for such instruction or how long the effects last, although even preschoolers have seemed to benefit. It will be important to find out how to balance developmental limitations (formal keyboard instruction is not generally recommended for preschoolers) with information about possible sensitive periods for this type of development.

Collecting inspires many budding scientists, and **exploring nature** with an interested adult has kindled the interest of many future biologists. Microscopes, magnifying glasses, measuring instruments, binoculars, and "kitchen chemistry" with simple ingredients are all motivators when introduced at the right age.

Measuring and weighing activities are appropriate even for young children. Making diagrams of rooms in the house or maps of the yard or neighborhood is fun. You might try introducing nonstandard measurements such as "How many Daddy-shoe-lengths wide is the kitchen?" and estimating, as in "How many steps do you think it will take you to get to the garage?" The *Guinness Book of World Records* is a rich source of relative measurements.

Using time is the best way to learn about it. Relate time to events that are meaningful for the child and use appropriate terms ("What are we doing *now*?; What will we do *after/while* we eat lunch?"). Pasting or drawing pictures of activities on a daily calendar while discussing past and upcoming events makes "then" and "soon" more understandable than using abstract concepts of days, weeks, months, or seasons. Incidentally, telling time on digital and analog watches are totally different mental exercises. I suggest using a clock with hands to establish temporal-spatial concepts.

Following directions is one of the most important skills to learn at home. Taking steps in order, planning ahead, and talking about what to do before tackling the task can all be encouraged. Cooking, as noted above, treasure hunts, building models, and some computer games are sequential, step-following activities. For older children, map and compass skills are very helpful.

Calculator games are a good source of problem-solving situations with numerical concepts.

These are only a few of the multitude of activities that are the natural base of math and science learning. They are essentially about the real world, which is the best place to learn about them.

Not long ago I was visiting a colleague on the farm that she and her husband have worked hard to develop. At the breakfast table I was struck by the rapt attention of her twelve-year-old daughter, whose head was bent with her father's over a page of figures that would have frightened most youngsters. "Doing your math homework?" I inquired. "Oh, no," she replied. "Dad needs my help figuring out where to put the fences in the new pasture." Not many of us have the mathematical challenges of a farm at hand these days, but any family can encourage real-life problem-solving and ask interesting questions.

As we move now into our final chapter, focusing on creative minds, it should become apparent that adult success depends as much on keeping curiosity alive as it does on mastering complex skills. Enriching environments give children reasons for learning the rules.

Chapter 12

The Toolshed Muse:
Creative Minds in Process

When talking with teachers about creativity, I always get their attention—not with words of wisdom, but with the jewelry I wear. My "creativity" necklace is an aged aluminum bottle cap suspended from a length of cotton string. Several lumpy knots unite the ends of the string with a rusted chain that started life on an anonymous piece of yard equipment. Embedded in white glue on the cap's inner surface is a wobbly heart made of dried kernels of Indian corn.

This treasure was ceremoniously presented to me many years ago by our eldest son, then eight, who found himself with nothing to do on a hot July afternoon except delve into the recesses of an old toolshed. It has become my personal symbol for the special muse of creativity that awaits discovery in the quiet corners of children's lives.

Parents tell me they are concerned about "developing creativity" in their children. They wonder how they can recognize early talent and worry about when the kids should start art, dance, or music lessons. Some have heard that schools neglect parts of the "creative brain" and wonder if there is any way they can help keep it stimulated. When they ask professionals in education and the arts, they get conflicting reports and more questions. Can creativity be taught? Can it be tested? What is its relationship to "giftedness"? Are schools stimulating original thinking in mathematics, science, social studies, and philosophy? Will today's students become "problem finders" who can come up with creative solutions for the world's needs?

Creativity—intellectual and artistic—is a timely topic, but studying it is somewhat like dissecting a flower. By the time all the pieces are examined, the essence of the whole has vanished. My favorite definition of creativity is a general one: *the ability to generate or invent, to approach problems in any field from fresh perspectives.* Creative brains seek out patterns of experience and new ways to put them together. Research suggests some practical questions and tentative answers for parents who would like to help with the search. The first question is, How do we recognize different forms of creativity in a child?

THE DIMENSIONS OF CREATIVITY
Gifted, Creative, or Prodigy?

Terms applied to talented children are confusing even to teachers. Here are some workable distinctions:

Gifted is a term that has most commonly been used for those who score near the top 3 percent on IQ tests. Thus, most students so labeled have primarily been adept at traditional, school-oriented tasks, and many have not turned out to be particularly creative. Intellectually gifted children flourish in an atmosphere that offers both academic challenge and the opportunity to expand their imaginative perspectives.

Broader definitions of giftedness now include exceptional abilities in any of the arts, visual-spatial reasoning, leadership skills, or psychomotor talent. Gifted individuals in any field tend to:

• Take more time to think strategically about problems and less time to solve them.
• Seek wholes, patterns, and relationships.

- "Web" knowledge (establish mental categories and connect new ideas to them).
- Prefer complexity.
- View learning as an adventure.
- Possess sufficient self-discipline to plan and implement projects.

Creative children may also be gifted, but many escape this classification because their talents lie in areas that are untapped by traditional school tasks or standard IQ measures. One large study found that 70 percent of highly creative students were not identified as "gifted" by IQ scores. Such children, who may even be labeled "learning disabled," often have several spheres of potential talent that don't show up in school. Many successful artists, filmmakers, and computer software "geniuses" fled from formal studies at the earliest opportunity.

My own bias is that *all* children are potentially gifted and creative in delightfully individual ways. It is up to parents and teachers to uncover those abilities and help the child make the most of them.

Prodigies exhibit a high degree of specialized ability at an unusually early age. A large part of their talent is believed to be innate, but its fruition requires exposure and encouragement. For example, a potential chess prodigy who grew up in an environment with no chess sets would doubtless go unrecognized. Most experts believe it is impossible to make a child into a prodigy; an unusual degree of native talent and a characteristic drive to pursue it are needed, for the path is not an easy one. Almost all child prodigies undergo an intense period of questioning and self-examination during adolescence, and many abandon their field of early promise.

Some so-called prodigies display "splinter skills," a poorly understood phenomenon in which one extraordinary talent accompanies severe deficits in other abilities. In one famous case, a three-year-old named Nadia began to draw strikingly realistic pictures; by the time she was five, her sketches were technically comparable to those of adult artists. Nadia, however, was severely autistic and unable to communicate. After she went to school, acquired some language, and began to socialize with other children, her interest and talent in drawing declined. Can we infer that her right hemisphere's visual capabilities were unusually advanced and dominant until she was taught left-hemisphere skills? This issue has been debated extensively but inconclusively.

The majority of creative people are not prodigies, however, and many who have achieved eminence in artistic fields were not even regarded as particularly precocious. Most parents wish to focus on broader definitions of creativity for their children.

Testing Creativity

Creativity by its very nature is difficult to test. Dr. E. Paul Torrance pioneered creativity testing by identifying four characteristics:

Fluency: Multiple relevant ideas generated about a topic. For example: In two minutes, how many uses can you think of for an empty pop bottle?

Flexibility: Different categories or shifts in thinking (e.g., switching types of uses for the pop bottle from a holder for flowers or pipe cleaners to a doorstop).

Elaboration: Use of details in working out an idea. Embellishing a story plot, for example, or weaving unrelated details together in some interesting way such as designing a pop bottle with futuristic details.

Originality: Creative and imaginative ideas that others haven't come up with. One student suggested that a pop bottle could be a battering ram for a gopher.

Teachers who have worked to encourage creativity in students would like to add a fifth criterion:

Evaluation: Selecting and refining ideas. Rather than accepting anything that sounds unusual or clever, truly creative people are able to apply a sifting process to glean the best or most relevant ideas.

"Creativity" tests have many weaknesses, however. One seven-year-old almost missed being included in an enrichment program the day she came home from school and announced, "Mom, you'll never guess what happened today. A crazy man came into our classroom and handed everyone a paper clip. Then he asked us how many things we could do with a paper clip. Isn't that the dumbest thing you ever heard!"

Antennae waving, Mom called the school. Yes, her daughter had "failed" the creativity exam because she didn't attempt to answer the question. Fortunately, the school reconsidered its decision.

Identifying Creativity

Let's look at some broader criteria. A child who exhibits several of these qualities may have unusual potential for creativity:

- Intense absorption in activities. Persistence in working or playing.
- An unusual ability to see patterns and relationships. ("Look, the legs on the picnic table and benches are all Xs—just like the lines on the kitchen floor." "Oh, I get how that gear made the other one turn; just like on my bike." "Monique and Abby probably act the same way because they both feel shy." "See the triangles in the tree branches?")
- An ability to combine things or ideas in new ways. ("If I turn my farmyard gate on its side and put it against the barn, it could be a ladder." "I invented a new dessert—maple sugar on rice with marshmallows on top!")
- The use of analogies in speech. ("I feel as bouncy as a ball.")
- Seeing things in a new or different way. ("What if the roads moved instead of the cars?") A sixth grade girl invented a unique wallet for the blind, which has been patented.
- A tendency to challenge assumptions or authorities because of a reasoned-out difference in opinion. One two-year-old boy informed his mother that he would like to wait until he was three to become potty-trained. A four-year-old girl dressed her kitten up in baby clothes and sat it in a high chair to circumvent the house rule prohibiting animals at the dinner table. Many creative teens study and may adopt divergent belief systems.

- Independent decision-making and the ability to take action.
- An ability to shift from one idea to another.
- Strong intuition. "Seeing" answers to problems.
- An ability to go "out on a limb," take risks.
- Insightful observations or questions. ("Where does the lotion go after you put it on your hands?" "What if we see different colors for the thing we both call 'red'?")
- A tendency to create and test hypotheses. ("I put my broccoli in the dog's dish and I found out that dogs don't like vegetables.")
- An ability to tolerate ambiguity while exploring alternatives. Creative people don't always expect an answer to be immediately apparent.
- An interest in new ideas. ("What if . . .")
- Enjoyment in thinking and working alone.

To the extent that we encourage qualities such as these in our children, we encourage the ability to think and act creatively. Does it surprise you that no emphasis has been placed on skill development? Those who study creativity don't talk much about teaching specific skills to children; in fact, they are seriously concerned that our culture is pushing them too hard too soon.

John Adams, a powerhouse behind the United States Constitution and its philosophy, certainly qualifies as a creative thinker. Yet, according to diaries quoted by biographer David McCullough, Adams's academic skills were very late-blooming. A ravenous reader and thinker in adult life, Adams until age fifteen "cared not for books or study," reveling in the ". . . bliss of roaming the open fields and woodlands of the town, exploring the creeks, hiking the beaches, of making and sailing boats, flying kites . . ." and socializing with his friends. Life was, of course, different for children almost two hundred years ago, but it does seem that their brains still managed to develop quite well. Is there a lesson here?

STAGE OF CREATIVE DEVELOPMENT
Growing Creative Brains

Dr. Howard Gardner, one of the most insightful current observers of children's creative development, has studied stages of development in the arts. He wondered what happens to the spontaneity of the elementary years and what would promote continued artistic development. He determined that creativity has distinct forms and different needs during specific periods of life.

Preschool children, in the *first stage*, are instinctively creative, delighting in original music, art, drama, and language. Gardner observed that the expressiveness of their paintings and drawings had much in common with those of talented adults, much like their ability to use simple poetic language to combine ideas or images in fresh, unusual ways. Preschoolers, however, are uncritical observers who have little perspective on artistic accomplishment. They might believe that a painting is finished "when the paper is filled up," or that an animal like a tiger could be a painter because he could hold the brush in his mouth. They may prefer "inferior" art or music simply because of familiarity. Lesson for parents: provide worthwhile models, such as quality picture books, child-length visits to museums, and good music. Gardner himself is a strong advocate of children's museums, where youngsters can explore ideas and experiment with hands-on problem-solving in a variety of different mediums. Don't pass up the opportunity to visit one, as you will learn a lot about what can really intrigue your child.

Around age seven the creativity pattern shifts. Children's imaginations seem to get stuck, and they stop engaging in those delightful flights of fancy. This *second stage* is characterized by concentration on rules and practical ideas. Gardner observed eight-, nine-, and ten-year-olds searching for literal meanings rather than for metaphors. Many prefer to copy or collect pictures rather than create their own. Have their creative spirits been crushed?

Some observers are ready to blame the schools; they claim originality and imagination get smothered by inexorable demands for accuracy, rule learning, and convergent thinking. Many teachers reward conformity, not creativity, and the first item cut in a budget is often the art, drama, music, or dance program. Sometimes parents join the anti-creativity movement with too much pressure for output and doing things the "proper" way.

Despite the validity of these concerns, schools and parents may not deserve all the blame. This period of literal thinking, with its emphasis on following the rules, may be an essential way station for growing minds. After ranging widely in imagination, children must solidify understanding and mastery of the physical world and feel the security of operating successfully within stated limits before they can venture on.

The years of middle childhood and early adolescence therefore become ideal for learning about nature, oneself, and other people, and also for lessons and practice in the skills of artistic achievement. Gardner points out that most successful artists in any medium must put in at least ten years of concentrated training before their talent can be fully expressed. Because he believes that different neural areas underlie various types of creativity, specialization and hard work are necessary—when the brain is ready.

The *third stage*, around ages fifteen to twenty-five, brings a convergence of abilities to plan a creative project, implement, and evaluate it. While most people are mastering information or skills in a field, the creative individual stands out as one who continues to take risks, attempt new projects, and preserve individuality. By ages thirty to thirty-five these patterns are even more evident.

If talent is specialized, should we expect a child to be good at everything? A potential artist, mechanic, dancer, or athlete may falter in school subjects. Can parents and teachers of such youngsters restructure their own value systems to accommodate nonacademic skills? Can they model open-ended approaches to problems? Can we all believe that time and energy devoted to creative skills are important?

Gardner says, "The ultimate flowering of artistry may require a society that has a genuine interest in its budding artists and values their creations."

Here are a few nodes in the budding process:

Stage One: Spontaneous Creativity

Ages one to two: Concrete mastery of simple artistic expression.
  Making marks on paper.
  Simple singing and musical chanting.
  Imitation of voice tones and pitch.
Two to three: Beginning use of symbols.
  Drawing geometric forms: circles, squares, crosses.
  Words standing for objects.
  "Pretend" play.
  Gestures, movement linked spontaneously to music.
  Awareness of and ability to imitate tunes.
Three to four: Beginnings of structure in creative efforts.
  Attempts to reproduce whole songs.
  Telling stories with simple structure.
  Simple dance sequences.
  Drawings of figures: human "tadpole" figures (circle and legs; no torso).
  Drawing a triangle.
Three to five: Beginnings of metaphor.
  Creating metaphors based on appearance of objects and personal action. ("The sunbeam is jumping.")
  Attempts to pick out tunes on musical instruments.
  Five to six: Original combinations of ideas, sensory impressions.
  Imitation of musical intervals; most six-year-olds can sing in key and pick up underlying musical rhythms.
  Grouping figures into scenes in drawings; shows sense of balance and color.
  Drawing a diamond.

Five to seven: "The golden age."

Love of drawing: may use art to express concerns and worries or to gain a feeling of mastery over the world.

Spontaneous enjoyment of music, dance, and poetic language.

Stage Two: Literalism

Eight to eleven: Craves competency, rules, feelings of mastery.

Ready to concentrate on lessons and skill practice. Needs exposure to varied types of creative expression and quality models of good artistic forms.

Enjoys enrichment experiences in science, math, and other fields of special interest.

Ready to begin learning structure and forms of writing.

Ten to eleven: Creative imagination beginning to broaden.

Practices making aesthetic judgments and evaluating creative efforts.

Appreciation of different types of literary forms (e.g., fairy tale, realistic fiction, opinion).

Needs good teacher, apprenticeships to mentors, for development of potential gifts.

Stage Three: Mature Creative Expression and Appreciation

Adolescence: Combining inspiration and execution.

Continued practice of skills.

Appreciation of others' artistic efforts.

Intense evaluation of own work.

Ability to create original artistic forms or ideas; challenges boundaries of standard disciplines.

Needs a teacher of high achievement in chosen field and/or mentors to inspire choices.

TRAINING YOUNG ARTISTS: WHEN AND HOW?
A Personal Lesson about Music Lessons

When our son the necklace-maker was completing first grade, his teacher held an afternoon program in which each child shared a talent or an interest. Some read original poems or stories, others displayed pictures or performed skits. At the end of the afternoon, Scott sat down at the piano and played a medley from *The Sound of Music*, for which he had arranged the chords by ear. As the program ended, I was surrounded by a clamor of mothers wanting to know my secret. "Where does he take?" they demanded. Somewhat sheepishly, I acknowledged that he didn't "take." Although our home had always been filled with music, rhythms, and movement, his only "formal" instruction had come during the previous year when Scott pestered his father to teach him basic keyboard positions and chording. He did the rest on his own—and he hasn't stopped yet! I have heard many similar stories from parents of children who later excelled in a specialized field. When the right time came, the youngster became self-propelled.

The "basics" of music and other art forms are best learned in a home where these skills are emphasized, but some parents, who may not have had musical or artistic training themselves, are unsure of how to start their child off. Experts in all forms of artistic expression, especially music, recommend that children have some sort of introduction to the art form while they are still preschoolers. Studies show that certain areas of the parietal lobes of trained adult musicians, for example, are larger than average, particularly if they had musical experience before age seven. This part of the cortex may account for perfect pitch, for which there may be a sensitive period during the early years. Make sure preschoolers have listening experiences with varieties of good music, rhythmic body movement, singing, and opportunities to make "music" with handheld instruments—or even pots, pans, and spoons. Music theory classes taught by a professional who understands the needs of young children may be helpful if parents are insecure about their own abilities.

Many programs for budding artists exist; the good ones are designed to be developmentally appropriate, incorporating plenty of fun, spontaneous expression, frequent changes of activities, and lots of emphasis on movement. Dalcroze, art enrichment, and Orff music training are only a few examples that broaden rather than narrow creative bases. One main criterion should be whether your child enjoys the experience. I once took a toddler to a music class where the teacher talked far too much, lacked suitable visual aids, had too few drums, rattles, or other rhythmic instruments, and rarely encouraged the children to stand up and move. Needless to say, most of these toddlers were soon wandering around the room, ignoring the "enrichment." When I suggested to the child's mother that she look for a different class, she was relieved.

"I thought maybe it was just my child who couldn't pay attention," she said. "I figured the teacher knew what she was doing." Not necessarily.

Preliminary studies of musical training affecting cognitive skills (see chapter 11) suggest that carefully designed experiences that link written notes with hand movements on the piano may increase visual-spatial skills and memory. The final verdict is not in, however, and for most children, even talented ones, there is little reason to rush into skill-and-practice-oriented lessons before about age seven, when the brain refines its ability to combine sequences from different senses. Traditional instruction in reading music demands an integration of visual, auditory, and motor patterns for which most preschoolers' brains simply are not equipped. Discriminating, identifying, sequencing, and playing notes from a written staff are far different from experimenting with finger movements for a simple tune. For most children, intensive music lessons should wait until after reading instruction is successfully underway. Even structured lessons without the demands of reading music, as on the violin, are very controversial among musicians who value "feeling" over mechanics for young children. They fear that forcing creativity may kill it.

Master teachers in the visual arts tell us that presenting advanced practices or theory in the hope of accelerating development is useless. Telling a child what to do to produce a pretty product will make him dependent on your direction and unsure of his own aesthetic choices. Children need to "own" all the steps of the learning process.

I'm glad our musician didn't "take" until he was ready and eager. When people ask me, "How did you get him to practice?" I have to admit it was the other way around. We couldn't keep him from practicing. Blessed with a talented child, we were happily too innocent of the dimensions of this treasure to steal the initiative from its rightful owner.

Flowing with Creativity

Mihaly Czikszentmihalyi, who has studied accomplishment in many fields, finds that highly creative people have certain characteristics in common. They tend to become immersed in the material at hand rather than focusing on some long-range product, and they concentrate so intently that they may lose track of time. They work primarily for the intrinsic satisfaction of the activity. He calls this experience "flow," noting how different it is from the externally generated absorption induced by electronic media.

Children often experience "flow" when they are at play, and highly creative adults retain their ability to "play" with new ideas and fool around with the raw materials of brilliance. They value creative exploration for its own sake. Don't make the mistake of trying to teach young children a structured set of facts or skills and mistake it for creativity. One of the most creative physicists at MIT recalls that his parents never pushed early learning, but always encouraged him to devise his own methods of playing with the materials at hand. He laughs affectionately when he remembers his mother patiently sweeping up the kitchen floor after his favorite game—pouring her flour from the canister and experimenting with different sizes and shapes of containers. Now he is experimenting with molecules that may someday lead to a treatment for cancer.

THE CREATIVE BRAIN
The Creative Brain Talks to Itself

Learning to think creatively is a process of making links: first between movement and the senses, then between ideas, and finally, between the human mind's most sophisticated achievements—inspiration and evaluation. At the heart of the system are the chains of neurons that make the connections. Although we have a great deal yet to learn about the brain's role in creativity, the gradual development of neurons' ability to "talk" among themselves probably explains a great deal about all intellectual talents.

In young children, the brain's inner communication systems are not well traveled. Perhaps because association pathways are immature, particularly in the left hemisphere and in the prefrontal cortex, preschoolers tend to react spontaneously, without careful analysis. Their approach to new situations reflects the first-strike capabilities of the right hemisphere. They can't evaluate details, put them in order, or plan ahead. They have trouble integrating the two sides of their bodies in complicated patterns. They enjoy creative activities that are restricted to demands on one or two sense modalities, such as spontaneous movement to music, free-form drawing, or dramatizing expressive poetry. Most need to use their bodies in creating; the motor cortex is one of the first high-level areas to mature in both hemispheres, providing children's first means of organizing their own brains. Multisensory experiences, such as having a child tell a story about a picture she has drawn, help make these connections.

For most children in the elementary years, development is active in the left hemisphere, but perhaps because the bridge of fibers that links the two sides is still in the process of completion, eight-, nine-, and ten-year-olds have trouble linking imagination, free expression, and visual imagery with demands for order, sequence, and analysis. Most schools emphasize these latter abilities because children need to master the technical tools of thought and a large store of specific knowledge.

Yet the arts, too, should be an integral and valued part of brain-building in every school, as they represent unique avenues for expanding intelligence. Instruction in the arts also energizes the brain's motivation centers, gives nontraditional learners another route to competence, and teaches attention and problem-solving skills—not to mention developing lifelong patterns of personal enjoyment. You can and should press your school district to support the arts, but until our culture gets the message, this all-important exposure to creative ideas and artistic expression may become the parents' responsibility.

Divergent Styles

Around the beginning of adolescence, integration of analytic and intuitive thinking becomes easier; an original idea can be analyzed and evaluated and its successful execution planned. Insight is followed by confirmation as the brain begins to move comfortably between holistic and analytical processing.

Individuals have different balances in the knowledge-imagination equation. Even toddlers show clear inclinations to be either "verbalizers" or "visualizers." Some are better at analyzing, some at synthesizing. Many highly creative adults prefer holistic and intuitive rather than verbal modes of processing. Isadora Duncan once remarked, "If I could say it, I wouldn't have to dance it." Picasso, who started painting realistically before he was in his teens, developed a mature style that portrayed figures as if he were looking at them from all sides at once.

The right hemisphere is involved in much artistic expression and is also in closer touch with the emotional "feeling" centers of the limbic system; thus the importance of a positive emotional climate for creativity. The right hemisphere may also generate more slow brain waves, called *alpha* rhythms, than vigorous *beta* waves of analytical thought. If the left hemispere is actively zapping an idea with beta waves, inspiration may not have much of a chance. Reflection, relaxation, biofeedback, and imagery techniques appear to be effective in activating calmer brain frequencies and reducing stress. Even simple movement activities work, too.

Here are some techniques that work for creative people:

Playing: Relaxation and enjoyment of spontaneous activities facilitates creative thinking, but many adults have forgotten how to play. Discarding the notion that a worthwhile product must lie at the end of every activity opens new mental avenues for adults and children together.

Humor: Invite humor to be a frequent visitor in your home—but be sure you laugh *with*, not *at*, each other.

Dramatizing: You can dramatize almost anything. Act out stories with your child. Pretend to be unlikely things. ("How would peanut butter act? Can you be a pair of scissors?") Learn new vocabulary by acting out words. ("Here's what 'vicious' looks like." "Do I seem 'tranquil' or 'perturbed'?") Help with school assignments by putting actions with ideas. ("Can you pretend to be Magellan? Cortez? You be the king and I'll be the serfs. How might we act?") This type of learning lets all parts of the brain talk to each other.

Moving: Some evidence suggests that rhythmic aerobic exercise subdues the pressure of beta waves and opens new avenues between the hemispheres. Runners swear that it works! Encourage spontaneous dance and creative movement. Invent dances in your living room for different types of insects, animals, birds, flowers, or objects. Dance to all varieties of music. For older children, you'll find that material "studied" in this manner sticks better, too. Pretend to be molecules when your child studies science, or words representing grammatical terms (adverbs dance with verbs; adjectives with nouns, etc.).

Imaging: The ability to "see" ideas in one's head is an important component of creative thinking. Start early, linking verbal ideas with pictures: First, read imaginative stories or fairy tales out loud while you show pictures; then let the children draw pictures of their own. After age five or so, suggest that they close their eyes and picture it inside their heads. Say, "Tell me about the queen's dress. What did the troll's house look like?" Don't be surprised if it takes a lot of practice. Some creative children have excellent visual memories for faces, objects, events, and scenes, but they bog down trying to link mental pictures with verbal material. Turn off the electronic screens and let the whole family use imagination for a change.

Listening: Melody, processed by the right hemisphere, is a catalyst for creativity in many people. A background of baroque music or Gregorian chant has been claimed to facilitate creative learning and memory. Listening to Mozart is worthwhile even if it doesn't raise your IQ. You might want to experiment with different types of melody as a background for thinking or learning in your home. Formal musical training develops more analytic, left-hemisphere abilities.

Expressing: Children need time and encouragement to be able to attach words to images and ideas. Encourage your child to make intuitive discoveries and then talk about them.

Originating: Think up new uses for common objects (e.g., a sponge, a hair dryer). Approach household tasks in divergent ways; experiment with different food combinations. Some parents keep a "prop" box of common objects such as old hats, scarves, flowerpots, kitchen utensils, or household "junk" and encourage children to play imaginatively with them. Keeping an open mind to new ideas is important because intuition gets stifled by a "one right answer" mentality. One teacher asks students to tell their troubles to a bowl of yellow Jell-O; he claims it loosens the imagination.

Incubating: Have you ever had a problem suddenly solve itself after you have "sat" on it for a while? Some of science's greatest discoveries demonstrate that intuition requires incubation time. Everyone needs time to be alone, to ponder, to contemplate. Sometimes doing "nothing" is the most creative activity of all. One childhood variable predicting later scientific achievement is time spent alone. Allowing children to be "bored" now and then gives them a chance to investigate toolsheds or other unlikely places where inspiration may be hiding.

CREATIVE PARENTS

Parents who produce creative children:

- Show them how to be problem-finders as well as problem-solvers.
- Have full lives themselves and do not depend on their children to meet their emotional or achievement needs.
- Are not in awe of the child and do not defer to his demands or feel compelled to entertain him.
- Tolerate divergent ideas and mistakes made "in the service of learning."
- Provide discipline and structure to give children security to explore.
- Set realistic standards and encourage pride in achievement.
- Show active interest in a child's thoughts and creative efforts.
- Encourage a child's interest in hobbies.
- Encourage a close relationship to nature and freedom of physical expression.
- Take children to plays, puppet shows, dance performances, interesting musical and cultural activities, and children's as well as adult museums.
- Give children early responsibility for making choices and taking appropriate responsibility for their own decisions.
- Permit children to have solitude and develop imaginative thinking by daydreaming.
- Encourage imaginative play.
- Show children how to be curious and observant.
- Allow honest expression of emotion.
- Encourage children to feel intuitively as well as to think logically.
- Do not put pressure on the school for "competency" that excludes intellectual creativity.
- Expose children to special artistic and intellectual pursuits: you might visit practicing artists in studios; find out how pianos are made; go backstage after a dance performance; obtain prints of interesting or important artistic works and enjoy them at home; or create homegrown musical, dance, or dramatic performances.

Sampling the Arts

What is the best way to get children interested in good artistic forms? One family planned a trip to a city with a well-known art museum, but the mother was worried because she knew her sons would be bored by a long tour through all the galleries. Before the trip she identified three special pieces they would see, one sculpture and two paintings, and she obtained prints of these works. The whole family examined, read about, and discussed them. They went to the library and on the Internet to find out more about each artist.

By the time of the museum visit, the excited boys had to be cautioned not to run through the galleries to find their "treasures." Once they had been located and savored, the family left the museum. These children could hardly wait for another visit! I suspect that a similar exposure to one single piece of music that has become familiar and understandable might be the key to preventing the "symphony ennui" learned from early concert attendance. A delicious sample is better than a smorgasbord overdose.

Complimenting Creativity

The way you praise your child's artistic efforts may be important in encouraging creativity and fostering pride of ownership. Compare these typical responses:

"That looks great; tell me about it," rather than, "What is it?"

"What an interesting cow!" rather than, "I never saw a purple cow."

"You certainly enjoyed using black!" rather than, "Why is it all black?"

"You must feel very proud of your project," as well as, "I'm proud of you."

This latter distinction is important for parents to get children to implement and evaluate their own ideas. Learning to depend on external praise or an adult judgment about whether something is good/bad, right/wrong may block creative circuits. One father started saying when his daughter was two, "Aren't you proud of yourself," and teaching her to clap for herself while her parents stayed in the background. He says the credit and the pride should belong to the child, not to him.

A teacher suggests that children's artwork come off the refrigerator and go into more "important" areas of the home. One mother who framed her children's paintings and stitchery and hung them in the living room got many compliments on her "modern art" while the children basked in the praise.

Evaluating "Creativity" at School

One question that bothers many families is whether children's creative needs are being accommodated at school. To prepare for a personally rich adult life, young people need aesthetic, open-ended experiences just as much as they need academic "standards." A culture that overloads youngsters with information and skills at the expense of imagination will soon work (and bore) itself to death. Here are a few questions you might ask your school:

1. Are the arts and innovative thinking esteemed and positively recognized?

2. Is "creativity" meaningfully related to curriculum and to the child's needs and interests rather than defined by work sheet or one-shot activities that are artificially cute or divergent?

3. Are all children viewed as being, in Howard Gardner's words, "at promise"? Do adults recognize unusual abilities and give children opportunities to develop them?

4. Is an effort being made to expand learning for academically gifted students rather than simply accelerating academic skill development, or ignoring their special needs?

5. Are children encouraged to share the fruits of their creative

mental explorations with a wider audience? Sharing adds an important dimension of meaning and responsibility.

6. Does the teacher have a creative spirit? Can he answer challenging questions without feeling threatened and accept divergent answers or approaches to his own lesson plan?

7. Are the arts well integrated with academic subjects?

8. Do students learn to work together in seeking answers to open-ended problems—good training for a technological age?

9. Is self-evaluation by students part of the evaluation process?

A creative classroom is not an excuse for mayhem or disorganization. Master teachers who focus on creative enrichment carefully plan and evaluate each activity. They realize, however, that an enriched setting and good plans are not enough. Creativity is a process that takes time, and often flourishes only after a process of trial and error. Does your child's school use any of these process-oriented activities?

- Hands-on science projects done by students, not by parents.
- Creative writing of all types in all subjects.
- Rap sessions and brainstorming of ideas.
- Studying "futuristics" (considering what the future will be like and how to anticipate and solve problems; Internet film or video clips can be provocative discussion starters).
- Simulation games (pretending to solve major challenges such as inventing a new civilization or planning a voyage to Mars) with or without computers.
- Thoughtful probing of philosophical or moral dilemmas.
- Use of many types of symbol systems.

One teacher linked symbolic use to personal interest by asking each child to come in with a bag of disposable "stuff" that would characterize his family members well enough for others to guess their main interests and personality characteristics. What would you use for your family?

Teaching creativity may not be possible, but *modeling* it is. Parents can help by not demanding a product from every learning experience. When the pressure is on to bring home a picture every week from art class, or a test instead of a project, the process of creativity—and of learning—is shortchanged. Support your school's efforts to expand creative thinking, and don't underestimate the importance of your job on the home front.

Now let's seek our own creative synthesis by returning to the fundamental idea that an "enriched" home environment can have profound effects in your child's brain.

A LIFETIME OF ENRICHMENT AND THE BRAIN OF A GENIUS
Enriched Rats

Neuroanatomist Marian Diamond, a pioneer in studying the effects of environmental enrichment on brains, is a living example of lifelong creativity. In her career analyzing the brains of laboratory rats, she realized that seeking out and pursuing interesting challenges is the brain's natural mechanism to keep neural connections exercised—and growing. For rats, "enrichment" consisted of interesting "toys" and exercise equipment that was changed often enough to provide ongoing challenges. The more active and curious the rats, the larger their brains grew. Nonetheless, rats in laboratory cages never reached the level of those raised among the natural challenges of their unartificial wild environments.

Diamond and her colleagues soon learned that "enrichment" works not only for youthful brains, but for aging ones as well—in rats or in humans. Current studies show that adults who keep their brains active with challenging and engaging work or new learning have larger and heavier cortexes and higher IQs. Even being married to someone who "pushes" you to get off the couch and try some new activities tends to keep your IQ higher. Thus Diamond plans her "retirement" activities to include enjoyment of new artistic, intellectual, and athletic pursuits.

At any age, stimulation enhances mental potential, up to a point. When does "good" become "too much"? An interesting and challenging environment is quite different from one that bombards the brain with too much of a good thing. At some point, laboratory rats, like humans, need relief. Don't lose sight of common sense in your efforts to produce children who have active and creative minds!

One amusing but cautionary note from Diamond's research: When young and old rats shared a cage, the older adults monopolized the enrichment objects and their brains grew more than did those of the offspring. Here's good evidence for creative "play"—*with* your child.

The Brain of a Genius

One of Dr. Diamond's studies departed intriguingly from rat brains. "If you could study any brain in history, whose would it be?" she asks.

"Einstein's!"

Einstein's brain had been preserved after his death, but no one had yet studied it when Dr. Diamond requested four special tissue samples. She was particularly interested in comparing two sections from each hemisphere with the same areas in more average male brains. By the intricate technique of staining cells and counting them under a microscope, she discovered that the brain of this genius was indeed different.

In small but critical areas of the frontal (executive centers, abstract thinking) and parietal lobes (the late-developing area where sensory information and bodily-spatial awareness intersect for meaning), Einstein's brain contained significantly more glial cells per neuron. Dr.

Diamond believes that this ratio is associated with more vigorous use of these particular areas for higher thinking and reasoning, since these support systems grow in response to cognitive demands.

We could speculate endlessly about what happened to that developing brain while, as a solitary child, Einstein played with his favorite toy, a compass, and listened to music, his other preferred hobby. Or when he was a young teen, as he reflected endlessly on the question: What would it be like to ride on a beam of light?—the impetus for his discovery of the theory of relativity.

"Imagination is more important than knowledge," was Einstein's credo, and it is one we might all do well to heed. Don't crush children's imagination with overscheduling, excess pressure for achievement, too much stimulation from outside, or insufficient time to play—both physically and mentally.

I asked Marian Diamond what her recommendation might be for parents interested in raising bright and creative children. Musing for only a moment, this scientist-mother, who has looked into the black box of thousands of growing brains and into the brain of a genius, replied, "I'd tell them to give children the broadest picture."

THE BROADEST PICTURE

Creative parents give children the broad picture of an interesting and loving environment with freedom to explore. Children get their own focus—in an old toolshed, a corner of a city apartment, or a suburban garden. I treasure my wobbly heart in its old bottle cap as a reminder that the truly creative mind is forged, not only from stimulation, but also from time—time to experiment, to discover, to understand, and to get acquainted with the very special muses of childhood.

The child's brain has an instinctive knowledge of its timetable, but the creative mind is more than a schedule of neural connections. I hope you will accept the suggestions in this book, and your role in your child's development, as part of a greater process, never perfect, never finished. Learning is something that children do, not something that is done to them. You have the wisdom to guide the process but not the power to control it. Listen, watch, have patience, enjoy the journey—and the product will take care of itself.

Select Bibliography

General References

Brooks, R., and Goldstein, S. *Nurturing Resilience in Our Children.* Chicago: Contemporary Books, 2002.

Byrnes, James P. *Minds, Brains, and Learning: Understanding the Psychological and Educational Relevance of Neuroscientific Research.* New York: Guilford Press, 2001.

Caine, Renate N., and Caine, Geoffrey. *Making Connections: Teaching and the Human Brain.* Alexandria, VA: ASCD, 1991.

Diamond, M., and Hopson, J. *Magic Trees of the Mind: How to Nurture Your Child's Intelligence, Creativity and Healthy Emotions from 6 through Adult.* New York: E. P. Dutton, 1998.

Gibson, K. R., and Petersen, A. C., eds. *Brain Maturation and Cognitive Development.* New York: Aldine de Gruyter, 1991.

Goldberg, E. *The Executive Brain: Frontal Lobes and the Civilized Mind.* Oxford: Oxford University Press, 2001.

Grigorenko, E. L., and Steinberg, R., eds. *From Environment & Intellectual Functioning: A Life Span Perspective.* Mahwah, NJ: LEA, 2001.

Gunnar, M. R., and Nelson, C. A., eds. *Developmental Behavioral Neuroscience* 24. Hillsdale, NJ: LEA, 1992.

Guthrie, E., and Matthews, K. *No More Push Parenting: How to Find Success and Balance in a Hypercompetitive World.* New York: Broadway Books, 2002.

Iran-Nejad, A., Wittrock, M. C., and Hidi, S., eds. Brain and education. Special issue: *Educational Psychologist* 27, no. 4 (1992).

Kandel, E., and Schwartz, J. *Principles of Neural Science.* New York: Elsevier North-Holland, 1981.

Kosslyn, S. M., et al. Bridging psychology and biology: The analysis of individuals in groups. *American Psychologist* 57, no. 5 (2002): 341–51.

Kranowitz, Carol Stock. *The Out-of-Sync Child.* New York: Skylight Press, 1998.

Luria, A. *The Working Brain.* New York: Basic Books, 1973.

Moore, Chris, and Lemmon, Karen. *The Self in Time: Developmental Perspectives.* Mahwah, NJ: LEA, 2001.

Olfman, Sharna, ed. *All Work and No Play: How Educational Reforms Are Harming Our Preschoolers.* Westport, CT: Praeger/Greenwood Publishing Group, 2003.

Pennington, B. F. *Diagnosing Learning Disorders: A Neuropsychological Framework.* New York: Guilford Press, 1991.

Pert, C. B. *Molecules of Emotion.* New York: Scribner's, 1997.

Rapin, R., and Segalowitz, S., eds. *Handbook of Neuropsychology* 6, Sec. 10: "Child Neuropsychology (Part 1)." Amsterdam: Elsevier, 1992.

Reichert, Heinrich. *Introduction to Neurobiology.* New York: Oxford University Press, 1992.

Rich, Dorothy. *MegaSkills.* Exp. ed. Boston: Houghton Mifflin, 1998.

Scientific American. "The Hidden Mind." Special issue (2002).

Segalowitz, S., and Rapin, R., eds. *Handbook of Neuropsychology* 7, Sec. 10: "Child Neuropsychology (Part 2)." Amsterdam: Elsevier, 1992.

Siegel, Daniel J. *The Developing Mind: How Relationships and the Brain Interact to Shape Who We Are.* New York: Guilford Press, 1999.

Spreen, O., et al. *Human Developmental Neuropsychology.* New York: Oxford University Press, 1984.

Webb, S. J., Monk, C. S., and Nelson, C. A. Mechanisms of postnatal neurobiological development: Implications for human development. *Developmental Neuropsychology* 19, no. 2. Lawrence Erlbaum Associates (2001): 147–71.

Wolfe, Patricia. *Brain Matters: Translating Research into Classroom Practice.* Alexandria, VA: ASCD, 2001.

Yakolev, P., and Lecours, A. The myelogenetic cycles of regional development of the brain. In A. Minkowski, ed. *Regional Development of the Brain in Early Life.* Oxford: Blackwell, 1967.

Chapter 1

Armstrong, E. The limbic system and culture. *Human Nature* 2, no. 2 (1991): 117–36.

Ayres, Jean A. *Sensory Integration and the Child.* Los Angeles: Western Psychological Services, 1991.

MacLean, P. A. Mind of three minds: Educating the triune Brain. In J. Chall and A. Mirsky, *Education and the Brain.* 77th Yearbook of the National Society for the Study of Education. Chicago: University of Chicago Press, 1978.

McClelland, J. L., and Siegler, R. S., eds. *Mechanisms of Cognitive Development: Behavioral and Neural Perspectives.* Mahwah, NJ: LEA, 2001.

Mostofsky, D., et al. Evidence for a deficit in procedural learning in children and adolescents with autism: Implications for cerebellar contribution. In *Journal of the International Neuropsychological Society* 6. (2000): 752–59.

Neville, H. J., and Bavellier, D. Neural organization and plasticity of language. In *Current Opinion in Neurobiology* 8, no. 2 (1998): 254–58.

Ross, Emma. "Without Proper Brain Exercise, London Cabbies Would be lost." Associated Press, March 15, 2000.

Schorr, A. N. *Affect Regulation and the Origin of the Self: The Neurobiology of Emotional Development.* Mahwah, NJ: LEA, 1999.

Sevenson, Larry W. *Brain Architecture.* New York: Oxford University Press, 2003.

Chapter 2

Barnett, A. B., and Barnett, R. J. *The Youngest Minds.* New York: Simon & Schuster, 1998.

Bradley, R., and Caldwell, B. The relation of infants' home environments to achievement test performance in first grade: A follow-up study. *Child Development* 55 (1984): 803–9.

Dawson, G., et al. Frontal lobe activity and affective behavior of infants of mothers with depressive symptoms. *Child Development* 63, no. 3 (1992): 725–37.

DeCasper, A. J., and Fifer, W. P. Of human bonding: Newborns prefer their mothers' voices. *Science* 208 (1980): 1174–76.

Eliot, Lise. *What's Going on in There?: How the Brain and Mind Develop in the First Five Years of Life.* New York: Bantam Books, 1999.

Gopnik, Allison; Meltzoff, Andrew; and Kuhl, Patricia. *The Scientist in the Crib: Minds, Brains, and How Children Learn.* New York: William Morrow, 1999.

Held, R. Plasticity in sensory motor systems. *Scientific American* 213 (1965): 85.

Honig, A. Mental health for babies. *Young Children* (March 1993): 69–76.

Mehler, J., and Fox, R. *Neonate Cognition: Beyond the Blooming Buzzing Confusion.* Hillsdale, NJ: Erlbaum, 1985.

Radell, P. L., and Gottlieb, G. Developmental intersensory interference: Augmented prenatal sensory experience interferes with auditory learning in duck embryos. *Developmental Psychology* 28, no. 5 (1992): 795–803.

Siegel, L. Reproductive, perinatal, and environmental factors as predictors of the cognitive and language development of preterm and full-term infants. *Child Development* 53 (1982): 963–73.

Tots and Toxins: Altered Brains. Symposium presented at LDA Annual Conference, San Francisco, February 1993.

Zuckerman, B., et al. Maternal depressive symptoms during pregnancy, and newborn irritability. *Journal of Developmental and Behavioral Pediatrics* 11, no. 4 (1990): 190–94.

Chapter 3

Belsky, J., et al. Assessing performance, competence, and executive capacity in infant play: Relations to home environment and security of attachment. *Developmental Psychology* 20, no. 3 (1984): 406–17.

Bronson, M. B. *Self-Regulation in Early Childhood: Nature and Nurture.* New York: Guilford Press, 2000.

Case, R. *Intellectual Development: Birth to Adulthood.* New York: Academic Press, 1985.

Denham, S., and Renwick, S. Working and playing together: Prediction of preschool social-emotional competence from mother-child interaction. *Child Development* 62 (1991): 242–49.

Flavell, J. H. Cognitive development: Past, present, and future. *Child Development* 63 (1992): 998–1005.

Gottfried, A. *Home Environment and Early Cognitive Development.* New York: Academic Press, 1984.

Holt, John; Farenga, P; and Farenga, P. *Teach Your Own: The John Holt Book of Homeschooling.* Boulder, CO: Perseus Publishing, 2003.

Kochenderfer, R., and Kanna, E. *Homeschooling for Success.* New York: Warner Books, 2002.

Layne, Marty. *Learning at Home: A Mother's Guide to Homeschooling.* Rev. ed. Victoria, BC, Canada: Sea Change Publications, 2000.

Lillard, P. P. *Montessori Today: A Comprehensive Approach to Education from Birth to Adulthood.* New York: Schocken Books, 1996.

Liss, M. *Social and Cognitive Skills: Sex Roles and Children's Play.* New York: Academic Press, 1983.

McNichols, J. C. *The Montessori Controversy.* Clifton Park, NY: Delmar Publishers, 1991.

Mostofsky, S., et al. Deficits in motor response inhibition and motor persistence in ADHD. Paper presented at 29th Annual INS Meeting, Honolulu, HI, February, 2003.

National Association for the Education of Young Children (a comprehensive resource on developmentally appropriate education). http//www.naeyc.org

Oldfield, L. *Free to Learn.* London: Hawthorne Press, 2001 (a description of Waldorf education).

Olfman, S., ed. *All Work and No Play: How Educational Reforms Are Harming Our Preschoolers.* Westport, CT: Praeger/Greenwood Publishing Group, 2003.

Parkinson, C., et al. Rating the home environment of school-age children: A comparison with general cognitive index and school progress. *Journal of Child Psychology and Psychiatry and Allied Disciplines* 23, no. 3 (1982): 329–33.

Petrash, J. *Understanding Waldorf Education.* Beltsville, MD: Gryphon House, 2002.

Rubin, K. Fantasy play: Its role in the development of social skills and social cognition. *New Directions for Child Development* 9 (1980): 69–86.

Segalowitz, S., and Hiscock, M. The emergence of a neuropsychology of normal development: Rapprochement between neuroscience and developmental psychology. In S. Segalowitz and I. Rapin, eds. *Handbook of Neuropsychology,* Vol. 6. Amsterdam: Elsevier, 1992.

Shonkoff, J. P. and Phillips, D. A. *From Neurons to Neighborhoods: The Science of Early Childhood Development.* Washington, DC: National Academy Press, 2000.

Chapter 4

Ames, L. *Is Your Child in the Wrong Grade?* Flemington, NJ: Programs for Education, Inc.

Armstrong, Thomas. *The Myth of the A.D.D. Child.* New York: Dutton, 1995.

Barkley, R. *Attention Deficit-Hyperactivity Disorder: A Handbook for Diagnosis and Treatment* (2d ed.). New York: Guilford, 1998.

———. *Taking Charge of ADHD: The Complete, Authoritative Guide for Parents* (rev. ed.). New York: Guilford Press, 2000.

Developmentally Appropriate Practice in Early Childhood Programs Serving Children from Birth through Age 8. Washington, DC: National Association for the Education of Young Children, 1997.

Hallowell, E. M., and Ratey, J. J. *Driven to Distraction.* New York: Touchstone, 1994.

———. *Answers to Distraction.* New York: Pantheon Books, 1994.

Jansky, J. The marginally ready child. *Bulletin of the Orton Society* 25 (1975).

Kagan, S. L. Readiness past, present, and future: Shaping the agenda. *Young Children* (November 1992): 48–53.

Kranowitz, Carol Stock. *The Out-of-Sync Child Has Fun: Activities for Kids with Sensory Integration Dysfunction.* New York: Perigee, 2003.

Levine, Mel. *A Mind at a Time.* New York: Simon & Schuster, 2002.

Pennington, B. F. *Diagnosing Learning Disorders: A Neuropsychological Framework.* New York: Guilford Press, 1991.

Rapp, Doris. *Is This Your Child?* New York: William Morrow, 1992 (children's diet and allergies).

Richardson, T. M., and Benbow, C. P. Long-term effects of acceleration on the social-emotional adjustment of mathematically precocious youths. *Journal of Educational Psychology* 82, no. 3 (1990): 464–70.

Shalice, T., et al. Executive function profile of children with attention deficit hyperactivity disorder. *Developmental Neuropsychology* 21, no. 1 (2002): 43–71.

Shepard, L., and Smith, M. L. Synthesis of research on grade retention. *Educational Leadership* (May 1990): 84–86.

Slavin, R. E., et al. Preventing early school failure: What works? *Educational Leadership* (January 1993): 10–18.

Solanto, M. V.; Arnstein, A. F.; and Castellanos, F. X., eds. *Stimulant Drugs and ADHD: Basic and Clinical Neuroscience.* Oxford: Oxford University Press, 2001. TV Turnoff Network. http//www.tvturnoff.org

Waber, D., et al. Diminished motor timing control in children referred for diagnosis of learning problems. *Developmental Neuropsychology* 17, no. 2 (2000): 181–97.

Chapter 5

Conger, J., and Peterson, A. *Adolescence and Youth.* 3rd ed. New York: Harper & Row, 1984.

DeGaetano, G., Director: The Parent Coaching Institute. http//www.thepci.com

Eccles, J., et al. Development during adolescence. *American Psychologist* 48, no. 2 (1993): 90–101.

Elkind, D. *A Sympathetic Understanding of the Child: Birth to Sixteen.* Boston: Allyn and Bacon, 1974.

Harter, S., and Monsour, A. Developmental analysis of conflict caused by opposing attributes in the adolescent self-portrait. *Developmental Psychology* 28, no. 2 (1992): 251–60.

Hasher, L., and Zacks, R. Automatic processing of fundamental information. *American Psychologist* 39, no. 12 (1984): 1372–88.

Kafka, R., and London, P. Communication in relationships and adolescent substance use. *Adolescence* 26, no. 103 (1991): 587–98.

Levine, Mel. *The Myth of Laziness.* New York: Simon & Schuster, 2003.

McCannon, R., Director: New Mexico Media Literacy Project. http//www.nmmlp.org

Paikoff, R. L., and Brooks-Gunn, J. Parent-child relationships at puberty. *Psychological Bulletin* 110, no. 1 (1991): 47–66.

Stuss, D., and Benson, D. Neuropsychological studies of the frontal lobes. *Psychological Bulletin* 95, no. 1 (1984): 3–28.

Tierno, M. The impact of cognitive change on personality development in middle schoolers. Paper presented at the Annual Meeting of Independent Schools of the Central States. Chicago, November 1984.

Chapter 6

Benbow, C. Physiological correlates of extreme intellectual precocity. *Neuropsychologia* 24 (1991): 719–25.

Bryden, M. P., et al. Hand preference in school children. *Developmental Neuropsychology* 7, no. 4 (1991): 477–86.

Dennis, M., and Whitaker, H. Language acquisition following hemidecortication: Linguistic superiority of the left over the right hemisphere. *Brain and Language* 3 (1976): 404–33.

Fagot, B. I., and Hagan, R. Observations of parent reactions to sex-stereotyped behaviors. *Child Development* 62, no. 3 (1991): 617–28.

Fox, N. A.; Bell, M.; and Jones, N. A. Individual differences in response to stress and cerebral asymmetry. *Developmental Neuropsychology* 8, nos. 2 and 3 (1992): 161–84.

Frankel, M., and Rollins, H. Does mother know best? Mothers and fathers interacting with preschool sons and daughters. *Developmental Psychology* 19, no. 5 (1983): 694–702.

Greenfield, P. M., and Cocking, R. R. *Interacting with Video*. New York: Ablex Publishing, 1996.

Kimura, D. Sex differences in the brain. *Scientific American* (September 1992): 118–25.

Lytton, H., and Romney, D. M. Parents' differential socialization of boys and girls: A meta-analysis. *Psychological Bulletin* 109, no. 2 (1991): 267–96.

Maccoby, E.; Snow, M.; and Jacklin, C. Children's dispositions and mother-child interaction at 18 months: A short-term longitudinal study. *Developmental Psychology* 20, no. 3 (1984): 459–72.

McCarthy, B. *The 4Mat System: Teaching to Learning Styles with Right/Left Mode Techniques* (2d ed.). Oak Brook, IL: Excel, 1981.

Meece, J., et al. Sex differences in math achievement: Toward a model of academic choice. *Developmental Psychology* 91, no. 2 (1982): 329–46.

Michel, G. F. A lateral bias in the neuropychological functioning of human infants. *Developmental Neuropsychology* 14, no. 4 (1998): 445–69.

Molfese, D. L., and Segalowitz, S., eds. *Brain Lateralization in Children: Developmental Implications*. New York: Guilford Press, 1988.

Springer, S., and Deutsch, G. *Left Brain, Right Brain*. 5th ed. New York: Freeman, 1997.

Vail, P. *Liberate Your Child's Learning Patterns*. New York: Kaplan, 2002.

Wilson, Frank R. *The Hand: How Its Use Shapes the Brain, Language, and Human Culture*. New York: Pantheon Books, 1998.

Chapter 7

Baron, N. S. *Growing Up with Language.* New York: Addison-Wesley, 1992.

Benasich, A. A. Impaired processing of brief, rapidly presented auditory cues in infants with a family history of autoimmune disorder. *Developmental Neuropsychology* 22, no. 1 (2002): 351–72.

deHirsch, K. *Language and the Developing Child.* Baltimore: Orton Dyslexia Society, 1984.

deVilliers, P., and deVilliers, J. *Early Language.* Cambridge, MA: Harvard University Press, 1979.

Diaz, R. M., and Berk, L. E. *Private Speech.* Hillsdale, NJ: LEA, 1992.

Garvey, C. *Children's Talk.* Cambridge, MA: Harvard University Press, 1984.

Kelly, S. D., et al. Putting language back in the body: Speech and gesture in three time frames. *Developmental Neuropsychology* 22, no. 1 (2002): 323–49.

McCartney, K. Effect of quality of day care environment on children's language development. *Developmental Psychology* 20, no. 2 (1984): 244–60.

McLaughlin, B., et al. Mothers' and fathers' speech to their young children: Similar or different? *Journal of Child Language* 10, no. 1 (1983): 245–52.

Molfese, D. L., and Molfese, V. J. The use of scalp-recorded evoked responses at birth to predict language performance at 3 years of age. Paper presented at the International Neuropsychological Society Annual Meeting. San Antonio, Texas, February 1991.

Chapter 8

Angier, N. Study finds region of brain may be key problem solver. *New York Times,* July 21, 2000, p. A11.

Boggiano, A. K., and Pittman, T. S. *Achievement and Motivation.* Cambridge: Cambridge University Press, 1992.

Brophy, J. Synthesis of research on strategies for motivating students to learn. *Educational Leadership* (October 1987): 40–48.

Ceci, S. J., et al. Memory, cognition, and learning: Developmental and ecological considerations. In S. Segalowitz and I. Rapin, eds. *Handbook of Neuropsychology,* Vol. 7. Amsterdam: Elsevier, 1992.

Coffin, L., and Cartwright, G. Brain-electrical activity profiles of special populations of children. Paper presented at International Neuropsychological Society Annual Meeting. Galveston, Texas, February 1993.

Feuerstein, R., et al. *Instrumental Enrichment.* Baltimore: University Park, 1980.

Friedman, M. ed. *Intelligence and Learning.* New York: Plenum, 1981.

Gardner, H. *Frames of Mind: The Theory of Multiple Intelligences.* New York: Basic Books, 1983.

Goleman, D. *Emotional Intelligence.* New York: Bantam, 1997.

Grolnick, W., and Ryan, R. Parent styles associated with children's self-regulation and competence in school. *Journal of Educational Psychology* 81, no. 2 (1989): 143–54.

Kohn, A. *Punished by Rewards: The Trouble with Gold Stars, Incentive Plans, A's, Praise, and Other Bribes.* Boston: Houghton Mifflin, 1999.

Lodico, M., et al. The effects of strategy-monitoring training on children's selection of effective memory strategies. *Journal of Experimental Child Psychology* 35, no. 2 (1983): 263–77.

Matarazzo, J. D. Psychological testing and assessment in the 21st century. *American Psychologist* (August 1992): 1007–18.

McCall, R. B., and Carriger, M. S. Meta-analysis of infant habituation and recognition memory performance as preditors of later IQ. *Child Development* 64 (1993): 57–79.

Perkins, D., et al., eds. New Conceptions of Thinking. Special issue, *Educational Psychologist* 28, no. 1 (1993).

Pintrich, P. R. Current issues and new directions in motivational theory and research. Special issue, *Educational Psychologist* 26, nos. 3 and 4 (1991).

Ratner, H. Memory demands and the development of young children's memory. *Child Development* 55 (1984): 2173–91.

Scarr, S., and Weinberg, R. The Minnesota Adoption Studies: Genetic differences and malleability. *Child Development* 54, no. 2 (1983): 260–67.

Shaywitz, Sally. *Overcoming Dyslexia: A New and Science-Based Program for Overcoming Reading Problems at Any Age.* New York: Knopf, 2003.

Squire, L. R., and Schacter, D. L., eds. *Neuropsychology of Memory.* New York: Guilford Press, 2002.

Sternberg, R. J. Ability tests, measurements, and markets. *Journal of Educational Psychology* 84, no. 2 (1992): 134–40.

———. *Successful Intelligence.* New York: Plume, 1997.

Van Strien, J. W., and Morpurgo, M. Opposite hemisphere activations as a result of emotionally threatening and non-threatening words. *Neuropsychologia* 30, no. 9 (1992): 845–48.

Wilson, R. The Louisville Twin Study: Development synchronies in behavior. *Child Development* 54, no. 2 (1983): 298–316.

Chapter 9

Adams, M. J. Beginning to Read: Thinking and Learning about Print. Cambridge, MA: MIT Press, 1994.

Bell, N. *Visualizing and Verbalizing.* Rev. ed. Paso Robles, CA: Academy of Reading Publications, 1991.

Cullinan, B. E. *Children's Literature in the Reading Program.* Newark, DE: International Reading Association, 1987.

Durkin, D. *Children Who Read Early,* New York: Teachers College Press, 1966.

Feitelson, D., et al. How effective is early instruction in reading? Experimental evidence. *Merrill–Palmer Quarterly* 28, no. 4 (1982): 485–94.

Finns do fine in worldwide study of reading literacy. *Reading Today* (October/November 1992): 7–8.

Fletcher, J. M. Neural correlates of learning to read. Paper presented at 53rd Annual Conference, International Dyslexia Association. Atlanta, November, 2002.

Healy, J. The enigma of hyperlexia. *Reading Research Quarterly* 17, no. 3 (1982): 319–338.

———, et al. A study of hyperlexia. *Brain and Language* 17 (1982): 1–23.

International Dyslexia Association (complete resources on dyslexia, reading, and learning development). http//www.interdys.org

Lyytinen, Heikki, ed. The Neuropsychology of Developmental Dyslexia. Special issue, *Developmental Neuropsychology* 20, no. 2 (2001).

Mills, J., and Jackson, N. Predictive significance of early giftedness: The case of precocious reading. *Journal of Educational Psychology* 82, no. 3 (1990): 410–19.

Molfese, D. L.; Molfese, V. J; and Siegel, L. S. Early brain and behavior measures reflect reading and mathematics skills. Paper presented at 53rd Annual Conference, International Dyslexia Association. Atlanta, November, 2002.

Pirozzolo, F., and Wittrock, M., eds. *Neuropsychological and Cognitive Processes in Reading.* New York: Academic Press, 1981.

Reid, G. *Dyslexia: A Practitioner's Handbook.* 2nd ed. New York: John Wiley and Sons, 1998.

Shaywitz, Sally. *Overcoming Dyslexia: A New and Science-Based Program for Overcoming Reading Problems at Any Age.* New York: Knopf, 2003.

Simos, P. G., et al. Dyslexia-specific brain activation profile becomes normal following successful remedial training. *Neurology* 58 (2002): 1203–13.

Spector, J. Predicting progress in beginning reading: Dynamic assessment of phonemic awareness. *Journal of Educational Psychology* 84, no. 3 (1992): 353–63.

Trelease, J. *The Read-Aloud Handbook.* 5th ed. New York: Penguin, 2001.

Vail, P. *Smart Kids with School Problems.* New York: NAL, 1989.

———. *About Dyslexia.* Rosemont, NJ: Modern Learning Press, 1990.

Vellutino, F., et al. Bridging the gap between cognitive and neuropsychological conceptualizations of reading disability. *Learning & Individual Differences* 3, no. 3 (1991): 181–203.

Weinstein, Lissa. *Reading David: A Mother and Son's Journey through the Labyrinth of Dyslexia.* New York: Perigee Books, 2003.

Chapter 10

Berninger, V., and Rutberg, J. Relationship of finger function to beginning writing. *Developmental Medicine and Child Neurology* 32 (1992): 198–215.

Frith, U., ed. *Cognitive Processes in Spelling.* New York: Academic Press, 1980.

Graves, D. *Writing: Teachers and Children at Work.* Exeter, NH: Heinemann, 1983.

Hodges, R. *Learning to Spell.* Urbana, IL: National Council of Teachers of English, 1981.

International Dyslexia Association (resources for spelling and writing development). http//www.interdys.org

Joshi, R. M.; Ocker, E.; and Schlagal, B. Spelling: Myths, realities, and classroom applications. Paper presented at 53rd Annual Conference, International Dyslexia Association. Atlanta, November, 2002.

Kirk, U., ed. *Neuropsychology of Language, Reading, and Spelling.* New York: Academic Press, 1983.

Rico, G. *Writing the Natural Way.* Boston: Houghton Mifflin, 1983.

Trieman, R. *Learning to Spell.* New York: Oxford University Press, 1993.

Walshe, R. *Every Child Can Write!* Rozelle, NSW: Primary English Teaching Association, 1982.

Welty, E. *One Writer's Beginnings.* Cambridge, MA: Harvard University Press, 1983.

Chapter 11

Briars, D., and Siegler, R. A featural analysis of preschoolers' counting knowledge. *Developmental Psychology* 20, no. 4 (1984): 607–618.

Clements, D. H. Creative pathways to math. *Scholastic Early Childhood Today* (January/February 2003): 37–45.

Copeland, R. *How Children Learn Mathematics,* 3rd ed. New York: Macmillan, 1979.

Hazen, A. Spatial exploration and spatial knowledge: Individual differences in very young children. *Child Development* 53 (1982): 826–37.

Hildebrandt, S., and Tromba, A. *Mathematics and Optimal Form.* New York: Scientific-American Library, 1985.

Hughes, M. *Children and Number.* London: Basil Blackwell, 1986.

O'Boyle, M., et al. Enhanced right hemisphere activation in the mathematically precocious. *Brain & Cognition* 17, no. 2 (1991): 138–53.

Rauscher, F., et al., Music training causes long-term enhancement of preschool children's spatial-temporal reasoning. *Neurological Research* 19 (1997): 2–8.

Van Scoy, I. J., and Fairchild, S. H. It's about time! *Young Children* (January 1993): 21–24.

Chapter 12

Amabile, T. *Growing Up Creative: Nurturing a Lifetime of Creativity,* 2nd ed. New York: Creative Education Foundation, 1992.

Boyarsky, T. Dalcroze eurythmics: An approach to early training of the nervous system. *Seminars in Neurology* 9, no. 2 (1989): 105–14.

Clark, R. *Einstein: The Life and Times.* New York: World Publishing, 1971.

Czikszentmihalyi, M. *Flow: The Psychology of Optimal Experience.* New York: Harper & Row, 1990.

———. *Creativity: Flow and the Psychology of Discovery and Invention.* New York: HarperCollins, 1997.

Davidson, Jan. *Genius Denied: How to Stop Wasting Our Brightest Young Minds.* New York: Simon & Schuster, 2004.

Diamond, M. *Enriching Heredity.* New York: Free Press, 1988.

———, et al. On the brain of a scientist: Albert Einstein. *Experimental Neurology* 88 (1985): 198–204.

Edwards, L., and Nabors, M. The creative arts process. *Young Children* (March 1993): 77–81.

Gardner, H. *Art, Mind, and Brain: A Cognitive Approach to Creativity.* New York: Basic Books, 1982.

———. *To Open Minds.* New York: Basic Books, 1989.

Horowitz, F. D., and O'Brien, M., eds. *The Gifted and Talented: Developmental Perspectives.* Washington, DC: American Psychiatric Association, 1985.

Hunt, M. *The Universe Within.* New York: Simon & Schuster, 1982.

McCullough, D. *John Adams.* New York: Touchstone, 2002.

Morrongiello, B., and Roes, C. Developmental changes in children's perception of musical sequences: Effects of musical training. *Developmental Psychology* 26, no. 5 (1990): 814–20.

Ostrander, S., and Schroeder, L. *Super-Learning.* New York: Laurel Books, 1979.

Silberstein-Storfer, M. *Doing Art Together.* New York: Simon & Schuster, 1982.

Sternberg, R. J., and Davidson, J. E., eds. *Conceptions of Giftedness.* Cambridge: Cambridge University Press, 1986.

Tait, M., and Haack, P. *Principles and Processes of Music Education.* New York: Teachers College Press, 1984.

Tomlinson-Keasey, C., and Little, T. Predicting educational attainment, occupational achievement, intellectual skill, and personal adjustment among gifted men and women. *Journal of Educational Psychology* 82, no. 3 (1990): 442–55.

Torrance, E. *Guiding Creative Talent.* Englewood Cliffs, NJ: Prentice-Hall, 1962.

Weikart, P. *Movement Plus Music: Activities for Children, Ages 3–7.* Ypsilanti, MI: High Scope Press, 1989.

Index

NOTE: Page numbers in *italics* indicate illustrations

About the Author

Jane M. Healy, Ph.D., is an educational psychologist who has worked with students from preschool through graduate school. A trusted authority on children's learning, she consults and lectures worldwide, helping teachers and parents understand the educational implications of current brain research. She is the author of *Endangered Minds* and *Failure to Connect*. Although Healy has received many honors, including being twice awarded the "Educator of the Year Award" by Delta Kappa Gamma, she claims that she and her husband have learned most of what they know from the process of raising three sons. She lives with her husband, Tom, in Vail, Colorado.